BLOWBACK

Also by Miles Taylor (as Anonymous)

A WARNING

BLOWBACK

A WARNING TO SAVE DEMOCRACY FROM THE NEXT TRUMP

★ ★ ★ ★ ★

MILES TAYLOR

ATRIA BOOKS

NEW YORK LONDON TORONTO SYDNEY NEW DELHI

ATRIA
BOOKS

An Imprint of Simon & Schuster, Inc.
1230 Avenue of the Americas
New York, NY 10020

First Atria Books hardcover edition July 2023

ATRIA BOOKS and colophon are trademarks of Simon & Schuster, Inc.

For information about special discounts for bulk purchases,
please contact Simon & Schuster Special Sales at 1-866-506-1949 or
business@simonandschuster.com.

The Simon & Schuster Speakers Bureau can bring authors to
your live event. For more information, or to book an event, contact the
Simon & Schuster Speakers Bureau at 1-866-248-3049 or visit our website
at www.simonspeakers.com.

Interior design by Dana Sloan

Manufactured in the United States of America

1   3   5   7   9   10   8   6   4   2

Library of Congress Cataloging-in-Publication Data has been applied for.

ISBN 978-1-6680-1598-8
ISBN 978-1-6680-1600-8 (ebook)

To Hannah, for saving my life

CONTENTS

BLOWBACK

PROLOGUE

October 30, 2020

The sky was cloudy and sullen, as if strewn with ash plumes. I exited the hotel, baseball cap and sunglasses in place, and crossed the street. Aware of everyone, talking to no one. A woman walked her dog. A man in a camouflage hat smoked a cigarette at the corner, while skateboarders weaved in and out of the bike lane. The smell of firewood smoke signaled the arrival of my favorite season, though on this morning, it barely registered. Around the block, I slipped into a bakery for coffee and a biscuit, keeping my sunglasses on while waiting at the counter. The food lived up to the description, slow-cooked.

Outside again, I walked back to the hotel. A pair of eyes stopped me. The same camo-hat guy from earlier was leaning on a truck, holding my gaze down the street. Something wasn't right. I changed directions as if I'd forgotten something, rerouting toward my parked car on the other side of the road. Settling into the driver's seat, I holstered the coffee in the cupholder and watched the man in the rearview mirror. He dropped his cigarette and flattened it with a twist of his boot.

I pulled out of the parking space, planning to do a lap around the block to shake the suspicion. Headlights lit up behind me, and the truck pulled out, too.

It's a coincidence. Calm down.

As I wound through the still-sleepy North Carolina town—knowing it no better than the distance covered by my high beams in the dim morning—the man seemed to stay with me. Right turn. Left turn. I was being followed, stalked maybe.

I sped a little faster along Asheville's streets and recalled advice from an ex-CIA mentor. *Time. Distance. Direction.* It was a technique called a "surveillance detection route." You tested whether someone was following you by measuring how long, how far, and how directly they remained on your tail. I tried to cool my nerves by running an ad hoc route, even though I had no idea where I was. I vectored away from downtown and took unusual turns, continually checking my rearview mirror.

On the outskirts of Asheville, the truck was still behind me. My heartbeat throbbed in my ears, racing so fast I worried that when it slowed I'd pass out at the wheel. I veered toward the shoulder and braked abruptly. My car shuddered to a halt over the gravel and kicked up a dishwater dust cloud. The truck drove onward and took the highway on-ramp, seemingly oblivious to my abrupt stop. I drove to a nearby parking garage and sat inside waiting, just to be sure. The street was quiet. The truck, nowhere to be seen.

You're losing it, man.

The paranoia was metastasizing. Before daybreak, I had received a note from a U.S. Secret Service agent: "You should get a security team, fast. I can connect you." And another from a Silicon Valley billionaire: "I'll pay your protection costs." While these were generous offers, I was five hundred miles from home, so for now, I was on my own.

It had started the prior afternoon. The president of the United States launched an "all-out assault" against me (as one news outlet put it) while in Tampa, Florida, at a campaign rally. Or was it a mob riot?

"Bad things are going to happen to him!" Trump warned ominously about the "horrible," "treasonous" Miles Taylor.

"Are you listening to me back in Washington? He should be prosecuted!" he roared, face contorted with rage, apparently directing his words at the Justice Department. The audience lapped it up.

"Traitor!" they shouted back gleefully. His followers began to search for me, online and in real life.

Why? Because I had just deliberately blown my own cover, revealing myself to be a longtime Trump detractor and—most infuriatingly to the president—one of his former aides. Internal dissent was one of Trump's worst fears. By his own admission, he had spent two years eyeing everyone who entered the Oval Office warily, wondering who in his midst was the elusive inside critic known only as "Anonymous."

It was me.

Years earlier, I had written an unsigned essay from within the Trump administration, blowing the whistle on White House misconduct. As the unknown author, I detailed the president's character defects, an administration in chaos, and the alarming views of Trump's own cabinet members—some of whom contemplated invoking the Twenty-Fifth Amendment to remove the commander in chief amid the instability. I knew these anonymous revelations would lead to a tidal wave of attacks, but I also hoped they would persuade other rational Republicans to tell the truth about the man in the Oval Office.

I was right, at least about the tidal wave.

As I hunkered down in a North Carolina parking garage, Trump's words from the rally—"Bad things are going to happen to him!"—replayed in my mind. I caught my breath.

No one is following you. You've taken all the precautions.

I had locked down my life before going public. While I will refrain from detailing the security measures or trip wires put in place (others are relying on the confidentiality of similar techniques to protect their families), I will note that I was obsessive. The process took months, and not all of it worked, as I soon found out. My accounts, devices, and phone numbers were all new, and my video backdrops became the peeling wallpaper of hotels, lest I give away my location while traveling the country to campaign against my former boss.

When I drove back into Asheville, the smoke-wood fog had burned off. It was light. An optimistic blue sky allayed my anxiety, until I got back to the hotel.

More vitriol had poured into my cell phone while I was gone, flooding the device. Emails, text messages, Twitter posts. They buzzed menacingly on the desk, each of them a digital grim reaper:

"Hope u die a slow painful death and suffer during the entire process, then burn in hell."

"Your blood will be in the streets traitor."

"Snitches get stitches."

My data was littered across the web—my home address, new cell phone number, new email addresses, personal details about family members, and surprisingly accurate guesses about where I was holed up.

Time to go.

I packed my belongings, reloaded the car, and drove several hours east to Charlotte. In the crucial swing state, I planned to get out and triumphantly persuade voters to "put country over party!" by opposing Trump. Now I was little more than a prisoner reassigned to a new cell, shuttling between rented rooms booked under fake names.

Nighttime brought the first in a series of reckonings.

I placed a pillow over the loaded pistol that was my sidekick on the road trip and settled in, eyes on the door. My new accommodations were cheaper than the last, marked by the permeating smell of mold and mildew and by a rust-stained sink and tub. Mattress wires poked through a threadbare comforter, and an increasingly familiar emotion—doubt—did the same.

You think you're clever? This was a mistake. You did this wrong. All of this.

Without the mask of anonymity, I felt exposed and, for the first time ever, hunted.

★ ★ ★

In September 2018, *The New York Times* published my anonymous opinion piece from inside the Donald J. Trump administration. I revealed publicly what Trump's cabinet members were saying privately: that he was unstable and unfit for office. While serving in top roles at the Department of Homeland Security, I had witnessed shocking acts

of corruption that led me to write the essay, "I AM PART OF THE RE-
SISTANCE INSIDE THE TRUMP ADMINISTRATION," and then to quit the
administration and write a book, titled *A Warning*, urging voters not to
re-elect Trump. I unmasked myself a year later and became a part of the
largest alliance of ex-officials in modern history to help take down the
U.S. president who had appointed them.

Trump lost. But in many ways, so did I.

You might question my judgment for blowing the whistle on Trump
from the safe harbor of anonymity. I don't blame you. Many nights I
questioned whether it was the right choice, even though my figurative
disguise was intended to be temporary. I pledged that I would take the
mask off before the 2020 election, but first I didn't want the truth to get
lost in a personal scuffle. Trump is a master at the politics of personal
destruction, I told myself, so I needed to find a way to deprive him of
the opportunity to distract public attention away from *the message* by
brawling with *the messenger.*

At first, withholding my identity seemed to work. Without a scape-
goat, the president was powerless in countering the narrative that his
own people thought he was incompetent. The essay led to a cascade
of questions about his mental state, new revelations, and a pressing
national conversation about Trump's fitness for office. He launched a
manhunt for the author.

"TREASON?" he tweeted after it was released, demanding the *Times*
hand over Anonymous for "national security" purposes, First Amendment be damned. Trump wanted more than to silence dissent. He wanted
revenge. By using the White House to get it, he unintentionally proved
my point about his corrupt use of power.

Despite sending the Justice Department after me, Trump's search
went nowhere. I continued issuing cloaked critiques to keep pressure on
the White House, even after I left the administration. Through secret
meetings, cutouts, safe houses, and burner phones, I smuggled a longer
tome out to the public, cataloging the reasons why the president lacked
the character for the job. I wrapped my justification in star-spangled
packaging, noting that the Founding Fathers had also crafted anony-

mous essays to promote the U.S. Constitution and to counter its nay-sayers.

The reasoning for keeping my identity a secret began to weaken, particularly as I tried to convince others to speak up. Outside of government, I set up an operation designed to enlist ex-appointees like White House chief of staff John Kelly and defense secretary Jim Mattis—the people Trump had fired or who had quit the executive branch—to announce their opposition to the president in the 2020 election. At the same time, a question nagged me: Why did I expect them to go to the microphone if I was still putting up a façade?

My two personas were at odds. "Miles" was begging his former bosses and colleagues to come forward, while "Anonymous" remained hidden, providing false hope of a resistance figure who might somehow bring down Trump from within, when in reality I was already gone from government. In truth, there were no heroes inside the Trump administration, only survivors. Anonymous couldn't protect anyone from a man so delusional that he once told reporters, "When somebody is the president of the United States, the authority is total, and that's the way it's got to be." Salvation was up to the voters—not Congress, the courts, or an unknown, unelected bureaucrat.

Staying in the shadows began to take a personal toll, too. Although I was trained in the national security community to safeguard classified programs, this was different than a government secret. Leading a double life became a ballooning moral conflict, a pressure cooker teetering at all times on the verge of detonation. The stakes in Washington kept getting higher as the president's behavior got more erratic, while outside calls for Anonymous to "come forward" kept rising, compounding my already-simmering anxiety.

I debated whom to trust and became paranoid about my security. I started drinking frequently and swept a drug overdose under the rug. Meanwhile, haunting self-criticism crept in, as Trump turned my anonymity into "proof" of a deep state out to get him.

With the 2020 election drawing near, I felt a renewed urgency to step into the light. I spent months thinking about it, yet I soon found out how unprepared I actually was. The public fight against Donald Trump cost me my home, my job and savings, friendships, a relationship, and my family's security, temporarily putting me on the run. Late one evening in a Virginia high-rise, it also nearly cost me my life. At the same time, the life of our nation was thrown into turmoil amid an attempted electoral coup and the lingering fallout.

No sympathy is needed for me. I went into this situation willingly; however, the same cannot be said for the civil servants, community leaders, poll workers, and local officials who also came forward and told the truth and in many cases are still fearing for their lives. Since the 2020 election, I have been traveling the country to meet with leaders on the front lines of the pro-democracy struggle—Republicans, Democrats, and Independents—who are trying to counter the rise of political intimidation that many of us have experienced. I'm disappointed to report that the situation hasn't improved. Rather, the system is blinking red.

"They did not listen."

That is what historians will write about American voters years from now, long after the Make America Great Again (MAGA) movement does the unthinkable and retakes the White House, either under the continuing influence of Donald Trump or led by a zealous understudy who adopts his agenda with gusto. Trust me, this isn't a political fantasy. It's a civic nightmare, and the skeletons in America's closet are conspiring day and night to bring it to fruition.

Donald Trump introduced a new brand of extremism to the Republican Party, and the thuggish populism has grown beyond his control. If corrective action isn't taken, the MAGA movement will reclaim the American presidency in the coming years and do irreparable damage to our democracy. I would know. I was once on the inside of it, naively hoping Trump would rise to the moment or that grown-ups would ameliorate the fanaticism of his movement. Neither happened, and America continues to pay a steep price for giving Trump the opportunity in the first place.

While Americans rightfully removed Trump from the White House in 2020, it wasn't without considerable effort. It also wasn't enough. I warned a year before the general election that even if the president was defeated, he would not concede.

"Trump relishes the cocoon he has built," I wrote. "He will not exit quietly—or easily. It is why at many turns he suggests 'coups' are afoot and a 'civil war' is in the offing. He is already seeding the narrative for his followers—a narrative that could end tragically."

It did.

The January 6 insurrection was the predictable outcome of Donald Trump's refusal to concede. In the aftermath, many more officials came forward and cautioned that our democratic institutions were so weakened by political extremism that if we did not unify to repair our republic, the understructure would collapse. Now it is happening. And if we don't act, the phrase "they did not listen" will be the watchwords of our time.

In the realm of national security, we have a term to describe unintended consequences, the failure to anticipate the repercussions when we make a choice: *blowback*.

This is a cautionary tale about how neglecting our guardrails—individually and as a democracy—can lead to self-destruction.

More specifically, it is a political forecast about how a deeply divided nation is setting the stage for the resurgence of Trumpism. In this book, you will glimpse the not-too-distant future of the blowback we will experience if we choose the wrong path. It's also a story about personal mistakes and why a failure of introspection can be fatal.

In the pages to follow, I will paint a vivid portrait of another term under a vindictive, twice-impeached, unconstrained commander in chief, or more likely under the rule of a savvier successor who will take his place—collectively referred to as "the Next Trump." Each section will assess a particular guardrail of democracy, toggling between how it was tested in the first Trump administration and how it could be dismantled next time. From remorselessly gutting the American judicial system to deploying U.S. combat troops in neighboring countries, you will see what "mega MAGA" really looks like and how it could endanger our lives, our livelihoods, and our way of life.

If we want to save democracy from the Next Trump, we need to fully understand the threat he or she will pose. Predictions must not be founded in fear but instead rooted in truth. In forming these projections, I have relied on first-person interviews with the people who know the MAGA movement's plans, never-before-told stories from the inside, and penetrating insights from the country's leading democracy doctors, who understand how dire the situation has become. Together, they provide a matter-of-fact prognosis for what to expect if we install another corrupt leader in the White House.

This isn't just about the next presidential election or a short-term hazard. Autocratic personalities will come and go, but the antidemocratic trend lines in our system pose lasting, generational peril. Trumpism is a political philosophy that seeks to achieve far-right, populist goals by defying democratic institutions and misusing government power for partisan purposes. It has spread like a disease, infecting a rising generation of copycats.

I know how ugly it can get. I sat in the Oval Office as Donald Trump fantasized about replicating North Korea's demilitarized zone on the U.S. southern border, replete with land mines, barbed wire, electric fences, and armed guards. Trump described in graphic detail the sharp, flesh-piercing spikes he wanted installed on the border wall, designed to maim climbers so bloodily that other migrants would be scared to follow suit. He mused about U.S. soldiers firing on civilians, knowing that if they blew the legs out from underneath pregnant mothers, it would keep them from reaching the border.

I listened aboard Air Force One as Trump lavished praise on America's adversaries and foreign dictators, waxing poetic about Vladimir Putin and Xi Jinping. Those men could do whatever they wanted, unconstrained by congresses and judges. *He* wanted the same power, ordering subordinates to send draft laws to Congress to eliminate appellate courts that overruled him and to write executive orders to invoke the Insurrection Act, allowing him to impose a version of martial law.

I heard gag-inducing comments about women, as Trump nitpicked their looks and television performances, including, most grotesquely, sexual references to his own daughter. Perversion aside, it was the ex-president's inclination toward illegality that led me to quit. I witnessed Trump tell border patrol agents to ignore the law and to send arriving migrants right back into the hot-sun desert where they could die despite their legal right to claim asylum, offering to pardon anyone who got arrested for carrying out his directive. That was the last straw. I reported the incident to government lawyers and resigned shortly thereafter, making sure news of the episode became public.

If another like-minded MAGA figure is given a shot at the presidency, these will not be anecdotes of near misses. They will be official U.S. government policy. I don't expect you to take my word for it. Many people who were close to Trump have shared with me—almost unanimously— their belief that the return of Trumpism will be more volatile than its initial rise, which is why we must act without delay. (Some Republicans I spoke with are so worried about retribution from figures inside the movement that they requested their names be withheld in these pages and/or that identifying details about them be modified, in part because of threats of physical violence from Trump's followers.)

Regardless of whether the ex-president has a shot at returning to the White House, his torchbearers intend to carry on his legacy by bringing the flame back into government. They won't allow political prudence to hold them back from weaponizing the very same democratic institutions that should serve as guardrails. As I write this, MAGA operatives are working in Washington to transform their hostile takeover of the Republican Party into sustained, multi-decade control over the levers of government.

These are not the national security dangers I expected to be worried about in the twenty-first century. I entered government service in the wake of September 11, 2001. Since that dark day, I have spent my career focused on protecting the country against foreign threats, from terrorists and transnational criminal organizations, to nation-states such as Russia and China. After witnessing Donald Trump's rise, presidency, and fall up close, I now believe that the greatest threat to American democracy in this century will come from within.

A widening cabal of antidemocratic leaders here at home have exploited our polarized political climate and are already mimicking Donald Trump. I have met them on the campaign trail as they run for local, state, and federal office. They are winning more elections than you think. The influence of Trump's example has created an opening for his apprentices to engage in abuses of power by using America's public offices to promote their own self-interest and to silence objectors.

We can halt the spread of political extremism, but it will be a once-in-a-generation challenge.

We didn't snuff out Trumpism. Rather, we looked the other way as its cinders lit the dry underbrush of our fraying society and spread like wildfire. Right now, the winds favor the fanatics, from a historically divided electorate to grim public attitudes about political violence. Recent surveys have found one in ten Americans—more than 30 million people—now support violence against the government. Such a combustible political climate is what MAGA-aligned figures need in order to burn down the system.

Democrats, reform-minded Republicans, and Independents can come together to create a symbolic "firebreak" to prevent the blaze's spread by taking three actions.

First, we must open our eyes. A victim mentality has overcome voters since the Trump presidency, with Americans lamenting the brokenness of our politics, as if the unwelcome situation were a faultless mishap. We must be candid with ourselves. This isn't happening to us; this is happening *because* of us. Our city streets are now the front lines in the war for the soul of our political system, and it won't end without a great civic awakening.

Second, we must proactively protect our institutions. The United States needs an insurance policy against political disaster, which means identifying the risks posed by antidemocracy figures and crafting mitigation strategies to safeguard the laws and traditions that made America the exceptional nation it is. I have identified some of the most crucial areas where we would expect the Next Trump to do damage, and I offer suggestions for how we can fortify our institutions against a would-be despot.

Third, we must not hide from a deeper menace. The stories you will read here—of illegal acts, long-lasting lies, misused presidential powers, conspiracies, assassination plots, and suicide attempts—are the consequences of a poorly understood bystander phenomenon, which I believe is the "hidden threat" to democracy.

For now, I will say I have arrived at an unexpected conclusion, given my background: anonymity is a gift to authoritarians. They thrive on fear and the suppression of dissent. My journey to the truth was painful—mentally, emotionally, and physically—and forced me to unlearn what I'd been taught in Washington.

In the end, I discovered that in politics, the real struggle is not *us-versus-them*.

It is *us-versus-us*.

Chapter 1

THE FACTION

The process of election affords a moral certainty, that the office of President will never fall to the lot of any man who is not in an eminent degree endowed with the requisite qualifications.

—ALEXANDER HAMILTON, FEDERALIST NO. 68, 1788

PART I

There is a front row to American democracy, and it can only seat four. In the U.S. House of Representatives, two nondescript desks positioned at the back wall offer the most revealing view of the magisterial chamber. Most Americans will never see these hidden perches. One is tucked away on the right corner, the Republican side of the chamber; the other on the left, the Democratic side. Young staffers assigned to these wooden tables mark opposite ends of a chaotic thoroughfare away from the cameras, where members of Congress mingle, laugh, argue, and cut deals to keep the country running. At fifteen years old, I was plucked from farmland obscurity in La Porte, Indiana, and dropped into one of these four seats. That is where I first learned about politics.

"Welcome to your new office."

I was lured to public service both as an escape and as a calling. As a boy, my obsession with superheroes imbued me with a simple good-against-evil worldview. I wanted to be one of the good guys. With a distant gaze at adulthood, government seemed thrilling compared to the drudgery of small-town life, especially after my parents divorced and home became a place of low-level turbulence. Washington was where actual superheroes lived, men and women elected with the noble purpose of rectifying the world's wrongs and confronting the real bad guys—criminals, polluters, dictators.

Sitting in the nurse's office one day at school, I listened through the curtain as a fellow student recounted his parents' struggle to afford food, while he and his siblings survived on trick-or-treat candy they had collected on Halloween. *Trick-or-treat candy.* That seemingly little moment changed my perspective. Suddenly, my own situation at home didn't look so bad, and I felt the faintest inklings of a calling. I devoured books about extreme poverty. An idealistic middle-schooler, I checked out tomes on history, economics, and the Millennium Development Goals.

Then terrorists struck. I was in the Twin Towers weeks before September 11, 2001, on a trip to New York City with my mom and aunt. At fourteen years old, I gaped down from the highest floor of the North Tower with a wide-eyed view of Lower Manhattan. The short passage of time between that moment and the implosion of the buildings made me feel a cosmic connection to the tragedy. Alone in my room, I sobbed looking at still photos of Americans leaping from the buildings' upper floors to escape flames ignited by men who had turned airplanes into missiles. "Never again," Americans vowed. I meant it, desperate to lend a hand in protecting the country against foreign enemies, while I compartmented clinical anxiety, which I couldn't name or understand until much later.

But what does a kid from a two-star town have to offer four-star military generals who are hunting down the bad guys? That was my

dilemma. My family didn't have a lot of money or major political connections. Without those, I couldn't see a fast path into government for a
high-school student and part-time restaurant dishwasher with scalded
hands and a restless mind.

When I heard about a minimum-wage job as a cub reporter at the
local radio station, I submitted an application. I got the gig. Luckily,
listeners couldn't tell I was a teenager unless my voice cracked on air,
something I carefully avoided by practicing a deep octave.

"And a pleasant good morning," I bellowed into the foam-covered
microphone hanging from the studio ceiling. "This is Miles Taylor here
at the broadcast center, with a look at your *neewwwws* at this hour."

I elbowed past colleagues to land assignments covering visits from
political leaders.

"A word to the wise," the salty news director warned. "Don't meet
your heroes. They'll let you down."

As I brushed shoulders with Bush administration officials who were
visiting the Midwest and national media figures like MSNBC's Chris
Matthews, I was pretty sure my boss was wrong. These were the giants
of public policy, and I wanted to join their ranks.

My interview subjects weren't fooled, though. No matter how grown-up
I tried to act, I was still a kid wearing big-people clothes. Literally. Dad's
oversize Navy blue blazer gave me away with sleeves that were only
centimeters away from my fingers, and without a driver's license, I was
forced to rely on my mom to drop me off and pick me up from news
events. But what felt like intolerable indignities ended up leading to an
opening.

"Son, how old are you?" U.S. senator Evan Bayh asked skeptically one
night on the sidelines of a town hall he was hosting in our community.

"Fifteen," I admitted reluctantly.

He abruptly ended the interview and asked me to kill my handheld
tape recorder. I was discouraged. But then he whispered to an aide and
told me about something called the Congressional Page Program.

"You want to see politics in action?" Bayh asked.

His aide handed me a fancy business card. I rubbed my thumb reverently over the gold-embossed eagle and probably emailed the staffer that same night. Several months later, I found myself on the ten-hour drive from Northwest Indiana to Washington, D.C., to join several dozen students for a job in the United States Capitol.

For two hundred years, young people have assisted with administrative proceedings in the nation's legislative body as congressional pages, or as we were sometimes called, "democracy's messengers." The errands ranged from mundane to momentous. We spent early mornings running packages around the Capitol complex and late nights putting bills and resolutions in the hands of hundreds of representatives, each of whom had a flurry of comments, edits, amendments, and rewrites to make to the people's paperwork. You rarely see congressional pages. We were trained to operate in the background, quietly supporting the country's leaders, except for every four years when pages are photographed delivering the Electoral College ballot boxes to the House to certify the results of the presidential election.

On my first day, I met a personal hero. U.S. senator John McCain greeted us in passing as he made his way to the other side of the Capitol. His handshake felt like a professional christening, and I watched the vaunted combat veteran and "maverick" presidential candidate disappear down a stately hallway. We were ushered onto the floor of the House of Representatives. The cavernous chamber was ornamented with Americana—busts, quotes, and frescoes of the country's Founders— and it struck me with the veneration that you'd reserve for a holy site.

"Welcome to your new office," Peggy Sampson, the businesslike page boss, told us as she pointed out the two desks in the back corners that would become our rotating perches.

The class was split between Republican and Democratic pages, a reminder of Washington's built-in divide. I was fortunate to be a Republican page. The GOP was in the majority, and soon I was selected to serve as the Speaker's page—the personal messenger for the most powerful figure in Congress: Speaker of the House Dennis Hastert.

Washington was enveloped in a sober urgency in those post-9/11 years, which became clear by the weighty atmosphere. Access to the Speaker's office was strictly controlled, and distractions weren't tolerated in his quiet sanctum. One day an aide found me using the office phone for a personal call to a girlfriend back in Indiana, and as punishment, I was sent back to the page desk on the House floor to run errands for junior members of Congress. (To me, getting sent back into the middle of the action wasn't exactly punishment.)

We trained as apprentices to wartime legislators who were grappling with an existential threat. You can't overstate the palpable fear vibrating through Washington at the time, from worries about biological weapons to whispers of nuclear dirty bombs. A gas mask was hidden under every seat in the U.S. House. But fear gave way to cooperation, as members of Congress crossed the aisle to compromise on sweeping legislation.

The master class in bipartisanship culminated, for me, in President George W. Bush's 2005 State of the Union Address. Despite having just come off of a contentious presidential campaign, he entered the chamber's arched doorway to applause and handshakes from Republicans *and* Democrats.

"We have known times of sorrow and hours of uncertainty and days of victory," he declared, as I stood by the page desk in the back. "In all this history, even when we have disagreed, we have seen threads of purpose that unite us."

The room applauded in agreement.

I had found my tribe. Roaming the musty marble passageways of Congress, I grew surer of my views as a Republican. I was a "compassionate conservative," the kind George W. Bush spoke about when he called for a government that used the free market to eliminate poverty, that openly welcomed immigrants who sought to join our country, and that championed freedom and human dignity around the globe. Joining the GOP tribe also seemed like the best way to defend the country; Republicans, after all, portrayed themselves as the party that was ready to stand up against enemies to our democracy.

What was meant to be a year turned into a whirlwind decade.

I could hardly stay in school, although I was obsessed with good grades. From elementary to graduate school, I was a straight-A psychopath (except for a lonely B+ on my seventh-grade report card). Valedictorian. Indiana State Debate Champion. Full ride at Indiana University as an undergrad. Full ride at Oxford University as a grad student. But I was bored. I dropped out of school multiple times to take jobs in Washington because I was more interested in sitting in secure briefing rooms, digging into intelligence gathered overseas by U.S. spies, than sitting in classrooms. I trained my strengths—and anxieties—toward supporting national leaders, from preparing research memos at the White House and Pentagon to briefing CIA directors and Homeland Security secretaries.

The stainless boy from a Midwest flyover state was awestruck at having a top-secret security clearance. I grew up fast and learned to stay in the background safeguarding information, knowing that lives were in the balance and that I was responsible for protecting the "sources and methods" of our spy agencies. Just as the kid inside me had yearned, I was working alongside the good guys to fight the bad ones, or so I thought.

Washington changed in the years after 9/11. After spending time in the executive branch, the private sector, and grad school, I returned to Capitol Hill in my late twenties and found a very different place. Some of the people I looked up to had turned out to be not-so-good guys (including House Speaker Dennis Hastert, who'd been arrested, charged, and later convicted in a hush-money scheme related to sexual misconduct with minors). The spirit of unity had also worn off, giving way to fermenting animosity. The Republican Party was focused on undermining Democratic President Barack Obama, while a confrontational Tea Party movement sought to take over the GOP by launching an insurgency.

I tried to ignore the partisan rancor that followed me up the career ladder. As the national security advisor on the House Homeland Security Committee, I told people I was focused on policy, not politics.

Then Donald Trump emerged.

"I want a Trump inoculation plan."

In early 2016, a small group of Republican congressmen and aides, my-self included, huddled around a conference table inside the U.S. Capitol. Afternoon sunshine illuminated untouched cookies and sodas in front of us. The faces around the table hung low.

"I want a Trump inoculation plan," House Speaker Paul Ryan de-manded, making eye contact with each of us.

Paul Ryan had been elected Speaker only months earlier and was eager to move the GOP toward a big tent, hopeful, ideas-driven party. I was a fan for this reason. We millennials prided ourselves on being fiscally conservative and socially liberal, and Ryan was going to be our figurehead. Trump was putting it all at risk in his unexpected quest for the GOP presidential nomination.

"We can't let him trash the GOP," Ryan fumed, noting that Donald Trump was not representative of the policies or the people in the Re-publican Party.

House majority leader Kevin McCarthy nodded in agreement. When it was his turn, McCarthy joked that Trump had switched parties so many times he couldn't tell a donkey from an elephant.

Party leaders had failed to knock out Trump early, so now they were trying to coalesce around someone who could stop him. In the mean-time, Paul Ryan wanted House Republicans to distance themselves from the New York businessman, who they all expected would lose any-way. It wasn't just that Trump was hostile to GOP orthodoxy; he was breathtakingly ignorant about the rule of law, the Constitution, and the democratic system. The select group of lawmakers and staff were tasked with developing a platform that was the antidote to Trumpism.

Rarely does anyone other than the Republican nominee release a party strategy during an election year. Speaker Ryan's "Better Way Agenda" was billed as a right-leaning response to eight years of a Dem-ocratic administration. In practice, though, we were drafting an alter-native to the ideas Trump was spewing on the campaign trail, where he was badly hurting the GOP brand.

We talked about what the document should say. It should repudiate the TV personality's vitriolic rhetoric, isolationist tendencies, protectionist economic ideas, disparaging comments about our allies, affinity for America's adversaries, and divisive anti-Muslim views, among other appalling comments. More broadly, it should reflect a party that was focused on the future and not relitigating the culture wars around guns, abortion, sexual orientation, and gender identity.

I went to work, charged with co-drafting the national security portion of Ryan's plan. For me, Donald Trump was number seventeen out of seventeen of the major candidates in the GOP primary race, a foul-mouthed imbecile who was doomed to fail. I was happy to do anything to separate *us* from *him*. He wasn't a part of our tribe; he was just trying to create a small faction to infiltrate the Republican Party for personal gain. I'd already seen the Tea Party movement do the same, and so far, we'd kept them at bay.

In fact, I didn't know any legislator on the GOP side who seriously supported Trump. Senator Ted Cruz called the man an "utterly amoral . . . narcissist." Texas governor Rick Perry said the businessman was a "cancer on conservatism," defining Trumpism as "a toxic mix of demagoguery, mean-spiritedness, and nonsense." Senator Lindsey Graham equated the man to an "evil force," and openly referred to him as a "jackass" and a "kook." Representative Mick Mulvaney had an even simpler summation: Trump was "a terrible human being."

Then the unthinkable happened. Donald Trump surged forward in the primaries and effectively clinched the nomination. A schism erupted within the party. While most establishment conservatives begrudgingly decided to coalesce behind the nominee (who still seemed destined to lose in the general election), a "Never Trump" wing formed to sink him using any means necessary. Former mentors and colleagues from the Bush administration signed letters disavowing Trump, but because I was a GOP official, I rationalized that it would be inappropriate to add my name to a public list.

Paul Ryan's policy project took on greater urgency. He advised us not to openly attack Trump—and risk pushing him away from the GOP mainstream—but to quietly point him in the right direction by giving him a plan that sounded Republican, not reckless. We foolishly thought we could guide Trump.

We weren't writing the "Better Way Agenda" anymore; it was the "Make Trump Better Plan."

In May 2016, I traveled with a group of GOP senators and congressmen to the Middle East. One evening in Bahrain, I went to dinner with Kansas representative Mike Pompeo. Over lamb shank and hummus, we talked about the dilemma, and I reiterated what was quickly becoming conventional wisdom: in the months ahead during the presidential race, Trump would set the GOP back years with his sensationalistic comments.

"What if—in a fluke—he actually wins?" I wondered aloud. Maybe we should do more than we were doing.

"Miles, he's a coward and a bully," Pompeo responded bluntly. "The American people will see through it, and when this is all over, he'll be a fucking afterthought."

He was so sure Trump couldn't win that we spent most of our dinner talking about what we could do from Capitol Hill to fix U.S. foreign policy during a Hillary Clinton presidency. Obama had backed away from America's allies, we lamented, and was bowing down to its adversaries. Pompeo was considering a run for chair of the House Intelligence Committee, where he could have more influence on U.S. foreign policy. I offered to help him angle for the job once the election was over.

Still, in every country we visited, foreign leaders expressed grave concerns about what a hypothetical Trump presidency might mean for the world, especially given the man's anti-Muslim commentary.

"There's no reason to fret," Texas senator John Cornyn told a group of diplomats in the region. "Trump was loud and unpredictable to win the primaries, but his tone will start changing for the general election. He'll calm down. You'll see."

The cowboy boots poking out from under the senator's khakis spoke louder than his words, as if to say, *Trust me, I'm from the land of rodeos.*

This is all part of the show. But was he reassuring them, or himself? None of us actually knew whether Trump would moderate his tone.

In late May, former New York City mayor Rudy Giuliani reached out for help with exactly that topic. He was having conversations with Trump and wanted the presumptive nominee to adopt more traditional GOP policy positions before the general election race, starting with reversing his crude comments about Islam. Giuliani asked my boss— House Homeland Security Committee chairman Michael McCaul— and me to assist.

Early in the campaign, Trump had shocked the world by calling for a "Muslim ban" on travel into the United States, falsely equating billions of everyday Muslims with the small population of terrorists who perverted the religion to justify violence. As a counterterrorism professional, I feared Trump's words would be exploited by militants to convince others that we were at war with Islam. As an American, I found his words disgusting. Most worshippers of Islam were just like Christians, Jews, or Hindus—people of faith who practiced their religion peacefully.

Giuliani convened an ad hoc group (including former U.S. attorney general Michael Mukasey, Chairman McCaul, and former prosecutor Andy McCarthy) to draft a memo to get Trump to stop saying "Muslim ban" and to talk about reasonable counterterrorism policies. While I didn't agree with everything in the document, the final draft condemned Trump's comments and rightfully made clear that a Muslim ban would "run afoul of our constitutional principle against religion-based discrimination," emphasizing to the candidate that most Muslims who came here were "patriotic and productive Americans . . . precisely the kind of immigrants our policy should encourage to come to the United States." In place of a ridiculous "ban," the memo proposed "intensified vetting" of U.S.-bound travelers to weed out the real terrorism suspects. Giuliani briefed Trump.

To our surprise, it worked. Donald Trump never said the words "Muslim ban" again on the campaign trail, although apparently the word "intensified" wasn't enough for him. He began to talk about "extreme vetting" and how he would implement harsh measures to keep terrorists out of the United States. While I wasn't sure he really understood what we wrote, I was buoyed to see he was shifting back toward the mainstream. Maybe Trump could be guided after all.

The relief was fleeting. When Paul Ryan released his forward-looking GOP agenda in June, Donald Trump accepted it like a buzzsaw accepts timber. He had no interest in policy nuance, crafting an optimistic Republican Party, or restraining his antagonistic tendencies. Within days, Trump attacked a federal judge who ruled against him in a fraud case as "biased" because of his "Mexican heritage." Ryan rebuked the GOP nominee's words as the "textbook definition of a racist comment," and after that, any hope that Trump would listen to Speaker Ryan faded.

Our Make Trump Better plan was dead.

"Maybe there is no hacking!"

My consolation that year was the feeling of certainty that Donald Trump would never, ever be president of the United States. It was October 9, 2016, the night of the second presidential debate, and I watched it with my girlfriend Anabel in our row house on Capitol Hill. Anabel wasn't in politics—she was a Southwestern transplant to D.C. who worked in banking—and her tolerance for sleazy politicians was even lower than mine. With a fire roaring in our exposed-brick fireplace, we mocked the GOP candidate's meandering performance.

There was good reason to think Trump's campaign was finished. As he roamed the town hall stage that night like a caged animal, he gave us another. During the debate, Donald Trump angrily denied Moscow was behind ongoing interference in the 2016 election, and that the interference was even happening in the first place. Trump was lying to the American people. I knew it because I'd helped brief him on the threat days earlier.

Russia's plot consumed me throughout the election. In mid-2016, an urgent bulletin sent to Capitol Hill from a U.S. security agency flagged a disturbing development: foreign actors might be launching digital attacks on the 2016 election, including cyber intrusions targeting U.S. political figures and institutions. The alert didn't identify the culprit, but within days, I arranged briefings for members of Congress to get the details.

The DNC announced weeks later that it had been hacked by Russia. My worry grew, in part because Moscow was breaking into a U.S. political party but also because one of the two major candidates in the election was seemingly ambivalent about it. Trump accused the DNC of making it up and then publicly goaded the Russians to hack the emails of his opponent, Hillary Clinton.

A fellow GOP aide on Capitol Hill, Evan McMullin, found Trump's behavior so offensive that it inspired him to quit his job and actually challenge Trump. The forty-something foreign policy advisor announced he was running for president as an independent, a quixotic last-ditch attempt to block the Republican nominee. Evan and I had come up in the GOP around the same time. We entered government service after 9/11 and both were convinced someone in our party would emerge to counter Trump. When no one did, Evan told me he had no choice but to do it himself, even if the odds were impossible.

The "Never Trump" movement had gone from the majority of the party to a small, faltering faction led by a no-name congressional staffer. Evan asked if I wanted to join his campaign. I gave him the reflexive excuse that I could be more effective from inside the party than outside of it. In truth, by then I'd concluded that Hillary Clinton was the only way to end Trump's candidacy for good.

Then in the summer and fall, Russia leaked emails and released disinformation to undermine Clinton. Both Trump and Clinton were briefed on the very sensitive intelligence about Moscow's ongoing operation. Yet Trump continued to dismiss it.

A handful of congressmen asserted themselves in Trump's orbit to get him to wake up, including my boss, House Homeland Security chairman McCaul. He agreed to prepare the nominee for the presidential debates in September and October 2016. Beforehand, I pulled together in-depth briefing materials for McCaul to take with him—background, charts, maps, talking points, the works.

Our singular goal was to get Trump to admit that America was under attack and to warn Russia that they would face our wrath.

At the debate prep, McCaul walked through the details. He assured Trump that the information about Russia was valid, that we'd been briefed on it for months, and that it was critical for Trump to publicly acknowledge the situation and vow that—regardless of who the Russians were trying to support—the United States would punish them. My dial-in connection was unsteady, so I phoned McCaul afterward to see how it went.

"Not good." The chairman recounted Trump's visceral reaction. "He didn't want to hear it."

The candidate interrupted McCaul repeatedly.

"It's all bullshit," Trump allegedly retorted, waving his hands dismissively. "Totally politicized bullshit, right Mike?"

Trump turned to another Michael in the room, Lieutenant General Michael Flynn, the former head of the Defense Intelligence Agency, who'd been forced out of his job for alleged misconduct and was now a Trump campaign advisor.

"You're right, sir," Flynn affirmed. "It's politicized, intelligence community BS."

McCaul tried again, but Trump ended the conversation.

Days later, the candidate lied in the presidential debate about what he knew.

"I don't think anybody knows it was Russia that broke into the DNC," he said. "[Clinton is] saying Russia, Russia, Russia . . . but it could also be China. It could also be lots of other people. It also could be somebody sitting on their bed that weighs four hundred pounds, okay?" He went further in the second debate, suggesting that the cyber breach might not have happened at all. "Maybe there is no hacking!"

The falsehood was sickening. Trump knew the truth, so why was he covering for one of America's adversaries, Vladimir Putin? Another controversy erupted at the same time. An old video recording surfaced of him making denigrating comments about women, sending his campaign into free fall. It was time to stop "managing" Trump within the party and start maligning him. This was the opening I'd been waiting for.

While on a road trip through the New Mexico desert a few days after the debate, I called and texted GOP members of Congress to encourage them to turn against the nominee. Now was the time to distance themselves from Trump's campaign or, better, to un-endorse the candidate altogether. Of course he wouldn't win the presidency, and if we didn't isolate him, we'd be associated with his lies and toxic politics for years to come.

"There's an awful lot of reasons to rescind your support," I texted one legislator, trying to convince him to ditch Trump. "Politically the scandals are destroying his chances and folks are going to use this as a litmus test in the future, i.e. 'what did Representative XX do when he had the opportunity to rescind his endorsement?' But the most compelling one is that it's probably the right thing to do."

The congressman said nothing.

The next day, he sent a meme of three faces and three quotes: former president Franklin Delano Roosevelt ("The only thing we have to fear is fear itself"), John F. Kennedy ("Ask not what your country can do for you but what you can do for your country"), and Trump ("Grab them by the pussy"). To him, it was funny.

While some Republicans denounced the nominee's comments, most quietly stood behind Donald Trump in the end. I couldn't understand why. Until he won.

"Sure, he's a dick, but now he's *our* dick."

Everyone remembers election night 2016 and the shock of Trump's comeback victory. But what I remember is the gloating, specifically from one GOP representative.

A Southern legislator leaned against a gold railing on the House floor several days later, trying to convince me Trump wouldn't be so bad. The party would benefit from his brash antics, the congressman reasoned. Trump would keep the pressure on "the libs."

"Sure, he's a dick, but now he's *our* dick," he quipped, ebulliently.

The vodka-soaked frat culture of Capitol Hill was already making me feel disillusioned, but the state of denial in the party was worse. The same people who had equated Trump to an "evil force" were now giddy about the prospect of a drain-the-swamp disruptor in the White House. After sneaking away to celebratory happy hours, congressmen would return to the House floor smelling like booze. During votes, they passed out their ID cards so someone else could register the "yeas" and "nays" for them. They were too busy to vote, placing bets on which of them would end up in the new president's cabinet.

Then came the pilgrimages to Trump Tower. To be fair, some sober-minded Republicans hoped to convince the incoming president to re-cruit serious leaders and statesmen and -women to replace the island of misfit advisors he'd assembled. But far too many alighted from the tower's golden escalator to pitch themselves for top spots.

One of them, Congressman Mike Pompeo, had just been picked to be CIA director and reported back confidently that Trump wasn't look-ing for "yes men." I hoped he was right. More so, I hoped people like Pompeo—who'd been blunt about his disdain for Trump—would serve as a check on the man.

I flew up to New York with a delegation of GOP figures a week later, in late November 2016.

Kellyanne Conway greeted us like a carnival barker welcoming circus-goers into a tent, as a gaggle of current and former officials came and went; Steve Bannon glad-handed donors in a corner, grinning ear to ear; General Flynn quietly escorted foreign visitors out, offering hushed farewells and promising to be in touch; and Ivanka and Jared made a brief appearance with an air that said, *The family is in charge.*

I squeezed onto a couch next to former vice president Dan Quayle, who brought ideas to help the untested president-elect think about gov-erning. The atmosphere was too surreal to ignore.

"Did your transition look like this?" I asked.

He scoffed and whispered from the side of his mouth: "No. This place is a fucking circus." Exactly what I was thinking.

If it were a circus, Vice-President-Elect Mike Pence was the ticket boy, dutifully shuttling back and forth to the waiting area to tell another newcomer it was his or her turn to enter the lion's den. We were next. Clutching policy papers on national security, Chairman McCaul and I were ushered into a meeting room.

Donald J. Trump—Secret Service codename "MOGUL"—was in full form. The braggart chief executive had just closed the biggest real estate deal of all time: the acquisition of the White House. An oversized suit jacket and wrinkled pants hung over his large frame, accented by a red necktie that dangled too far below his belt line.

"Look at that! Isn't it beautiful? *Just. Beautiful.*"

He waved his hand at a map of all the counties he had won across America, as if the congressman and I hadn't seen the results. A sea of red with occasional pockets of blue. The conversation never got to counterterrorism or cybersecurity; Trump wanted to talk about how much of a winner he was and how he was going to bring other winners into the new administration.

An aide escorted me out to meet with a staffer on the transition team. I introduced myself and started to talk about the national security issues the incoming president would need to start thinking about. He cut me off. We weren't there to talk about policy. He wanted names. Which prominent figures from Capitol Hill would be loyal lieutenants to the incoming president?

"Loyal," he repeated.

I had brought a list with me, but it wasn't a list of congresspeople. The legislators I knew weren't showing backbone, so I handed over a spreadsheet of leaders who I thought actually had character. The staffer crossed out most of the names. "Bushie," he said. Another. "Never Trumper."

"John Kelly?" he asked, stopping at a name on the list. "You think he's experienced enough to be defense secretary?"

"He's a four-star Marine general," I replied. Kelly had met with Trump recently, and I had been floored that serious people were being considered at all.

"We'll see," the aide responded.

We were interrupted. McCaul's meeting was over, and Pence was ready to walk us out. On the elevator ride down, the vice-president-elect gave us a knowing look. He'd seen others leave with the same worried faces, the type that commuters make when passing a fiery roadside crash.

"It's going to be all right," he offered. "Here's my personal information if you need anything." Pence handed me a scrap of paper with a mobile number and an obscure Gmail address scrawled on it.

"It's not as bad as it looks. It's a hell of a lot worse."

These aren't the words you want to hear from your soon-to-be boss. Yet John Kelly stated them matter-of-factly. It was March 2017. He'd been serving for two months as Trump's Homeland Security secretary. The job I'd hoped he'd take—running the Pentagon—had gone to another man I regarded as a rare living legend, General Jim Mattis.

Kelly dealt with a flurry of crises after taking office, including Trump's surprise executive order blocking millions of people from Muslim-majority countries from coming into the United States. The shock order certainly looked like the "Muslim ban" we thought we'd talked Trump out of. Worse still, Trump didn't consult John Kelly or other agency heads before releasing it. The results were disastrous.

At the time, I was still on Capitol Hill and asked Chairman McCaul to condemn the policy. It was highly unusual for a top Republican to criticize a new president from his own party, only days into the administration, no less. But McCaul agreed. He called on the Trump White House to roll back the executive order, using my words to admonish them: "Don't undermine our nation's credibility while trying to restore it."

I was wary of any job in the administration and turned down a White House post during the transition period. However, I admired Kelly. The plainspoken, no-nonsense operator wasn't interested in partisan politics. He was one of the leading military figures of his generation and the highest-ranking officer to lose a child in the wars in Iraq or Afghanistan. He continued to serve despite the family's loss.

If anyone could be a check on Trump, I hoped, it was hardened soldiers who tended to be immune to politics and wary of unlawful orders. Word got out that Kelly needed more people to bring order to the chaos at DHS. I was open to working for one of the "adults in the room," though a breakaway part of my conscience argued otherwise. Anyone could see this wasn't going to end well. I buried the internal dissent under layers of careful reasoning about how "good people" were going inside to do what was right.

By March, I'd come around. I accepted a position as Kelly's counterthreats and intelligence advisor. I was just entering my thirties and would be the youngest counselor on his team. Days before I was slated to take the post, another crisis hit. A man jumped the fence at the White House and evaded Secret Service agents for seventeen minutes before he was caught. Trump was furious at the breach, and so were members of Congress from both parties.

Kelly was called up to brief the House Homeland Security Committee, and I waited to catch him in the hallway before he went in to see the representatives.

"Leatherneck inbound," an agent whispered into his sleeve. The Secret Service codename—an old slang term for U.S. Marines—captured Kelly's aesthetic perfectly. As he rounded the corner, he had the imposing presence of a general, and his face was carved with weathered battle lines that spoke as loudly as his record.

We were in a secure facility several stories underneath Congress. No cameras, no reporters. While I was still technically working for the room of angry congresspeople, I would soon be one of Kelly's deputies, and I felt an obligation to brief the man who would be my boss about what he was walking into.

"Mr. Secretary, they're frustrated—not just about the White House intruder," I warned him. "Democrats are probably going to grill you about the president's missteps on everything else."

"That's okay. It's not as bad as it looks," Kelly responded. "It's a hell of a lot worse."

I laughed. "I'm not sure I'd frame it that way in the room, sir." Kelly wasn't joking.

He patted me on the shoulder. "I've got this, Miles. Hang back for a minute afterwards, okay?"

The briefing went as expected. The secretary played security camera footage of the intruder scaling multiple fences, dodging sensors, and taking advantage of a comedy of errors as Secret Service agents tried to locate him before he nearly made it inside the president's residence. Kelly announced that he was boosting protection at the White House complex until long-term corrective action was taken, starting with a request for Congress to give him more money for a bigger fence.

The representatives were unified in their concern over how easily the guy had entered one of the most high-security facilities in the world. If he'd detonated a bomb, God forbid, he could have destabilized the entire federal government.

Representative Bennie Thompson pressed Kelly: "How could this happen?" (Incidentally, Thompson would be asking the same question years later while investigating a far bigger breach of the U.S. Capitol.) Before long, attendees were off-topic and the meeting devolved into partisan bickering.

Kelly was the first Trump lieutenant to brief the group, and Democrats in particular were still coming to terms with a whiplash White House. Trump's preposterous travel ban; his denial of Russian election interference; an obsession with a hulking concrete "border wall"; already frosty relations with Congress; and his apparent disregard for his own cabinet. Republicans jumped in to defend the president, though most barely knew the man.

Kelly calmly told the representatives that everything was copacetic. There was an adjustment period in every new administration, and President Trump *was* taking the advice of his team. The general understood the importance of this assurance. Skeptics of Trump were only comforted by the hope that the businessman would somehow assemble a credible cabinet, a group of grown-ups who would provide stability in the executive branch.

Then another topic came up.

Days earlier the administration had made a cryptic announcement that carry-on laptops would be banned on certain flights to the United States from several Middle Eastern countries. What was happening? Members of Congress demanded to know, reminding John Kelly that we were sitting in a secure environment and could discuss sensitive issues. For the first time, Kelly looked uncomfortable. He demurred, offering up only the fact that the decision was based on "evaluated intelligence" that he hoped to share at the appropriate time.

A buzzer screeched from behind the members of Congress and lights flashed on a wall clock. It was time for votes on the House floor. The meeting was over.

As the room cleared, I waited for Kelly. I told him that he had handled the back-and-forth well.

"You still on board?" he asked with a grin.

"Yes, sir. But you spooked me on the way in," I joked.

"About that . . ." The secretary's smile faded. He lowered his voice. "I want you to know something. I swore an oath to protect this country against enemies foreign and domestic. Foreign and domestic, Miles. You'll be doing the same by joining my team. Take it as seriously as a heart attack, okay?"

"Yes, sir, of course," I affirmed.

Kelly waited a beat before his face lit up again. He reminded me that I had one day of freedom left. "Don't fuck it up."

The secretary disappeared down the hall followed by staff, agents with earpieces, and a military aide carrying a black briefcase, leaving only silence in his wake.

I closed up the briefing room by punching in a code, sealing the vault-like door, and spinning the lock. The hallways were empty. The House was a vacuum that hoovered up bodies from around the Capitol when it was time to vote. I headed that direction, returning above-ground through a maze of passageways, staircases, and elevators, thinking about what the general had said.

Foreign and domestic.

PART II

The American system was designed to prevent a tyrant (or, more specifically, a would-be king) from becoming president. With the heavy-handed British monarchy fresh in their minds, the Founders wrapped a protective layer around the U.S. executive branch. They placed strict legislative and judicial checks on the presidency, curtailed the president's powers, and put a four-year term limit on the office. Most importantly, they designed a presidential selection process that was meant to block bad leaders from winning.

The emergence of fringe politicians was inevitable. "The latent causes of faction are thus sown in the nature of man," James Madison wrote, and have "divided mankind into parties, inflamed them with mutual animosity, and rendered them much more disposed to vex and oppress each other than to cooperate for their common good." Rather than try to fix this ugly side of human nature, Madison proposed using it to help *protect* democracy.

Put another way, warring factions could be pitted against each other as a check. In small societies, political movements tended to merge and trample the rights of the minority, Madison wrote. However, in a country as vast as the United States, various parties and factions would have trouble combining forces, and instead they'd compete with one another, preventing any one group from becoming too powerful.

America's most famous anonymous author sought to reassure the people. The Founding Fathers wrote a series of unsigned essays to sell the public on supporting a new constitution, using the alias "Publius."

Under the pen name, Alexander Hamilton declared that "talents for low intrigue and the little arts of popularity" were not enough to get someone elected president. To capture the top job, a person would need to appeal to the country's broad swath of political groups. As a result, "it will not be too strong to say, that there will be a constant probability of seeing the [presidency] filled by characters pre-eminent for ability and virtue," he wrote.

In 2016, Hamilton was proven wrong.

THE LONG-TERM CONDITIONS ARE HIGHLY FAVORABLE FOR A VOLATILE POPULIST FIGURE—THE NEXT TRUMP—TO RECAPTURE THE WHITE HOUSE.

Our system of government allowed an observably unqualified man to win the U.S. presidency. Democracy's electoral guardrails were tested, and they failed. I witnessed the futile efforts of Donald Trump's early opponents as they tried to stop him and his breakaway MAGA faction, the naivete of a Republican Party apparatus that attempted to guide him, and the GOP advisors—like me—who hoped we could manage Trump on his way to inevitable defeat. That is not what happened. Trump won and held the White House for four chaotic years.

Afterward, many continued to think Trumpism was an aberration. When Joe Biden defeated the one-term president in 2020, it was supposed to mark the death of MAGA. Since that time, however, Trump-inspired candidates have popped up across the country, assumed party leadership positions, and taken control of an entire ecosystem of groups that shape the GOP's direction.

What began as a small faction within the party now commands the entirety of it. The MAGA movement—or Trumpism, which I use interchangeably—remains the fastest-growing political coalition in America, regardless of how damaged its namesake is. The coalition has been able to unify disparate groups of Republicans—Tea Party, libertarian, small business, establishment, Evangelical, and beyond. Various factions within the GOP no longer compete and balance each other out. They've been subordinated to Trumpism.

The prospect of a MAGA comeback in the White House goes far beyond the next presidential election. The electoral guardrails that were supposed to stop someone like Donald Trump from getting elected have not been hardened to prevent a repeat. They have been corroded. Far-right figures like Representatives Marjorie Taylor Greene and Lauren Boebert are now in the mainstream of the Republican Party, and they are using intimidation to silence remaining opposition, while persuading the masses to believe conspiracy theories that are tilling the fertile soil for a new crop of antidemocratic populists.

We have seen this story before in history, and it doesn't end well.

First, MAGA forces are purging internal opposition with striking efficiency.

One of the best checks against the emergence of a dangerous figure in a free society is the ambition of his or her opponents. Almost every senator, congressperson, or cabinet secretary I know in Washington has fantasized about becoming something more, namely the president of the United States. Most coyly deny it, but the glint in their eyes when they cross the threshold into the Oval Office betrays their true desires. The fact that scores of politicians are always considering presidential bids is good for our political system; their ambition makes the presidential contest more competitive and weeds out defective candidates.

This is how Trump should have been stopped. He faced a wide array of competitors more qualified to hold the nation's highest office, most of whom repudiated the New York tycoon. Nearly all observers expected the combined ambition of Trump's opponents to smother his candidacy. As we know, that didn't happen.

Today, we should have little confidence that the ambitions of moderate politicians will prevent MAGA acolytes from seeking and eventually winning the presidency again. Few dissenters remain in the party. Pro-Trump forces are silencing dissent and eliminating internal opposition using a three-pronged approach: threaten, defeat, and destroy. For hundreds of moderate Republican officials around the country who have been driven out of office or even into hiding, this has become a grim reality.

It starts with a warning.

Former GOP congressman Denver Riggleman, who was elected from Virginia in 2018, recalled that it felt like a hostage situation on the House floor. He was expected to support the MAGA movement, or else.

"As soon as I won, I realized what I'd gotten myself into," he shared with me. "I found that votes had nothing to do with policy but with complete loyalty to the president. I just found it amazing that [other representatives] were so subservient," while they privately mocked Trump as "probably high on meth," he said.

At first, Riggleman toed the party line. He campaigned as a Trump supporter and was a good soldier, following the guidance of party leaders. But one day, he decided to vote against a Trump bill that would throw the government into chaos by shutting it down. Riggleman was admonished by Republican leaders.

"I was told I would have a primary opponent," he said. The congressman shrugged off the threat and voted his conscience anyway.

Representative Mark Meadows, who eventually became Donald Trump's fourth White House chief of staff, aggressively confronted Riggleman on the House floor afterward with a foreboding message: "You're done."

Meadows was right. The next year, Riggleman lost the support of GOP leaders in his primary race—the same race he had won overwhelmingly two years earlier—and was defeated by a vocal Trump supporter who derided COVID-19 as a "phony" pandemic.

Why did he lose? I asked Riggleman.

"I refused to kneel at the altar of Trump," he responded plainly. "That is really what it comes down to."

★ ★ ★

The threat of political alienation is not enough for MAGA forces to keep the coalition in line. They are trying other tactics to intimidate opponents of Trumpism and discourage other dissenters from joining the rebel ranks. The ten House Republicans who *did* vote to impeach Donald Trump experienced this viscerally.

Several months before she was defeated in the Wyoming Republican primary, Liz Cheney told me that the fear of physical harm was working. Flanked by armed guards at a fundraiser, she said that Republican colleagues rejected Trumpism but were afraid to come forward after witnessing her experience. She was no stranger to Secret Service protection, given that her father had been vice president of the United States, but this was different. A security detail was not a mark of status for the Cheneys anymore; it was reflective of the fact that people were making violent threats against her family back in Wyoming, where she couldn't go out in public the way she used to.

Her fellow dissenters felt the same.

"You know, it puts you at risk," said Michigan congressman Fred Upton, who decided to walk away from a thirty-year career in Congress after his impeachment vote, "particularly when they threaten not only you—and I like to think I'm pretty fast—but when they threaten your spouse or your kids or whatever, that's what really makes it frightening."

Ohio congressman Anthony Gonzalez decided to quit, too, confessing to receiving threats and fearing for the safety of his wife and children.

In February 2022, I reached out to hundreds of former GOP officials to join a public statement condemning party efforts to silence dissent. More than 140 Republican leaders signed on. Many more than that declined.

A former U.S. congressman apologized that he couldn't add his name to the list, citing the fervor of MAGA supporters in his area.

"I can't do that," he lamented. "These people are fucking crazy."

Second, the takeover of the GOP apparatus is largely complete.

The people who opposed Donald Trump in 2016 are either gone or converted. The Paul Ryans of the Republican Party have been sidelined or have made their way to the exits, along with their illusions about breaking a populist wave with oceanic words about a big-tent party. The Trump inoculation plan failed. Today, the GOP that tried unsuccessfully to stop the man has been overtaken by his staunchest allies, all the way down to the precinct level.

"Trumpism has taken over the party machine almost entirely," one retired Republican congressman told me. "You have party chairs who cannot advance in their positions unless they pledge themselves to Trumpism." The former elected official had helped lead a libertarian insurgency in the GOP in the 2010s and regretted that the movement had been commandeered by the ex-president.

The evidence of a MAGA takeover of the Republican Party could fill several volumes. For example, GOP state legislatures are fervently advancing Trump-like agendas, passing extremist laws on everything from elections to abortion that were inconceivable only a few years ago. Previously mild-mannered policy wonks such as Representative Elise Stefanik now speak in a combative Trumpian tone. Even the adjacent Libertarian Party has been seized by MAGA-friendly operatives who scorn moderation and compromise.

Arizona is an illustrative case.

Donald Trump won the state by a few percentage points in 2016, but that didn't make it a MAGA safe haven. Home to longtime Trump critic and Republican U.S. senator John McCain, the Southwestern state is known for its political nonconformity. Arizona boasts as many independent voters as Democrats or Republicans. Trump lost the state in 2020, and when pro-Trump forces tried to overturn the election results, they were thwarted by election officials within their own party.

Bill Gates was one of them. The Republican (not to be confused with the Microsoft billionaire of the same name) was serving as supervisor for Maricopa County, the fourth most populous county in America. At fifty years, Gates still had the eyes of a kid who sported a "Reagan-Bush '88" shirt before he had car keys and who joined the college Republicans rather than thinking about pledging a fraternity. His folksy demeanor struck me as the mark of a man who took his local position seriously. No kid dreams of becoming county supervisor.

Gates was surprised to find himself at the center of a firestorm in November 2020. "The system held after the election," he explained. In his position, he was charged with overseeing Maricopa County's election procedures. Despite several days of uncertainty, public outcry, and a changing vote tally that kept the nation on edge, "the results got certified," Gates said. "And Joe Biden won."

Gates respected the results. Others didn't.

"Trump's allies started trying to get their hands on the ballots and the voting machines [after the certification]," he recalled, "and it took a very ugly turn."

Three phone calls changed his career forever.

The night of November 12, Gates was picking up food when a colleague rang to warn that his personal information—and that of the other county supervisors—had been released online, doxxed by Trump voters angered by the election results. Gates tried to lie low, but the hate mail arrived anyway. It got worse in the weeks that followed, as Trump claimed the election was stolen. Gates knew the allegation was false, at least in Arizona, where he'd personally overseen the voting procedures.

He hoped the anger would dissipate, but Arizona's GOP lawmakers were riled up by the outgoing president, including Congressional representatives Paul Gosar and Andy Biggs. They demanded an audit of the vote. State legislators agreed and wanted to get their hands on the raw materials themselves. The GOP-dominated assembly requested Maricopa County give up its voting machines, administrative passwords, and all ballots that had been cast in the November election as part of a "forensic investigation." Gates didn't believe he was allowed to hand over 2.1 million private ballots. If he did, surely there was a serious risk of tampering or manipulation.

The issue came to a head when Arizona Senate Republicans subpoenaed the Maricopa County Board of Supervisors, demanding that the request be fulfilled. The supervisors went to court to challenge the subpoena. Gates was cautiously optimistic that a judge would settle the issue definitively in the county's favor, leaving the votes alone while the political winds died down.

He got another call on January 6, 2021. This time, a friend in the business community phoned to report that armed protesters had constructed a full guillotine—a wooden structure for beheading criminals—on the grounds of the Arizona state capitol. The device was meant to send a menacing signal to those who were upholding Biden's victory.

"You gotta get out of your house," the friend told him.

Gates rented an Airbnb in Scottsdale.

"I moved my whole family. We took the dogs," he recalled. "They wanted us killed."

That night Gates, his wife, and his daughters watched the television coverage of what happened in Washington, D.C. as rioters stormed the United States Congress. The violence was real. Republican officials were being targeted by their own base for defying Trump's effort to remain in office. The Gates family remained cautious until Joe Biden was sworn in as president.

On Super Bowl Sunday 2021, they were back at their home. The beleaguered county supervisor planned to take a much-needed break from the smoldering controversy, which had put him at odds with long-time friends in the party.

Then one of his daughters called him.

"Dad, are you going to jail?" she asked after seeing a post on Twitter. In a bid to pressure the Maricopa County Board of Supervisors, state Republicans had drafted a resolution that would give the legislature power to arrest anyone who defied their subpoenas. What's more, the measure had the sixteen cosponsors it needed to pass. If Gates and his colleagues didn't hand over the 2020 ballots, they now faced the prospect of jail time.

Gates sprang into action to stop the bill before it was too late. After a flurry of behind-the-scenes calls and the release of an emergency public message to condemn the measures ("We shot a video here in my office," Gates noted, "and it was like a prison video"), they caught a break. One lawmaker decided to pull his name off the bill, effectively killing it.

"The State Senate came within one vote of jailing us," Gates mused. "We were thrilled we were not being detained, but we had real concerns that MAGA people would come to the house. . . . We were worried they'd come take us into custody on their own."

So that night two sheriff's deputies were dispatched to guard his home. Arizona Republicans were effectively at war with one another.

A judge ultimately ordered the Board of Supervisors to turn over the voting machines and the ballots. A person familiar with the case believes the judge privately agreed with Maricopa County—and didn't think there were legal grounds for an audit—but approved it anyway under pressure and fear that his family might also be targeted by the MAGA crowd if he didn't order the county to hand over the ballots.

Gates became a vocal critic of the review, earning him national attention—and scorn. He appeared before a U.S. congressional committee to speak out against the partisan audit: "This is without a doubt the biggest threat to our democracy in my lifetime."

The contractors hired to comb through the election results, known as the "Cyber Ninjas," were inexperienced. Yet right-wing social media viciously trolled Gates and others who tried to point out the review's failings. The final report released in fall 2021 was filled with unsubstantiated claims but no real evidence of widespread fraud. The election was free, fair, and accurate. Joe Biden had clearly won the state, and it was time to move on.

A year later, Bill Gates still didn't feel vindicated.

Sitting behind his desk in Phoenix—the same place he recorded the "prison video" to protest the legislature's power grab—Gates reflected anxiously on the future of the Republican Party. In recent primaries, MAGA types had defeated GOP moderates up and down the Arizona ballot. Normally the state GOP apparatus stayed out of hotly contested primaries, letting voters decide the party's direction. That wasn't the case anymore, Gates said.

"Now the party is putting its thumb on the scales," he explained at the time, noting that the Arizona Republican Party was openly favoring pro-Trump figures over centrist alternatives. "Even the people who aren't endorsed by Trump . . . are still falling all over themselves to be MAGA. The movement is permeating the entire party."

Is the intimidation working? I asked.

He thought for a beat and looked out the window, as if expecting someone to show up when I said it. "Anyone who would dare speak the truth to these people is in danger."

Third, much of the GOP base is now radicalized.

The state-by-state MAGA takeover of the Republican Party machinery will make it easier for the Next Trump to emerge. But the transformation of the GOP base is what will actually propel such a volatile figure into the White House. The increasingly reactionary views of grassroots Republicans virtually guarantee that the movement will maintain its dominant influence on the party for the foreseeable future.

A yard sign I saw in rural Pennsylvania tells the story. Driving through the Midwest during the 2020 presidential campaign, I saw planted in front of a house a homemade poster with the words RONALD REAGAN IS A LOSER written on it in bold. Former President Reagan's face was crossed out with an X, with Donald Trump's smiling face next to it. Presumably this was a Trump supporter, but why attack Reagan? The fortieth president was beloved by Republicans, not on the ballot, long dead, and certainly not a threat to Trump. The last assumption is where I was wrong.

Trump fixated on his predecessors and so did his supporters.

"You go around Pennsylvania and you see Trump signs everywhere," he once tweeted, proceeding to quote a supporter. "The Donald Trump situation is bigger than the Reagan Revolution. Donald Trump has inspired us."

The same year: "94% Approval Rating in the Republican Party, an all time high. Ronald Reagan was 87%. Thank you!"

And again: "Wow, highest Poll Numbers in the history of the Republican Party. That includes Honest Abe Lincoln and Ronald Reagan. There must be something wrong, please recheck that poll!"

To be seen as powerful enough to restore the country to what it was—to Make America *Great* Again—his identity requires that others see him as equal to, or greater than, those who came before him. I used to think such comparisons were a farcical insecurity. Now I believe Donald Trump was *understating* the comparison. In truth, there is no comparison. He created a cult unlike any of his predecessors, inspiring throngs of supporters to create deeply personal—sometimes spiritual—connections with his movement.

Tribalism is as strong as it's ever been within the Republican Party. Whether or not Trump remains the tribal leader, the power of group loyalty has radicalized the base. Tens of millions of people now believe conspiracy theories that are provably false, a reality that will shape the American political system in unknowable ways for many years to come.

In summer 2022, former Republican congressman Reid Ribble did a test. He was a founder of the Tea Party movement, though he was disillusioned by Trump. Speaking to a group of several hundred church-goers in Wisconsin, he decided to poll the congregation.

"How many of you believe the 2020 election was stolen from Donald Trump?" Ribble asked.

A sea of hands went up. It was almost the entire room. Ribble disguised his shock by shifting to a second question, which he hoped would cause most of the hands to go down.

"And how many of you believe Donald Trump is still the rightful president of the United States?"

Some hands dropped, but roughly half the room kept their arms in the air. It was worse than he had realized.

"Populism—in almost all of its historical iterations—tends toward authoritarianism," he told me. The test he did with the congregation reminded him of another dark period in history: pre-Nazi Germany.

In the 1920s, Adolf Hitler rose to power on a Big Lie. He alleged that Germany had been on the path to victory in World War I, but its leaders surrendered prematurely. Victory was seized from Germans by corrupt politicians, Hitler said. The people had been "stabbed in the back." In reality, the German military had been defeated and the country had no hope of winning the war; nevertheless, millions believed Hitler's lie amid the harsh conditions of postwar life, from political gridlock to inflation. Anxious Germans welcomed the rise of a disruptor who could upend the institutions they believed had failed them, which paved the way for Nazism.

"He created a whole class of victims," Congressman Ribble explained, "and then he told them he would vanquish the villain." Similarly, Ribble worries Trump's lies have created an opening for another dangerous leader. The untruths have created an angry and restless electorate.

In poll after poll, a majority of U.S. Republican voters say that Joe Biden was not the winner of the 2020 election—that it was stolen from Donald Trump. As one of the officials appointed by the Trump White House to oversee election security during his administration, I can confirm (once again) that this is entirely false. The 2020 election was the most secure in modern history. Yet such attestations have failed. In the aftermath of the Trump presidency, GOP-dominated legislatures in more than thirty states have put forward or passed measures to make it easier to interfere in the vote in the GOP's favor—teeing up the possibility of legal civil war in future elections.

This isn't the only falsehood reshaping the system.

The MAGA movement has promoted the QAnon conspiracy theory of an evil deep state running the government. An Economist/YouGov survey found that half of American Republicans now believe in core QAnon concepts, such as the assertion that a single group of people "secretly . . . rule the world" and that "top Democrats are involved in elite child sex-trafficking rings." In 2016 a man shot up a Washington, D.C., pizza parlor that he believed was used as a Democratic sex-abuse lair. GOP leaders have fanned the flames of these theories. The number three House Republican referred to Democrats as "pedo grifters" in 2022, and the party backed candidates who were open QAnon believers.

Likewise, millions of Republicans subscribe to the Trump-fueled "Great Replacement Theory." The conspiracy alleges that the Democratic Party is attempting to "replace the current electorate" of white Americans with "Third World" voters, as Fox News host Tucker Carlson claimed. A gunman cited this race-baiting theory in a manifesto before murdering nearly a dozen black Americans in a New York supermarket in 2022, not to mention the mass shooter who killed two dozen people in an El Paso Walmart in 2019, echoing Trump's words about an "invasion" at the U.S. southern border. An AP poll found nearly half of Republicans believed in the theory, while a University of Chicago poll found that tens of millions of MAGA supporters agreed with the statement that "African American people or Hispanic people in our country will eventually have more rights than whites."

It would be willful delusion to think these conspiracy theories won't have lasting repercussions. These highly motivated voters are hungry for MAGA candidates who share their views. And such views will not change overnight. The Next Trump will be a product of this beast because he or she will have to feed it to win, which means keeping the base radicalized on a steady diet of conspiracy theories about existential threats to their way of life.

"There's a soft totalitarianism coming into play," Michael Steele professed. He spent two years leading the GOP as chairman of the Republican National Committee. "Modern-day conservatism meant lower taxes, less government, free markets. What we are witnessing now is a deconstruction of that. . . . I think the rational side is losing, if not having already lost.

"For a party that's all sensitive about the Left canceling them, they do a pretty good job of canceling their own," he added. "That's why the hammer came down so hard on Liz Cheney—to send a message of fear. No one wants to be targeted the way she's been targeted, which makes this period we are in perhaps the most dangerous."

Observing what has happened to the party of Lincoln, we can make one conclusion with confidence: we've only seen the beginning of Trumpism. The rational faction of the GOP has been put down by the radical one and is no longer a check on the system. The conditions are right for the Next Trump to emerge. Worse still for our democracy, when he or she enters the White House, the rest of the guardrails will be weaker than ever.

Chapter 2

THE DEPUTY

Once an efficient national government is established, the best men in the country will not only consent to serve, but also will generally be appointed to manage it.

—JOHN JAY, FEDERALIST NO. 3, 1787

PART I

Today the Department of Homeland Security sits on a hill just outside of the nation's capital, a behemoth visible from the Potomac River. But the original Homeland Security headquarters was nestled in the sleepy D.C. neighborhood of Tenleytown, largely unnoticed by pedestrians. The network of interconnected brick office buildings had previously been a secret National Security Agency hub and, later, a naval research facility. After 9/11, it became the home of DHS and almost blended in with nearby American University, were it not for two layers of barbed-wire fence and a fleet of armored SUVs that regularly transited the premises, flashing red and blue lights.

I was awed to work there during the Bush administration, proudly swiping my badge each day to enter the compound. HQ was responsible for overseeing the department's nearly 250,000 employees—helping them do their jobs and protecting the American people by responding to everything from natural disasters to cyberattacks.

When I returned years later during the Trump administration, little had changed at the compound, except that now the government's third-largest department was more worried about *one* person than the many thousands in its ranks. DHS was in a constant battle with the president of the United States. I soon found out why.

"The 'adults' are winning."

The DHS Visitor Center was backed up when a group of anxious bureaucrats arrived on March 22, 2017. They cut to the front of the line at the magnetometers—shuffling past framed photos on the wall of President Donald Trump and the newly confirmed DHS secretary, John Kelly—and discreetly flashed blue badges at the guards. In my mind, the matching tote bags gave these spy community employees away. CIA, maybe NSA. They were clutching otherwise unremarkable nylon pouches with thick zippers and pick-proof locks, the kind used to deliver classified material to decision-makers.

Was it good news or bad news in the bags? The visitors' impatience suggested the latter. They vanished into the facility almost as suddenly as they'd arrived. Before long, I'd be on the receiving end of such deliveries every day.

Hours earlier, I had been sworn in to be John Kelly's top intelligence and counter-threats advisor, overseeing the vast efforts under way at DHS to catch violent extremists, root out foreign spies, and detect weapons of mass destruction (WMD). For now though, I was trapped in a mundane waiting area, watching a silent parade of public servants remove their belts and empty their pockets at the metal detectors. My own paperwork had gotten lost.

"We don't have a Miles Taylor in the system," the security guard had explained. "Please call your supervisor for guidance."

My boss's photo was hanging on the wall behind the guards. I imagined how they'd react if the secretary of Homeland Security himself came to get me. Instead I rang the personnel office to figure out what happened, and an hour went by before I got a call back. I was told it would be a while longer.

If I wanted to bail on the job, this was probably my last chance. An old mentor had reached out earlier in the week to ask me if I was sure I was making the right choice. Jim Kolbe had served as a congressman for more than twenty years in the House (until 2007) and was one of the rare Republican leaders to oppose Trump in the general election. To him, it looked as if only bootlickers were going into the administration, and I should keep my guard up. At a minimum, Jim told me I should carry a draft resignation letter at all times.

"Don't stay too long," the ex-lawmaker advised.

I assured him I was joining a team that understood the situation. Secretary Kelly was the right leader for DHS and would shield the department from Trump's never-ending political controversies. No draft resignation letter was needed.

I scrolled through Twitter while I waited in the Visitor Center, catching breaking news in my feed. A driver on the Westminster Bridge in London had just mowed down dozens of pedestrians before crashing into the gates outside the UK Parliament. Twitter users reported a nearby knife attack on police. Details were murky, but it looked like a terrorist attack in progress.

I got a call.

"Where are you?" Kirstjen Nielsen, the DHS chief of staff, was looking for me to brief the secretary on the attack.

She was flustered when I told her I was stuck at security, and promptly hung up. Minutes later an assistant from the secretary's office arrived on a golf cart and told the guards to let me through. They obliged. I was whisked into the complex, toward one of the many red-brick buildings, through several checkpoints, past a skeptical Secret Service agent, and beyond frosted-glass double doors. I was in.

The secretary's suite hummed with activity. A group of staffers huddled on phones and military aides moved purposefully between offices. Kirstjen emerged from their midst. Shoulder-length blond hair and not an inch taller than five-four, she wasn't exactly intimidating, unless you knew how seriously she took her job. I did. We had worked together briefly during the Bush years, and she had no tolerance for wasted time. She waved me impatiently into John Kelly's office, without a "How are you?" or "Welcome to DHS!"

"Hey Miles." Kelly greeted me from behind a large brown desk. "Whatta we got?" He and Kirstjen wanted the latest on the London attack.

I explained that I'd just arrived and only knew what I'd seen on Twitter—not from any intelligence reports, calls with law enforcement, or any official sources whatsoever.

Anything was better than nothing, Kelly said. He was expecting Trump's call any moment since this was the first terrorist attack in the West during his presidency. Kelly was worried Trump might pin the blame on Syrian immigrants, post about his Muslim ban, or criticize UK police for failing to stop the attack—none of which would be helpful and would probably cause a diplomatic rift in the middle of a crisis.

So I gave Kelly the latest information and my best advice: the suspects were most likely ISIS-inspired locals. Not operatives deployed from the Middle East (but we should talk to our UK counterparts before saying so). The president should call Prime Minister Theresa May and offer condolences and assistance. Not immigration critiques. And DHS should take the lead away from the White House so this looked operational, not political. We'd review the intel and reassure the public that we didn't see any imminent threat to America—if, indeed, that was true.

"Mr. Secretary," a military aide interrupted through the doorway, "the president is on the line." I stood up to leave, but Kelly motioned for me to stay.

"Yes, Mr. President," the secretary answered.

I could hear the irritation in Trump's voice on the other end. He was clearly itching to comment on the news. Trump didn't like waiting or being managed by staff when something was making headlines.

But he responded differently to John Kelly. The president was awed by military generals and listened quietly as Kelly briefed him on the situation, urged Trump to offer assistance to the British, and said the White House should let DHS take it from here. The president agreed.

After some back-and-forth, the call ended.

"Now go make it happen," the secretary told me. This is what I was hired for.

As the door closed behind me, I thought I should have asked where my desk was. I was greeted by a smile that seemed to anticipate the question. Elizabeth Neumann, the deputy chief of staff, gave me a warm hug.

"Heeeyyyy! Welcome. We're so excited you're here!" She offered an impromptu orientation around the office.

The blond Texan was the type you see in the movies who proudly says, "I serve at the pleasure of the president." Only in Elizabeth's case, she had known what she was walking into, understood that the president was unsteady at best, and had spent weeks since the inauguration expertly putting out fires. Nonetheless, she remained optimistic that these were just the growing pains of a new administration and that Trump could be tamed, eventually.

Six of us were appointed to help the secretary lead DHS: the chief of staff (Kirstjen Nielsen), two deputy chiefs of staff (Elizabeth Neumann and, soon, Chad Wolf), and three senior counselors—one for border and immigration (Gene Hamilton), one for cybersecurity (Chris Krebs), and one for threats and intelligence (me).

We shared important similarities. All of us were former Bush officials (a rarity in Trump's world, since the president hated "Bushies"), and we all acknowledged that our biggest challenge wouldn't be tornados or terrorist attacks, but Trump himself. He was more fixated on DHS than any other department in the federal government, because of his immigration priorities. Dealing with his impulsiveness in the coming months would forge us into a close-knit family, for a time anyway.

Elizabeth took me to the "bullpen" to meet my fellow counselors. Gene Hamilton, the border advisor, greeted me while on mute during a conference call.

"Howdy, my friend," he offered in a genial Georgia drawl. The tall, mid-thirties lawyer had previously worked for Senator Jeff Sessions on Capitol Hill, and his reputation as a bureaucracy-busting immigration hardliner stood in contrast to his upbeat attitude and Southern charm.

Chris Krebs, the cyber advisor, had a different energy. Fresh out of Microsoft, his surfer-swoop hair was closer to Silicon Valley than Washington, D.C., while his zero-to-sixty attitude about everything had earned him the nickname "Catastrophe Krebs." Until our offices were ready, he and I shared a tiny workspace. He could tell by my face that I didn't think we could both fit inside the matchbox of a cubicle.

"How's your first day?" Chris asked. I told him what had just happened with Trump and the frenetic terrorism briefing based solely on what I'd read on Twitter. He looked at me knowingly, like he'd seen it a thousand times.

"Ride the wave, man," Chris advised. "Ride the wave."

Back in Elizabeth's office, she filled me in on the dynamics between DHS and the White House. Yes, it was more erratic on the inside than it looked. But General Kelly was taking charge.

For instance, Trump's right-wing strategist, Steve Bannon, had recently been appointed to the National Security Council (NSC)—the body that advises U.S. presidents on matters of war and peace. The NSC was no place for political hacks. Kelly had teamed up with General Mattis at the Pentagon to reverse the decision, Elizabeth explained, and it would soon be announced that Bannon was being kicked off the NSC.

Even on immigration, the secretary was having a positive impact. Kelly told the president that it was impractical to build his wall "from sea to shining sea," and a few weeks ago, the General had traveled to Mexico with Secretary of State Rex Tillerson to make sure Trump's bluster didn't blow up relations with our neighbor. The president had been teasing "mass deportations" and unspecified "military operations" at the border. Much to the relief of Mexican officials, Kelly and Tillerson denied that any such actions were planned.

Of course there was the ongoing Russia investigation. Trump's behavior toward Vladimir Putin vexed everyone, including Kelly, who worried we didn't fully know whether the Trump campaign had colluded with Moscow or not. A lot of us were acquainted with FBI director James Comey and trusted him to run an impartial investigation.

A briefer with a courier tote knocked on Elizabeth's door. I noted his impatient expression (bad news in the bag).

"What is it?" she asked.

The man seemed unsure if he should say. He mumbled two words reticently in my presence. Her face fell.

"I have to kick you out for this. Codeword clearance only." She could tell I was put off. I was supposed to be the intelligence advisor, after all.

"Don't worry. You'll be 'read in' soon, and you'll wish you hadn't been."

I spent the rest of the afternoon handling the response to the UK terrorist attack. There were no off-the-wall presidential tweets about the crisis, and to my surprise, the White House followed our cues, just as Kelly had requested. After I spoke to my British counterpart on the phone and reviewed a threat assessment, we put out a statement that DHS didn't see any reason to change America's security posture. We would help with the investigation and remain vigilant.

That evening we gathered in the secretary's office. Me, Gene, Chris, Elizabeth, Kirstjen, and Secretary Kelly. In honor of my arrival, they opened a bottle of mescal, given to Kelly by Mexican officials weeks earlier.

He raised a glass of the smokey spirit and toasted—to me and "to another day of dodging bullets."

Not long after starting, I caught up with a reporter friend. We sat outside drinking cocktails not far from the White House, enjoying unseasonably warm April weather. I confidently told her there was an "Axis of Adults" emerging inside the Trump administration—comprised of Kelly, Mattis, Tillerson, and others—who were keeping it on track. She pushed back gently.

"They know what they're up against?" she asked.

"They realize this is a tumultuous White House," I explained, "and they are serving as a leveling influence over fractious personalities . . . protecting the country from enemies both foreign and domestic."

The reporter ran a story in the *Daily Beast*—"New Power Center in Trumpland: The Axis of Adults"—and asked to use the quote. I agreed, hoping others would take comfort in knowing it wasn't all chaos in Trumpland. In hindsight, I was probably sending the message to a few particular people—like the mentor who'd reached out to warn me against going into the administration. And maybe, I was still trying to convince myself.

Steve Bannon's recent removal from the NSC, the reporter wrote, should be "seen as a sign the 'adults' are winning."

The job was all-consuming. I returned home most nights after my girlfriend Anabel was already asleep, and left before she awoke, so I took to staying in the guest bedroom. DHS personnel transformed it into a miniature secure facility, complete with a special phone to reach me during emergencies. I fell asleep easily in those early days knowing I'd made the right decision. The Trump administration was starting to function, thanks to capable deputies who knew how to run the government.

Like most bedtime stories, this turned out to be fiction.

"Watch your backs."

The helicopter banked left—hard—pushing me against the window. I gripped the armrests. We were low, so low that the downdraft spun up an artificial sandstorm in the Jordanian desert while we buzzed the ground. Another sharp turn, right. The seat belt revolted against my chest and waist, as inertia tried to yank my body out of the seat.

Distress flares erupted from the side of the aircraft. I could see the dazzling red fireballs out the window as they raced away from the helo, leaving behind thin smoke trails.

What had begun as a sightseeing trip was now one of the most turbulent flights of my life, and I'd volunteered for it.

"Wooohooo!" one of the copilots cheered in my headset after setting off another flare.

We were on a joyride, courtesy of King Abdullah II.

Secretary Kelly and I were in Jordan for sensitive discussions with the Middle Eastern monarch. At lunch I'd made a joke about taking a spin in the leader's rotorcraft. He was a pilot, and I knew he had state-of-the-art helos. The king flashed a mischievous grin. Thirty minutes later, two limousines pulled up outside the palace to take us to a helipad. Kirstjen shot me a sternly disapproving look, Kelly gave me a thumbs-up, and off we went.

A lot had happened in the two months since I swore my oath. But the most pressing issue on my plate had brought us halfway around the world to the desert. After I started, I got "read in" on some of the issues Elizabeth had warned me about, especially the panoply of terrorist threats. It was worse than I had imagined.

A few hours away from Jordan, in neighboring Syria, ISIS militants were plotting sophisticated global attacks. For instance, terror masterminds were designing bombs that could pass through security undetected and had already shipped packages with hidden explosives around the world to test the system, as a West Point counterterrorism report and law enforcement authorities revealed after several plotters were arrested.

Before our trip, I traveled to a secret facility outside of Washington to get up to speed.

A veteran spook—we'll call him Rob—boasted a lengthy career of putting bad guys in the ground, or "warheads on foreheads," as he put it. We sat in a room with a dozen television screens. Each carried a feed from somewhere abroad. Behind some of those cameras, I guessed, were warheads.

"Guys like you and I get asked, 'What keeps you up at night?'" Rob remarked. "For me, it's this," he motioned to the screens.

Rob shared details of plots that intelligence agencies were tracking. The schemes under way could rival 9/11, and that's just what we knew about. The reach of ISIS was far greater than al Qaeda, and we were in a real-life race against time to stop attacks that could hypothetically involve anything from chemical weapons and homemade drones to carry-on luggage bombs and vehicle-ramming attacks. The full magnitude of the danger covered me like an oversized gravity blanket.

The military was playing offense. DHS was expected to play defense. I remember calling the acting TSA administrator afterward to say, *I get it now.*

In the months that followed, I convened DHS leaders to wrestle with one particular plot that spanned multiple cells, multiple countries, and multiple attack vectors. We had only pieces of the puzzle, and I understood why John Kelly was hesitant to tell Congress or European allies too much. If the details got out, terrorists might speed up their plans before we uncovered the full conspiracy.

We were also cautious about telling the president too much.

The Oval Office wasn't the highly controlled environment I remembered from the Bush years. It was a crowded New York bagel shop. Donald Trump stood behind the counter chattering with disheveled patrons who ducked in and out, rushing between meetings and showing little reverence for the president's schedule or the regal decor lining the rounded walls. The president's notorious reputation as a gossip made us nervous to talk about classified information.

Still, he was the commander in chief. Stopping a complex international terrorist plot would require presidential powers, so we shared information and impressed upon Trump the sensitivity of it.

Thankfully the president avoided the topic in the press, but we chafed at the White House's private micromanagement. We logged hours and hours inside the Situation Room with Trump aides, debating what to do. DHS wanted to take swift action to elevate global aviation security across the board to prevent an attack, while White House staffers were worried about upsetting the airline industry. In Kelly's words, it was "time to stop admiring the problem" and do something—fast.

The secretary and I flew to the Middle East to meet with allies who understood the seriousness of the danger, including the Jordanians and the Saudis. They'd implemented their own heightened counterterrorism protocols in recent years. We sought their help with the spiderweb of lethal threats.

Inside the helicopter over the Jordanian desert, the copilot came back on the radio.

"Are you ready to head back?" he asked. For the past twenty minutes, my answer had been yes, but the Jordanians were obviously proud to show off the aircraft.

Back on the ground, the king gave me a high five, smiling behind aviator sunglasses.

"Thank you, Your Majesty," I offered.

"No, thank *you*!" He laughed. These weren't Jordanian helicopters. They were American ones, funded by U.S. support to the kingdom.

The relationship was hardly one-sided. As I learned in future meetings with King Abdullah, the Jords were willing to take enormous risks for us and had lost lives gathering the kind of information used to protect Americans from groups like ISIS. They had our backs.

Former soldiers known for their integrity, Kelly and the king wordlessly understood the somber bond. We left the royal compound as the sun melted into blood-orange sand dunes, and I saw a handshake between the two men that was more valuable than any press conference or economic deal or helicopter. You couldn't put a price on trust.

After a stopover in Saudi Arabia to meet with the country's leaders, we returned home with a skeleton of a strategy to deal with the danger we were facing.

Tom Bossert, the president's lanky homeland security advisor, met us in Riyadh. He rode back with us on our modified air force 757, normally reserved for the vice president. Tom was known for lengthy philosophical conversations, and we got hours-deep into one, workshopping a counterterrorism plan for the White House. Aside from the pilots, he and I were the only people awake for the overnight flight.

I walked Tom through a proposal for how to deal with the threat, based in part on conversations with Middle Eastern allies. I referred to it as the Global Aviation Security Plan, or "GASP." The melodramatic acronym was fitting because it would be the biggest increase in airport security in years. Airlines and passengers wouldn't love it, but it would make it far more difficult for terrorists to advance their attack plots.

Would the president stand behind it?

Tom was typically circumspect in his commentary about Trump. He rarely criticized the president. But at thirty thousand feet, with everyone around us passed out, Tom was candid.

"Miles, the details don't matter to him," he admitted. "He is the most distracted person in the world. He has no fucking clue what we're talking about."

The president wouldn't read anything, Tom said, which is why we needed to take our jobs extra seriously. The next steps were up to us. The homeland security advisor admitted that he almost hadn't joined us overseas; Tom was worried about leaving Trump unsupervised. Something was going down back home, but he wasn't sure what.

We landed at Andrews Air Force Base, and the secretary's motorcade pulled up next to the plane. Kelly could tell I hadn't slept and told me to take the day off. I accepted the order.

Rather than nap, I spent the afternoon of May 9 with Anabel, taking advantage of a rare chance to decompress. We went to a lunch spot on Capitol Hill. On top of my slow-burn exhaustion, a glass of wine felt like three.

My work phone vibrated on the table. It was the secretary.

"Yes, sir," I answered.

Kelly had bad news. The president had just fired FBI Director Comey in an apparent attempt to obstruct the Russia investigation. The secretary had called Comey to express his disgust and, so far, was the only person in the cabinet to reach out to the director. Conditions inside the executive branch were worsening.

The wood-paneled room was tense while we waited for the secretary the next morning. A half dozen of us huddled with him at the start of each new day. When he finally entered the room, his face bore quiet anger and resolve.

John Kelly made his views clear. He thought the president's firing of Comey was undignified; he was deeply disturbed by how the White

House was operating, and he warned us: "watch your backs." He didn't know where this administration was headed, but he wouldn't allow political meddling inside his department. Going forward, we should be cautious about any White House intrusions into DHS business, he said.

"I'm the only person here who was confirmed by the U.S. Senate to run this department," he instructed, "and if someone at the White House tells you to do something, you tell them to have the president of the United States call me. He's the only person I report to. I'm the only person *you* report to. Is that understood?"

We all agreed.

Comey's firing loomed large over the month of May. The only person who seemed undisturbed was Trump, who tweeted gleefully. "Comey lost the confidence of almost everyone in Washington, Republican and Democrat alike," he wrote. "When things calm down, they will be thanking me!"

Perhaps not coincidentally, Trump was slated to meet the morning after the FBI director's removal with Russia's foreign minister, Sergey Lavrov, and the country's ambassador to the United States, Sergey Kislyak. Firing Comey and embracing the Kremlin in the same week felt eerie, if not sinister.

A few days later, I went to an event with a mix of national security officials. The outdoor bar near the White House was the same one where I'd persuaded a reporter the month before that there was an "Axis of Adults" inside the Trump administration. Incidentally, one of those Adults—Tom Bossert—rang my phone while I was sipping a cocktail.

The homeland security advisor wanted to give me a heads-up. When President Trump met with the Russians in the Oval Office days earlier, he apparently had chatted them up about the "great intelligence" he was getting and shared sensitive details with them about an ISIS terror plot. The news was about to be in the headlines everywhere, Tom warned.

Before I could tell the secretary, *The Washington Post* broke the story. The president had given "code-word information" to the Russians, a top official familiar with the episode told the paper. Trump "revealed more information to the Russian ambassador than we have shared with our own allies." In one meeting, the president had broken the trust of our international partners, possibly tipped off our adversaries, and put U.S. lives in danger. I needed to get back to the office.

"I may last a day . . ."

With the arrival of summer, whatever cautious optimism there had been inside the Trump administration burned off like water on hot asphalt.

Every few days, John Kelly and I descended into a secure room in the basement of DHS headquarters for virtual meetings. We spent a lot of time in these "SCIFs" (secure compartmented information facilities), on the phone with Secretary of Defense Jim Mattis, CIA Director Mike Pompeo, Secretary of State Rex Tillerson, and others, notionally to talk about threats to the country. By midyear, I had begun to dread the meetings. We spent less time talking about international developments and more time figuring out how to fix crises of President Trump's own making.

One day, he might insist that America pull out of the North Atlantic Treaty Organization (NATO), the defense alliance that is the backbone of U.S. security. Another day, it might be an errant demand to cancel a free trade agreement with a top ally Trump was mad at for a perceived slight, regardless of whether it might hurt the economy or create diplomatic upheaval.

After his first meeting with Russian president Vladimir Putin, for instance, Trump tweeted that he had made a deal with the Kremlin leader to jointly form an "impenetrable cyber unit" to protect elections. Let me clarify: Trump wanted to cooperate on anti-hacking with the very same man who'd just hacked the 2016 vote in the United States. It was like agreeing to host an anger management class with a serial murderer.

I showed Kelly the tweet.

The Secretary fumed. "I don't know what the hell he's talking about," he said. Our cybersecurity chief, Chris Krebs, was beside himself.

Secretary Kelly's mood began to change. I watched him at Trump's first cabinet meeting in June. One by one, the president went around the room to his deputies for an update, basking in their words of praise.

Vice President Pence said it was the "greatest privilege" of his life to serve Donald Trump.

White House Chief of Staff Reince Priebus waxed poetic about how the president's agenda was "a blessing."

UN Ambassador Nikki Haley gushed about the New York tycoon's "strong voice" on the international stage.

The two generals at the table, John Kelly and Jim Mattis, kept straight faces, declining to fawn over the president before, during, or after the meeting. When Trump turned to them expecting tribute, they said little about the man. Mattis praised "the men and women of the Department of Defense," while Kelly noted the honor of representing a "quarter of a million men and women that serve the country in DHS." Afterward, I told Kelly that two spectators would notice his choice of words: a grateful DHS workforce and a seething Donald Trump. He smiled.

Privately, deputies to the president were questioning more than just Trump's thirst for adulation. They worried about the commander in chief's mental state. Trump was becoming more irascible in meetings, lashing out at staff, frequently repeating himself, and displaying a maddening inability to focus.

On June 23, Kirstjen and I went with General Kelly to the White House for a series of meetings. Kelly, Mattis, and Tillerson planned to confront Trump about the creeping state of chaos inside the West Wing, and the scene that morning appeared to prove the point. Unable to get the conversation on track as aides darted in and out of the Oval Office, Secretary Kelly raised his voice, demanding that anyone who wasn't confirmed by the U.S. Senate needed to leave to room. Staffers shuffled out into the hallway where I was waiting, until the only people left in the Oval were the cabinet members.

The president bristled at criticisms of how the West Wing was run, Kelly later recounted.

"If it's so screwed up," Trump shot back at the general, "come fix it yourself."

It was at least the second time Trump had suggested that John Kelly become his chief of staff at the White House. The secretary declined, in addition to turning down Trump's request that Kelly take Comey's place as FBI director. Kelly reassured us he was closer to resigning than accepting a role at Trump's side, but someone needed to take command soon, or the ship would sink.

Trump's shortcomings stood out particularly during emergencies. I remember briefing the president in the Oval Office on the projected storm track of an Atlantic hurricane. At first, he seemed to grasp the devastating magnitude of the Category 4 superstorm, until he opened his mouth.

"Is that the direction they always spin?" the president asked me.

"I'm sorry sir," I responded, "I don't understand."

"Hurricanes. Do they always spin like that?" He made a swirl in the air with his finger.

"Counterclockwise?" I asked. He nodded. "Yes, Mr. President. It's called the Coriolis effect. It's the same reason toilet water spins the other direction in the Southern Hemisphere."

"Incredible," Trump replied, squinting his eyes to look at the foam board presentation.

We needed him to urge residents to evacuate from the Carolinas, where it looked like the storm would make landfall, but the president mused about another potential response.

"You know, I was watching TV, and they interviewed a guy in a parking lot," Trump leaned back and recounted. "He was wearing a red hat, a MAGA hat, and he said he was going to 'ride it out.' Isn't that something? That's what Trump supporters do. They're tough. They ride it out. I think that's what I'll tell them to do."

Sometimes his irreverence could be funny, even charming. That day it wasn't. Worried looks filled the room.

A clever communications aide piped up. "Mr. President, I wouldn't take that chance. This is going to be a pretty bad storm, and you don't want to lose supporters in the Carolinas before the 2020 election."

The president thought about it for a moment. "That's such a good point. We should urge the evacuations." You couldn't write such a stupid scene in a movie, but it always got a little worse.

The president told John Kelly that he wanted to take the Marine One helicopters down to the Carolinas to view the expected wreckage. The visual of him flying over leveled houses in a helicopter would be much cooler than him viewing the damage from a motorcade, he said.

"Mr. President," Kelly interjected. "We can't travel down that far on Marine One for this."

"No, no, no," Trump protested. "When I was in New York, I would take helicopters much, much further. I would take them everywhere. That's what we should do—we're taking the Marine One helicopters."

Kelly stated the obvious. "Sir, the helicopter can't carry your whole team. We don't travel that light."

Marine One held a handful of people. In contrast, when the president's motorcade was assembled in a new location, it included forty to fifty vehicles packed with staff, armed agents, and medical personnel in the event of an emergency. The image of squeezing all of that into a couple of helicopters was beyond cartoonish.

As Trump looked at the faces in front of him, he seemed to know the idea wasn't going anywhere. He couldn't pilot the choppers himself. Suddenly, he changed his tune.

"Actually, you know what, it's probably not a good idea to take them. Helicopters always break down. Do you know why?" The president paused and looked around the room for guesses. I shook my head. "Because there are too many parts!" he exclaimed. "That's right. It's true. Helicopters have too many parts, so they're always breaking down—it's *this* part, then it's *that* part, then it's *another* little tiny part. So we won't do it."

I felt secondhand embarrassment for the briefer in circumstances like this. He or she would stand there awkwardly waiting to get back on topic, while witnessing in person—often for the first time—how genuinely incompetent our president was. It was one of many reasons General Kelly was circumspect about who had access to Trump.

Word came down from the White House in mid-2017 to stop providing the president with lengthy documents. If there was a staple in it, the briefing paper was probably too long and needed to be cut. Fifteen-page updates on complex issues were chopped down to one. Bold fonts. *Simple words*. BIG pictures. Know your audience, they say, and the "audience of one" (as we called the president) had the temperament of a child, albeit a child with a finger lingering over the nuclear button.

We were forced to dumb down life-and-death decisions. Nowhere was this more relevant than on Afghanistan and Syria, two places Trump knew nothing about. The president was dismissive of his national security team's advice. He wanted out of foreign countries altogether, was eager to please the people who had applauded him on the campaign trail for saying so, and balked at the idea that he needed to give the concept of a massive U.S. military withdrawal any thoughtful deliberation.

Military leaders reminded Trump that he liked boasting about how hard we were fighting terrorists. Well, *Afghanistan and Syria* just so happened to be the places where we were fighting terrorists, they told him. If we pulled out too fast, extremist operatives would be able to carry out their plots with impunity, and Trump would get blamed for it by the public. The national security ramifications didn't matter to the president, but the political implications mattered to him a great deal.

I could tell that Trump's careless handling of military decisions weighed on General Kelly. Amid the internal debates, he made a speech in New York City about honoring U.S. service members. As Kelly spoke, I was sitting close to the stage, reviewing his written remarks, when I realized he was going off script. He brought up the death of his son Robert, who had been killed several years earlier by a land mine in Afghanistan.

The room went quiet.

When a parent loses a son or daughter in combat, Kelly explained, they are visited in person by a U.S. military casualty officer who delivers the news. In November 2010, there was a knock on John Kelly's door from his close friend, Joseph Dunford, who was then the number two of the Marine Corps. That morning General Dunford had volunteered to personally break the terrible news to Kelly and his wife Karen. As soon as they saw their friend's face at the door, they knew that it meant their lives would be forever changed.

"It's a kind of grief that is unbearable to the mind and antagonizing to the heart," Kelly recounted.

He had been on the other side of the doorway many times in the past, comforting families. In those moments, grieving mothers and fathers asked him whether the sacrifice was worth it—"worth the life of someone they brought into the world, raised and nurtured, and looked forward to seeing grow up . . . meeting husbands and wives . . . having kids of their own," he said. Kelly had felt ill-equipped to answer such a heartbreaking question without having experienced it himself. "I learned I was right," he said. Until he received the knock on the door himself, he had no idea how deep the grief could go.

The day Kelly buried his own son at Arlington National Cemetery, he described the feeling of emptiness in his heart. He arrived at an answer to the question other parents asked themselves in mourning. Was it worth it?

"Robert volunteered to risk everything—including himself—to serve our country," Kelly explained. "So was it worth his life? That wasn't up to me. My son answered the question for me."

When it came time to deliver options on Afghanistan, Kelly was worried that Trump was unprepared. The thick briefing memo that had landed on the president's desk was beyond the man's comprehension or reading ability, truly. I was asked to boil the fifty- or sixty-page document down to a page or two—in the president's voice. So overnight in my office, I stayed awake writing a Wikipedia-style 101 about why America was in Afghanistan and what was at stake, all in the Trumpian vernacular.

The title of the unclassified version felt like a parody: "Afghanistan: How to Put America First—*And Win!*" If we pulled out of the country too fast, I wrote, we would be mocked as "losers" by terrorists. If we wanted to be "winners," we needed to fight smarter and harder, then cut a "great deal" to hand over security to the Afghans. A career DHS expert helped me workshop the absurd document so that it sounded like Trump but also made sense from a national security standpoint, strident rhetoric notwithstanding.

The memo went to Camp David with the president for decision day. After hours of waiting, we got word. Trump reluctantly agreed with our recommendation to keep U.S. forces in place. He wanted to be "a winner."

Left unsaid in the memo was the solemn promise the U.S. government had made to the families of the fallen, like the Kellys. America had pledged to memorialize their service and sacrifice by ending the conflict, in due course, in the same spirit that their loved ones had fought and died: honorably. I couldn't figure out how to put that in Trump's words.

★ ★ ★

In July, Kelly told the president we were moving forward with the aviation security plan in response to the spiderweb of terrorist plots we were tracking. The White House was worried about the massive scope of the "GASP" proposal, spanning nearly three hundred airports in more than one hundred countries; I was more worried about going too slow, fearing that Trump's alleged comments to the Russians in the Oval Office might cause terrorists to accelerate their attack plotting. Kelly didn't exactly ask for permission and announced the far-reaching measures in a speech from a hotel in downtown D.C., televised live on the major networks.

Weeks later, the secretary's decision was validated. Authorities in Australia disrupted an ISIS plot to bomb an international flight with explosives hidden inside a meat grinder and to develop chemical weapons to kill civilians. Police revealed that the Sydney-based plotters were in touch with operatives in Syria. Our enemies were on the move, and we had to take decisive action to protect Americans.

With the GASP announcement out of the way, I felt like it was almost time to depart the administration. I told Anabel the job might kill me. After nearly six months of late nights and full-workday weekends, I was more exhausted than I'd ever been. The only way I could sleep was with a glass of whiskey (or two) before bed, and I was immediately saddled with an unshakable anxiety every morning when I woke up.

What would each day bring? I had push-alerts on my phone for all of the president's tweets. At any moment the posts could throw the day into turmoil, let alone the threats we read about in our daily intelligence briefings. John Kelly seemed to have adapted to managing Trump while also managing DHS. As long as I could find a suitable replacement, I decided I'd leave in the fall. Yes, it would be an early departure, but this place wasn't for me.

"This administration is a fucking nightmare," then deputy chief of staff Chad Wolf lamented late one evening. Neither of us had taken a proper day off since we started. In normal times, Chad appeared more like a TV actor than a DHS bureaucrat—high-and-tight haircut, five-o'clock shadow, and designer clothes. But we spent far more time in the office than at home, and it was starting to show. He looked gaunt.

At the end of July, Secretary Kelly told everyone to take a week off. I gladly complied, flying to a friend's wedding in Texas. That's where I got the phone call that changed everything. I was standing in my swimsuit at a water park outside of San Antonio embracing the warm sunlight when Kirstjen rang.

She said Kelly had just gotten off the phone with the president. Once again, Trump had appealed to him to come run the White House as chief of staff, an offer the secretary had rebuffed twice already. The secretary had decided to fly back early from the West Coast, where he'd been spending time with his family.

In the past, Kelly had told me there was "zero chance" he'd take the White House job. But, given how unstable the White House had become, Kelly wasn't dismissing the possibility this time. I had a bad feeling in the pit of my stomach.

For thirty minutes, our core front-office team was on a conference call to talk about it. Kelly tried to calm everyone down. He hadn't committed to the job, was fifty-fifty about the idea, and had convinced the president to discuss it first, man to man, in the coming days. Kelly would see if Trump was willing to do what was needed to restore order in the White House. I couldn't imagine Trump showing the discipline a four-star general would demand.

Then the president tweeted while we were on the call. We paused to read it.

"I am pleased to inform you that I have just named General/Secretary John F Kelly as White House Chief of Staff. He is a Great American . . . and a Great Leader. John has also done a spectacular job at Homeland Security. He has been a true star of my Administration." In a subsequent tweet, Trump fired his existing chief of staff, Reince Priebus.

A moment of stunned silence was broken by the realization that someone—Kelly, Nielsen, anyone—needed to call the White House immediately to figure out where the breakdown had occurred. Kelly hadn't formally accepted the job. If we acted fast enough, we might be able to put the announcement back in the box, which turned out to be another foolish miscalculation.

The president had appointed (ordered, really) his homeland security secretary to become his chief of staff, and the manner in which he'd done it was a forewarning of how John Kelly's tenure would play out.

★ ★ ★

The next day I was on a plane back to Washington.

I was crestfallen that the secretary was leaving DHS, but there was no time to complain or use in protesting it. I sent along ideas for what needed to happen in Week One at the White House, from personnel changes to suggestions for resetting bipartisan cooperation on Capitol Hill. I also wrote the secretary a parting note about the "turbulent moment" in which he was taking the job and how much we were counting on him.

I shared a Thomas Paine quote: "An army of principles can penetrate where an army of soldiers cannot." The president didn't need a general. He needed a conscience, and I told the secretary I hoped he'd be one for Trump.

"I may last a day or five years in this job," he wrote back, "but no matter [what], every day I will work hard to live up to your words."

Back in Washington, Kelly literally had only a handful of belongings to pack up to take to the White House. His sparse office symbolized the impermanence with which he viewed his role. I sat on the black leather couch in front of his desk watching him place a few items in a single cardboard box.

He threw me a parting "gift"—a pair of wacky socks that had been given to him by some visitor. John Kelly didn't wear wacky socks. The black stockings were emblazoned with white pineapples, a symbol of friendship.

"When it's time to do the right thing, don't get cold feet," he joked.

Three days after the tweet, our team drove to General Kelly's swearing-in ceremony, entering the White House gates in a somber procession of government vehicles. The atmosphere inside was subdued as we made our way to the Oval Office. White House staff who joined us—Steve Bannon, Sean Spicer, Kellyanne Conway, Anthony Scaramucci, and others—weren't enthusiastic either, worried how a new regime would affect their stature. Jared Kushner glared at the Kelly team from across the room.

Trump was the only buoyant person in the Oval. Proud of his latest acquisition and eager to show him off, the grinning president motioned for the general to say a few words. In a few moments, Kelly would no longer challenge him from outside the White House walls. He would loyally serve him right here, in Trump's mind, as a compliant deputy. I saw it differently. A good man was jumping on a grenade thrown by a bad one.

Kelly chose his words carefully. He reminded everyone in the room about the importance of swearing an oath to *the Constitution* instead of to a person. If we swore allegiance to a particular man or woman, he said, we'd be living in a despotism. Not a democracy.

With that, a black-robed judge in front of the Resolute desk asked the general to raise his right hand and led him through a civic ritual that felt like last rites.

Everyone who came with Kelly to the ceremony shared his view of the oath of office. He'd hired us for that reason. Kirstjen Nielsen, Elizabeth Neumann, Chad Wolf, Gene Hamilton, Chris Krebs, and me. We stood together feet from Donald Trump, united against the turbulence he was creating in the executive branch.

The unity wouldn't last. In the years to come, our group would fracture, as the commander in chief tested whether we were loyal to the Constitution—or to him.

PART II

The Founders intended for executive branch employees to be an internal guardrail for democracy. Although the chief executive was empowered to personally nominate the "assistants or deputies" to run agencies, the Senate would confirm them to ensure responsible leaders were picked. In addition, the Founders envisioned "the steady administration of the laws" by a workforce of duty-minded public servants who would faithfully operate the daily functions of government, regardless of who was president.

"The true test of a good government," Hamilton wrote under the pen name Publius, "is its aptitude and tendency to produce a good administration."

Donald Trump thoroughly dismantled this guardrail. He systematically sidelined or eliminated anyone who objected to his agenda or sought to restrain his impulses. By the end of four years, only the sycophants remained. It will be worse the next time around. In my interviews and conversations with former Trump officials, the most oft-repeated view was that a future MAGA administration would not be led by "the best men in the country," as Publius hoped, but by the worst.

THE NEXT TRUMP WILL INSTALL ONLY DEVOUT LOYALISTS IN TOP POSITIONS, WHILE PURGING DISSENTERS FROM THE EXECUTIVE BRANCH.

The MAGA movement learned a hard lesson in Donald Trump's first term: people are policy. The president appointed a vast array of public figures to key government posts, most of whom didn't know the mercurial businessman. And they certainly weren't willing to carry out policies that were plainly irresponsible, immoral, or illegal. In some cases, the internal resistance set Trump back years in carrying out his true intentions.

John Bolton saw himself as one of those people. The former ambassador agreed to serve as White House national security advisor partway through Trump's term. For a time, Bolton thought he was shielding agencies from Trump's disruptive mood swings and sudden changes in policy direction. But the more the ambassador objected to the president's bad ideas, the more he got left out of the conversation.

"There would be secret meetings at Mar-a-Lago on national security issues," a former aide to Bolton told me, "and [John] would call me and say, 'What the fuck is going on? Why am I not in this meeting?'"

Afghanistan was the tipping point. Trump was angry about the modest Afghan War plan we'd persuaded him to adopt in 2017 and returned to demanding a sudden pullout. He wanted to host Taliban leaders—the same people who'd harbored the al Qaeda terrorists responsible for 9/11—on U.S. soil at Camp David for talks just days before the anniversary of the tragedy. Bolton objected strenuously. Trump cut him out of the decision-making process, tweeted the summit into existence, and fired his national security advisor soon after.

Then Trump put in motion a hasty framework for exiting Afghanistan. What was the point, I wondered, of the months, the meetings, and the misery we had endured trying to get Trump to do the right thing, only to have him reverse the decision?

I put the question to Tom Warrick, the DHS civil servant who had helped me put together the infamous memo, "Afghanistan: How to Put America First—*And Win!*" Tom was less defeatist.

"We bought an extra two years of the United States staying [in Afghanistan] and killing terrorists and protecting the country," he said.

John Bolton agreed that moments like this—when staff persuaded President Trump to take the prudent course, even if only temporarily—bought just enough time to protect the country from the worst possible outcomes.

"The damage Trump did in the first term is reparable," Bolton told me.

But a second MAGA administration "would do damage that is *not repara-ble*, especially in a White House surrounded by fifth-raters," he predicted.

Nearly every Trump appointee I spoke with made a similar predic-tion. Another MAGA president won't hire a stable of experienced pub-lic servants. From the start, he or she will populate the administration with a "D Team" of political operatives who pledge allegiance to a cult of personality, not the Constitution.

"[Trumpism] is like a progressive disease," Bolton explained. "It might remit for a while, but it never gets better." Or as a Pentagon leader under Trump told me: "In Round Two, you won't see Jim Mattis and John Kelly. It will be the fucking enablers."

A future MAGA cabinet will be led by unapologetically un-confirmable figures and Trump look-alikes.

The U.S. Department of Veterans Affairs (the VA) is a prime exam-ple of an institution that will be targeted by the Next Trump. VA leaders were on the receiving end of withering White House pressure during the Trump years to manipulate the department's budget and programs for political purposes. While public servants fought back against the constant interference, the writing was on the wall: in a successor MAGA administration, America's veterans won't be so lucky.

"What the Trump folks wanted to do . . . was 'turn it upside down,'" recalled Tom Bowman, who served as Trump's deputy secretary of Vet-erans Affairs. Bowman explained that the White House wanted to push veterans into the private healthcare marketplace, a move that would potentially have left millions of vets out in the cold or abandoned amid a monumental bureaucratic transition. The White House ignored the warnings of medical personnel and agency leaders. The VA, Bowman said, "had a tremendous amount of authority to manage and deliver changes to veteran healthcare. . . . [T]he White House knew it, and they were ready to force VA leaders to disrupt and even dismantle the veterans' healthcare system without a medically competent and safe follow-on plan to implement."

In particular, the president was tempted to reallocate the department's $250 billion budget, which was second only to the Pentagon in magnitude. Even if the administration shifted 25 percent of the VA budget to other priorities, that would have been more than $60 billion. "That's real money for a president, and the White House wanted to spend it somewhere else," a former VA official told me.

In other words, the VA could be a piggy bank for Donald Trump. When he interviewed candidates for the department's top positions, he quizzed them about how they could whittle down the size of the VA and reallocate its resources. VA leaders (especially those who had served in uniform) were appalled by proposals to overhaul healthcare for America's 19 million veteran population. They worried the Department would be demolished under the guise of "modernizing" healthcare programs.

"The veterans' social safety net is extremely complex," explained Jim Byrne, another former deputy secretary of the VA and previously the department's general counsel under Trump. "If you suddenly privatize all veteran medical care, it will have deadly consequences. First, despite the valiant efforts of the [VA's healthcare officials], millions of veterans would fall through the cracks during the transition to the private sector, which is mostly unable to handle the surge, and veterans will not get the care they need. Second, it would disrupt the entire United States healthcare system, where much of our nation's medical training and research is conducted in VA medical centers. If you break that system, it's not just a healthcare problem. It becomes a major national security concern."

Most of the VA officials I interviewed acknowledged that the department's unwieldy bureaucracy needed to be slimmed down. They were not averse to reform. But the wrecking-ball approach Trump wanted to take could have been extremely dangerous.

"To put a fine point on it, if the VA's existing integrated medical system were to be turned upside down overnight, the lives of veterans would be at serious risk," Byrne explained matter-of-factly. "Veterans would die by the thousands, maybe hundreds of thousands. That's why any reforms have to be done deliberately. And any talk about 'dismantling' or discrediting the VA to facilitate privatization is abhorrent."

VA leaders told me that they tried to thwart White House efforts to dismantle the department. But as they did, they got relentless pushback from the president's aides. They were constantly berated for not being "loyal enough," and Trump assigned a zealous watcher named Darin Selnick to keep tabs on the VA and its leadership team.

"He was the Stephen Miller of Veterans Affairs," one official said. "He thought he was a five-star [general]." Selnick once allegedly drove up to the VA headquarters and parked in a reserved spot where the secretary's motorcade was typically positioned.

"Sir, you can't park there," a guard told him.

"Yes I can. I work at the White House," Selnick reportedly shot back.

A former official described the aide's perceived micromanagement of the VA as a shadow war to implement Trump's plans by going around the department's leaders and pressuring junior appointees. Ironically, political considerations ended up protecting the department against implosion during Trump's tenure.

"Their ultimate hope was upending the existing VA healthcare system," Tom Bowman explained, "but they were worried about doing too much before the election." Department executives played into this fear. They warned the White House about alienating the veteran community by saying major changes would hurt the president electorally, which led Trump to change his tune. He held off on "gutting" the VA until he could win reelection.

"Trump talked about veterans, veterans, veterans," one former VA leader commented. "But at the end of the day, he thinks they are lazy malingerers." In a second term, the former official speculated, a MAGA White House "wouldn't care about flipping them out on the street."

The Next Trump will carry forward plans to disassemble the Department of Veterans Affairs without any resistance from the agency's leadership team. That's because, as one interviewee told me, "the Darin Selnicks will be in charge."

★ ★ ★

Few people understand the personnel drama that will overtake another MAGA White House better than Anthony Scaramucci. He was once a take-no-prisoners Trump backer. Then he witnessed the MAGA machine from the inside. Scaramucci said that although a surprising number of high-profile leaders joined the Trump administration, it won't happen again. "I don't think good people are going to make that decision next time," he remarked. Cabinet roles will be awarded to "a lower breed" with "lower intellect" who are "more malevolent," he predicted.

In conversations with dozens of former Trump aides, a range of controversial figures were repeatedly mentioned as people who would dominate the cabinet of a successor administration. For instance, the National Security Council might include people such as: Pam Bondi (attorney general), Michael Flynn (defense secretary), Richard Grenell (national security advisor), Peter Navarro (treasury secretary), Robert O'Brien (secretary of state), Kash Patel (director of national intelligence), Erik Prince (CIA director), and Stephen Miller (DHS secretary), all of whom are MAGA figures unlikely to be appointed to top government positions in "normal times."

One former NSC official called this a "doomsday org chart," since the list includes people who were accused of politicizing intelligence, couldn't be trusted with secret programs, or defended Trump's mishandling of classified material. The MAGA names and faces will change as time goes on, but their moral code—and commitment to subverting democratic norms—will not.

Conservative think tanks are preparing slates of MAGA figures to fill top administration posts. No group was more active in placing people in the Trump administration than the right-leaning Heritage Foundation, which is now running a 2025 Presidential Transition Project, overseen by the ex-president's former personnel chief Kevin Roberts. A Republican familiar with the project told me the organization's list is composed almost exclusively of pro-Trump personalities—a "nightmare slate"—and that Heritage is expected to pressure any Republican president to accept the list of loyal recruits, or else.

"Heritage will help provide not just the intellectual firepower to policymakers," project leader Roberts wrote, "but also do everything we can to ensure the right people hold positions of influence in Washington."

Perhaps the most influential GOP group attempting to staff up the next Republican presidency will be the America First Policy Institute (AFPI), described by some as MAGA's "White House in waiting." Many of the group's 150-plus staff members are former officials in the Trump administration, and its American Leadership Initiative is dedicated to filling the next GOP White House with the most MAGA-friendly people. They've already held conferences focused on avoiding the mistakes of the first term, with AFPI leaders bemoaning the fact that Trump's orbit was infiltrated by cabinet heads who weren't nearly MAGA enough.

It doesn't matter that many of their prospective nominees are un-confirmable. On several occasions, I witnessed Trump extol the virtues of naming "acting" officials, since he knew they would be more compliant than those confirmed by the Senate. He wanted his lieutenants to sense a guillotine blade hanging over their heads, and to know that he held the rope. The desire to be formally nominated into a prestigious position, coupled with the constant fear of being publicly humiliated and replaced, was just enough to coerce them into displaying fealty to Trump. As a result, a historic number of officials—nearly thirty in four years—were placed in nonpermanent roles running cabinet agencies during the Trump administration.

MAGA forces plan to exploit work-arounds in the law once again to put extreme figures in positions of power without congressional approval.

"Expect a return of the acting secretaries," a senior congressional staffer told me. He predicted the movement would be prepared to subvert the Senate's "advice and consent" role on presidential nominations if given another opportunity to do so. Indeed, Trump's Office of Presidential Personnel developed elaborate schemes for rotating people between top positions in order to avoid congressional authorization, while still technically complying with federal vacancy laws. His former lawyers are looking to take these measures even further in order to staff a future administration with faithful agency heads.

One of Donald Trump's earliest senior campaign aides, George Gigicos, worked closely with these figures.

"You wanna talk about what a second term would be like? It would be dangerous," he shared. The hangers-on from Trump's orbit would be put in charge in the senior-most government positions during a MAGA comeback in order to carry the movement forward, he said, regardless of whether the former president plays a kingmaker role.

"We have a system of checks and balances," he said. "We can survive bad policy, but we can't survive bad people."

In addition to the cabinet, the second layer down in government will be packed with a "rising generation of assassins."

Incoming presidents have roughly four thousand jobs to fill. Before they step foot in the Oval Office, they start working with their teams to identify who will take these political appointee positions. They must find chiefs of staff, assistant secretaries, deputy assistant secretaries, and others to operate U.S. agencies day-to-day on behalf of the White House.

In the Trump years, many of the incoming appointees were moderate Republicans from Capitol Hill or the Bush administration and didn't necessarily share Donald Trump's populist fervor. In a future MAGA administration, GOP moderates will be weeded out in favor of "a rising generation of assassins." This is how Trump strategist Steve Bannon described the young professionals who are being groomed as "shock troops," charged with remaking the federal bureaucracy "brick by brick."

Josh Venable, who served as chief of staff to Trump's education secretary Betsy DeVos, exemplifies the kind of Republican who will be shut out. Venable is no RINO (Republican in name only). A rock-ribbed conservative who led Michigan's Republican Party, he served as an aide to Florida governor Jeb Bush and later as the GOP's deputy finance director before coming into the Trump administration in 2017. Despite his credentials, Venable earned his way onto the MAGA blacklist the way others did: by bucking a bad presidential idea.

On Valentine's Day 2018, a gunman entered a Parkland, Florida, high school and murdered seventeen students. The tragedy prompted the White House to announce a Federal Commission on School Safety to protect classrooms. To some Trump staffers, it was a political necessity to show that the administration was doing something on gun violence, but to the Education Department's chief of staff, it was the most important task they'd been assigned yet. DeVos and her team were hearing from parents around the country and felt school safety was an urgent priority.

"It was set up for disaster from the get-go," Venable recalled.

In ordinary times, it would be a political challenge for any agency to produce a report on an issue as sensitive as gun violence. The Trump White House put four different agencies in charge: Education, Health and Human Services, Justice, and Homeland Security. Venable took the reins, hoping to corral the disparate organizations. West Wing aides assured him that the commission would not be micromanaged. So he carefully shepherded a multi-month process that—surprisingly—resulted in all four agencies agreeing to a series of recommendations on how to make U.S. classrooms safer and prevent shooting tragedies like Parkland.

That's when the trouble started. The group ran its draft recommendations by the White House, including a proposal to explore whether to raise the "minimum age" for firearms purchases to twenty-one years of age, the same as alcohol. The commission was *not* recommending the minimum age actually be raised—only that the idea be further studied. However, Donald Trump was terrified of losing the support of the National Rifle Association (NRA), an organization that would object to any discussion of the topic whatsoever. Trump's staff demanded that the NRA review the draft report before it was issued.

What's more, White House staff told Venable that they didn't want the report to mention "firearms" at all. He thought this was an absurdity. The whole purpose of the commission was to look at classroom safety in the wake of a mass shooting. It would be like writing a report about flood protection without mentioning rain or hurricanes.

This led to a curt back-and-forth between the Education Department and the White House. Venable objected strenuously. He was uncomfortable with allowing gun lobbyists to have veto power over a supposedly independent report on mass shootings, especially when teachers, chief state school officers, and mental health professionals weren't being extended the same privilege. And he definitely wasn't going to avoid the topic of "guns" like they wanted him to.

"If you want me to do *that*, I'm done." That's how Venable said he felt. He was already frustrated over Trump's reluctance to meet with the parents of Parkland shooting victims (the president had shown up late to one of the conversations). Now Trump was suddenly happy to engage on school safety if it was with the NRA. Venable knew this would send a terrible message.

Education Secretary DeVos supported her chief of staff in pushing back, at first. But she began to waver under White House pressure. When Trump personally got involved to insist the NRA have a say in the report, DeVos caved. In the aftermath, Josh Venable quit. There were other reasons he wanted to leave, but this was one of the final straws. Donald Trump had begun using the department as a weapon in the culture wars. Venable was long gone by the time the commission released its findings, which had undergone a series of rewrites in his absence.

The final language on restricting firearms purchases was definitive: "Existing research *does not* demonstrate that laws imposing a minimum age for firearms purchases have a measurable impact on reducing homicides, suicides, or unintentional deaths." (Emphasis added.) This is the opposite of what experts were recommending internally. Ironically, the school shooting that prompted the report in the first place was perpetrated by a young man under the age of twenty-one, who had obtained the firearm legally.

(The commission's findings can still be found on the department's website, albeit with a disclaimer added after Trump left office: "Some statements in this report do not reflect the current positions or policies of the Departments of Education, Homeland Security, Justice, or Health and Human Services.")

The day the report dropped, I was actually in the Oval Office with the president. My job was to brief him on how DHS could help protect school buildings. Trump was uninterested. He used the allotted time to rant about the border wall ("I want it to be a work of art," he mused), whether it could be painted black to burn the hands of anyone who touched it ("How much would that cost?"), if Congress would fund it ("If they don't give me the money, we shut the whole fucking border"), and whether there were any ways to put more pressure on America's southern neighbor ("Let's stick it to the Mexicans!").

Down the hall, the parents of school-shooting victims waited to meet with the president. He was late, again.

★ ★ ★

The next MAGA administration won't welcome more "Josh Venables" into their ranks but will instead enlist "assassins." Already, young people interviewing for GOP jobs in Washington worry about whether they are Trump-y enough to get hired. Shaming the alleged RINOs has worked. Moderates are keeping quiet or changing their views, so they're not confused with the type of person who'd say "no" to the idea of putting the NRA in charge of school safety, for instance.

Appointees in the next GOP White House will be heavily vetted for obedience. Trump advisors blamed the president's inability to execute his plans on reluctant political appointees. Objections from conscientious staffers certainly slowed down the policy process. So toward the end of the Trump administration, the White House started to implement very strict criteria for new hires.

"That's what they regretted not doing . . . in the beginning," noted former NSC staff member Lieutenant Colonel Alexander Vindman, who testified at Trump's first impeachment trial.

Vindman recalled one particular episode. A job opened up on the NSC for a Russia policy expert—a role that involves handling supersecret intelligence and U.S. policy related to one of America's top rivals. Trump wanted to forge a warm relationship with Putin and his regime, but the effort was faltering. Alex Vindman's brother, Eugene, worked as a lawyer on the NSC and helped to screen the candidates sent over from the White House personnel office.

"He came across a guy who worked with the [Trump] campaign and was friends with the loyalists," Vindman explained. "He had no background in Russia." Eugene's instinct was to discard the candidate. He had résumés from seasoned intelligence officials and Russia specialists who in his view were far more qualified. The White House rejected his recommendations. They gave the job to the campaign aide.

In a second term, the loyalty tests are going to be rigorous. Before the 2020 vote, one of the president's HR chiefs admitted to me that, if Trump won, their plan was to demand resignation letters from all four thousand political appointees and force everyone to go through a political "re-evaluation" if they wanted to keep their jobs.

"We're gonna put 'em through fucking boot camp," he bragged at the time with a laugh.

The plan was creepy. He said they were exploring in-depth social media searches (web-crawler firms could "find shit no one else can find," he said), interviews with colleagues to find out whether appointees had privately said bad things about the president, and airtight NDAs and loyalty commitments. Even the music that staff listened to might be scrutinized. Not for taste, the operative clarified. Music could help reveal someone's true political leanings.

I found this farfetched until my former colleague Olivia Troye told me that she had been forced to turn off a Taylor Swift song playing at her desk in the White House. "Do you want to get fired?" someone warned her. Swift was seen as an anti-Trump celebrity. That year a junior staffer at the Department of Housing and Urban Development had been "caught" liking a Taylor Swift post on Instagram, an issue that was elevated all the way to White House Chief of Staff Mark Meadows, according to reporting from *The Atlantic*.

Future MAGA political appointees might have their phones monitored, too. This might also sound absurd, but the idea was raised at the highest levels. In Trump's second year in office, I had dinner with a cabinet member who shared that the president's paranoia was causing him to unravel, so much so that he wanted to spy on his immediate lieutenants. He allegedly told aides that he wanted to "tap the phones" of White House staff to find out who was leaking damaging stories about him to the media. Chief of Staff John Kelly quickly nixed the suggestion, knowing it would be illegal.

"What if there was no John Kelly?" I asked.

"Well, the careers would have stopped it," my dinner partner responded.

"Careers" is shorthand for civil servants. Millions of permanent *nonpolitical* employees are responsible for carrying out the inner workings of government. Tapping someone's phone isn't something a president can make happen by waving a wand. It requires a legitimate law-enforcement or intelligence justification, not to mention sign-off from a range of career officials, including law-enforcement officers, lawyers, compliance personnel, and technical staff. Those protective layers might not be in place in a second go-round.

The Trump advisors who were charged with hunting down the disloyalists are involved in efforts to shape the next Republican presidential administration. And they are hell-bent on weakening or eliminating the peskiest guardrail in the executive branch: the careerists.

In the name of countering the Deep State, MAGA forces plan to take a hammer to the government's career civil service.

The tone of government is set at the top and then echoed by midlevel enforcers. Nevertheless, the real action happens on the front lines. Almost 3 million civilian employees do the daily work of federal agencies—disbursing Social Security checks, managing hurricane recovery, conducting highway maintenance, researching life-saving vaccines, and much more. Strict regulations forbid government employees from taking politically motivated actions or allowing their work to be influenced by any particular political candidate or party.

A president cannot order these millions of employees to do whatever he or she wants. Since the 1800s, the American system has been built atop the notion of an *independent* civil service. When Congress passes laws, they do so with the expectation that the executive branch—regardless of who is in charge—will faithfully execute those laws, rather than wipe away statutes it doesn't like and enforce the ones that it does.

But a corrupt chief executive can try to skirt these protections. He or she might ignore the recommendations of the career civil service or badger employees and experts to act in ways contrary to their reasoned judgment. The Trump administration regularly pursued both strategies to bend the federal government to its will, frustrated by what they rue-fully labeled the "Deep State." MAGA leaders intend to destroy the civil service next time, and they have plenty of case studies to use.

The ex-president's hostility toward careerists was best captured in what became known as "Sharpiegate."

In September 2019, Hurricane Dorian was bearing down on the United States, and Donald Trump tweeted that Alabama and other states would "most likely be hit (much) harder than anticipated." It was true that the Category 5 hurricane was looking bad; the only problem was that Trump was wrong about where it would hit. He was basing his claim on an outdated storm forecast from the National Weather Service (NWS), which days earlier had predicted a slight possibility Alabama could be impacted by winds. But the state wasn't in the cross hairs any-more.

"Trump was following an old spaghetti chart. . . . He hadn't looked at a recent forecast in forty-eight hours," explained Rear Admiral Tim Gallaudet, who was the Trump administration's number two official at the National Oceanic and Atmospheric Administration (NOAA) at the time, which oversaw NWS. NOAA leaders were concerned the presi-dent was tweeting false information amid a public safety crisis.

An NWS branch in Alabama quickly corrected the president with a tweet: "Alabama will NOT see any impacts from #Dorian."

The issue could have died right then, but it didn't. According to Gallaudet, the White House was "angry that the 'Deep State' was coun-tering the President." So Trump doubled down on his claim publicly, sending Alabama's 5 million residents into a state of uncertainty and, in some cases, panic. Did they need to evacuate from the path of a massive CAT-5 hurricane or not? Alabama first responders explained again that the state *was not* in danger. Weather reporters churned out updated forecasts to prove the point.

Still, Trump wouldn't let go. He held a televised meeting in the Oval Office with FEMA before the hurricane made landfall. The chart he was using showed that Dorian would likely hit Florida, but then in black marker, there was an extra bubble drawn onto the jumbo map, falsely projecting that the hurricane would continue onward into Alabama. The storm track had been doctored. It was widely suspected Trump had drawn the bubble, though it couldn't be verified.

I spoke to two people present in the White House that day and involved in the meeting. Both confirmed that Trump did, in fact, adjust the forecast himself. The president overruled the government's extreme-weather experts with a Sharpie. As the White House got mocked, Trump got angrier. He directed NOAA to draft a press release saying that he'd been correct. The agency hastily issued an unsigned statement admitting there were earlier "probabilities" that Alabama might be affected by winds. Incredibly, the statement didn't say anything to emphasize the fact that the state was no longer in danger.

Television commentators thought the back-and-forth was comical. Trump's appointee at NOAA, Tim Gallaudet, was furious. He hadn't been consulted on the president's statements or his agency's press release.

"The hurricane track influences emergency management responses to what can be multibillion-dollar damages," he told me. "It was so reckless and so dangerous for him to politicize it."

Alabama was spared by the storm, while the weather service was roiled. A top NWS official emailed agency leaders in the aftermath: "Employees now fear for [their] jobs and are questioning whether they should post potentially life-saving info or check tweets first."

Gallaudet agreed, writing back to the NWS chief operating officer: "I'm having a hard time not departing the pattern right now"—military parlance for quitting. Some of his top scientists threatened to resign, too. "They were distraught," he said. I asked the retired admiral what would happen if there was another MAGA presidency.

"That shit will be commonplace," he sighed. "There will be a mass exodus from science agencies."

People I spoke with predicted widespread career resignations under another MAGA presidency. The result will be a younger civil service without the knowledge, experience, or wherewithal to run government agencies. White House appointees will be forced to fill in the gaps as a result. In a hurricane, for instance, you might have inexperienced political operatives trying to handle the crisis instead of experts.

Mass *resignations* will be made worse by mass *recriminations*.

A future MAGA president will purge careerists who dare to dissent against the commander in chief. Trump put such a plan in place in October 2020, issuing an executive order that would have allowed him to fire tens of thousands of career officials using an authority called "Schedule F." Through an obscure administrative power, the order would have enabled the president to strip large parts of the federal workforce of their employment protections. As a result, they could be fired without appeal.

Top Republicans have praised Schedule F. *Axios* reporter Jonathan Swan expertly documented how the plan was concocted and the enthusiasm for it among MAGA figures. Former secretary of state Mike Pompeo told *Axios* that "Schedule F was a step in the right direction . . . [to] hold the D.C. bureaucracy accountable"; Texas senator Ted Cruz applauded the Trump team for "thinking creatively" about how to "root out the Deep State" and wished the White House had "done more sooner"; and Missouri senator Josh Hawley expressed openness to the order and hit back at the "unelected" career workforce as a constitutional danger.

"It will be a revenge machine," explained Monte Hawkins, who worked previously on Trump's NSC. "They will go after careerists that were 'problems' last time. They know who they are. They have a list."

In particular, the intelligence community (IC) will be in the cross hairs. One former IC official, who served in Trump's White House, predicted the spy world "gets gutted" under another Trump. In his words, the community was already "a battered spouse" at the end of the administration.

"Career senior intelligence officers were afraid to go brief," the NSC staffer remembered. "Anybody who could find an assignment out of D.C. was getting out as fast as they could. . . . No one felt like they could deliver truth to power."

Brian Murphy, a former FBI agent and DHS intelligence chief under Trump, likewise painted a stark picture: "The pressure, the distortion, the megalomania would be so intense a second time around, it will be very hard for the federal government to withstand."

We've already had a taste of it. Trump over-hyped terrorist threats at the U.S. border and deliberately played down the danger posed by dictators he considered to be friends, despite intelligence briefings to the contrary. Another Trump-like figure will transform the IC into his or her "propaganda arm," Murphy said, cherry-picking intelligence to support a political agenda.

· "The MAGA movement has paved the way for a politicized intelligence community," added Fiona Hill, Donald Trump's former top Russia advisor. Hill believes that the partisan manipulation of the spy world will cause leaders in Washington to make cataclysmic miscalculations. "This will lead the United States into wars," she predicted.

Monte Hawkins forecast another chilling possibility closer to home. "They are going to send more [political appointees] into the IC, pulling FISAs and other things to support political aims and engage in political retribution," Hawkins speculated, referencing the Foreign Intelligence Surveillance Act (FISA). In other words, the White House will turn the powers of the American spy community inward. The FISA law outlines procedures for government wiretapping of civilians, including on U.S. soil. If law-abiding careerists are purged, the Next Trump will find it easier to use intelligence powers to monitor his or her own staff and, worse, to keep tabs on rivals.

We must urgently fortify the "deputy" guardrail of democracy. No American president should be able to pack the executive branch with unblinking loyalists and rewrite the laws of the land unilaterally. Independent public servants are an essential check on power. If laws are enforced selectively, democracy's diagnosis is terminal. Thankfully, President Joe Biden rescinded the Schedule F order, but it could easily be reinstated and expanded by a MAGA successor. Congress must forbid such reclassifications of federal positions, enshrine protections that allow careerists to do their jobs without fear of retaliation, and make it harder to circumvent vacancy laws to appoint un-confirmable diehards to lead agencies.

Still, no reforms can fully shield agencies from corrupt appointees. An incoming president chooses his or her team, and often those lieutenants are more conniving than the leader. GOP Congressman Denver Riggleman pointed to Soviet dictator Joseph Stalin. "Stalin was awful, but you had Little Stalins that were much more abusive and terroristic than he was because they thought that they were allowed to be that way," he said. The Next Trump will bring aides into government who lack character, experience, or both—and are ready for retribution.

Michael Karloutsos was surprised by the vindictiveness of staffers who swept into the State Department during the Trump administration. He was appointed by the president to serve as the head of diplomatic protocol, responsible for managing meetings with the world's most powerful people—kings, queens, presidents, and prime ministers. From the outset, Karloutsos witnessed the bizarre behavior of his fellow appointees, such as the day he walked into the State Department office that archives gifts given to the United States by foreign leaders.

"There was a bunch of young people scratching out Barack Obama and Hillary Clinton's names," he recalled. "Their job was to go through items from the last administration—cups, candlesticks, you name it—and deface them."

Karloutsos objected. Erasing history is what autocrats did, he said. "You'd think that I was advocating for reelecting [Obama]. People looked at me sideways. That set the tone."

Every administration is staffed by flawed souls who enter public service with conflicting motivations. Ambition, altruism, greed, goodwill, and love—of country, or of self. The Next Trump won't choose people who are conflicted at all. He or she will pick staffers who put the president first, above all else. There will be no treasonous conversations about the chief executive's mental state, let alone the thought of correcting him.

The best place to hear White House staff speak candidly is a tiny anteroom just down the hall from the Oval Office. Before important meetings, aides huddle in the cramped space adjoining the chief of staff's office to rehearse, vent, and sometimes to scheme. I spoke to one of the young aides who was assigned to a desk there during the Trump administration (a space later occupied by White House whistle-blower Cassidy Hutchinson).

"I characterize my time there as pure insanity," the junior official reflected.

At first, according to the person, the room was trafficked by people frantically trying to counteract bad Trump decisions. Appointees with a conscience. By the end, it was a waypoint for aides "fully unwilling to stand up to the president" and conspiring to thwart the Deep State on his behalf. These personalities—"the most extreme figures"—will return for another MAGA administration.

Next time, the aide clarified, "'Yes men' will rule."

Chapter 3

THE JUDGE

No man is allowed to be a judge in his own cause, because his interest would certainly bias his judgment, and, not improbably, corrupt his integrity.

—JAMES MADISON, FEDERALIST NO. 10, 1787

PART I

November 28, 2017

Relief hit me in a warm wave of goose bumps. As I drove away from DHS headquarters, I imagined the metal filing cabinet where we stored classified documents, and I pictured all of my internal stressors as specifically as I could. It was the start of a familiar exercise. One by one, I would drop the nagging anxieties into a file drawer before sliding it shut and spinning the combination dial. The ritual usually felt ridiculous. On that day, I told myself it was working.

My calendar listed the time as "HOLD—Offsite Meeting." No matter what assurance the HR people offered, mental health issues were still taboo for people with security clearances, so I kept the problems to myself and kept the doctor's appointments confidential. Without any obvious trigger, I was having near-fainting spells in meetings and large gatherings. My pulse would thump in my ears. My fingertips would get sweaty. My peripheral vision would darken until I excused myself to a restroom, waiting for the feeling to pass. I told my doctor, and he referred me to a therapist whom I'll call Courtney.

Courtney's "containment" exercise was really just a visualization technique, and I'd actually been using it for years for other purposes. In school or at the office, I retained reams of information by forming vivid mental pictures and placing them in a familiar place, like the house I grew up in or an old workplace. The memory trick had helped me win Indiana debate championships on no sleep and pass multihour exams at Oxford after months of procrastination. Now I was using the technique to forget.

As I drove to Courtney's Georgetown office on that crisp November afternoon, I let my worries sprout into detailed mental images, then fall into the metal office drawer like leaves: a tiny skyscraper of unopened bills; Anabel, sleeping alone; a sprained wrist, bruised purple (it was actually broken); a family member floating facedown in a hot tub; a man with a gun, crouched in a hotel window; a crumpled white pickup truck spattered with blood; and a projectile that landed in the filing cabinet, erupted into a fireball, and vaporized everything inside.

I felt a brief sense of release. Wisps of smoke faded from the filing cabinet's mangled frame.

I held on to the feeling during the drive and in the parking garage. Through the sterile lobby and up the elevator, I tried to hold tighter to the sense of calm. It was gone by the time I walked into the office, which was dressed up as a cozy living room. The decor didn't fool me. The cheap mauve carpet exposed the room's real purpose: it was a medical office like any other.

"Containment is working."

Courtney studied me through translucent purple frames. "I really do think containment is working," I shared with her from the couch, perhaps a bit too earnestly. I told her how the visualization technique was changing my daily life. Maybe I hoped she would smile approvingly and reward me with a clean bill of health, marking a conclusion to our pricey sessions. Several beats of silence told me she wasn't so easily fooled.

The technique was a Band-Aid, she said, not a permanent solution. Just like the backup Xanax my doctor had prescribed and which I kept close by in my backpack, visualization was a tool for coping until I could confront the underlying stresses. I needed to build real breathing space into my life, not just during occasional drive time to-and-from therapy appointments.

"Are you still planning to leave?" Courtney knew my plans to depart the administration were slipping. And she knew why.

After John Kelly went to the White House, I agreed to help Acting Secretary Elaine Duke run the place until a permanent DHS leader was announced by the president. To outsiders, Elaine's halting demeanor and cautious, deliberative style were incompatible with Trump. She was understated while he was belligerent. I knew the real reason the two were mismatched though: Elaine seemed like a pushover, until you pushed—and met resistance from an iron moral core.

Her first major decision put her at odds with the president. She never regained his approval. She didn't mind.

When Elaine took over for John Kelly in August 2017, she inherited a draft plan that would thoroughly piss off Donald Trump. I'd been monitoring it for months. The president would be furious when he found out that DHS wanted to gut his travel restrictions by fully replacing the "Muslim ban" that had reared its ugly head when Trump took office with something far different.

After federal courts struck down Trump's original order, he issued another order "pausing" immigration from several Muslim-majority nations while a new plan could be developed. The stated reason was to put in place more stringent screening to keep terrorists from slipping into the United States by posing as immigrants or refugees. That itself wasn't entirely controversial; the Obama administration had designated the same countries as terrorist hot spots.

But I was skeptical of Trump's motivation. Not only had he made anti-Muslim comments on the campaign trail, but he told aides he wanted a "massive" travel ban to replace the original one. Trump was expecting his agencies to come back with a proposal listing "dozens and dozens of new countries," his advisor Stephen Miller told us. He was trying hard to influence the process.

The DHS Office of Intelligence and Analysis objected. Blanket bans on U.S.-bound immigrants and travelers were foolish, they explained, since 99 percent of those people were harmless. I agreed. If this was really about combating terrorism, the process should be simple. First, career spies should rank the most dangerous terrorist hot spots. Second, State Department envoys should assess which of those places were cooperating with the United States to combat the threat (and which weren't). And third, DHS should recommend temporary screening measures or travel limitations from "high risk" locations—not based on religion, not based on politics, just based on threat assessments.

John Kelly approved the way forward. We'd call the White House's bluff and get them a small tailored list, knowing it wouldn't be the one Trump wanted. Secretary Kelly put me and Gene Hamilton in charge of monitoring the process, since one of us handled counterterrorism and the other handled immigration. Gene was a friendly guy whose office was next to mine, and while we disagreed on immigration policy, we agreed generally that the White House needed to stay out of this.

But through the thin drywall separating us, I could hear the phone calls to Gene from Stephen Miller. There were a lot of countries Trump didn't like—Somalia, Haiti, El Salvador. Were they on the draft list? Miller wanted to know. The president would be "upset" if the process didn't produce the correct results. Although Gene and I had our differences, I was heartened to hear him push back on the demands. If we cherry-picked countries Trump wanted to block, the courts would surely strike down the plan.

We were aided in elbowing out political meddling by an analyst named Olivia Troye. When I met the seasoned intelligence officer, I was told she was one of the best in the entire department—hardworking, apolitical, by-the-book. Olivia exceeded the description. Over several months, she ran aggressive interference, blocking attempts by political minions at the White House to tip the scales on certain countries, while making sure the outcome of the process was driven solely by the analysis of intelligence personnel and diplomats.

Secretary Kelly was gone by the time the plan was finalized, and Elaine Duke had taken his place. Career officials presented her with a plan to lift travel restrictions on countries that were cooperating with the United States, to add new ones (including Venezuela and North Korea, both of which refused to help America catch terrorists), and, most important, to end blanket travel bans in favor of narrower, country-specific restrictions. While imperfect, it was better than allowing Trump to personally block travel from whatever country he disliked on a given day.

Very late one night, Olivia and I huddled in the SCIF looking over the updated country chart her team had developed. Short of getting Trump to rescind his executive order, this was probably the best we could do.

She confessed that when we'd first met she was worried I was "one of the MAGA ones." Now, she said half-jokingly, we'd probably both get fired for defying Trump. Olivia wanted to know if Acting Secretary Duke would stick to her guns and defend the weakening of the travel ban.

I told her I wasn't worried at all.

"Trust the experts." That was Elaine's maxim. She may not have been a terrorism specialist, but in three decades of managing government programs, she had been a fierce defender of the career civil service. She promised to get the president to accept the outcome. Or she'd leave.

Her conversation with Donald Trump went as expected. He was seething. At his golf resort in Bedminster, New Jersey, the president railed against Elaine and the other cabinet members who were present. The "weak-ass travel ban," in his words, was too small and went too easy on his least favorite countries

"Somalia? Come on, they have fucking pirates!" he vented. To be sure, there was a piracy threat from armed militants off the coast of Somalia, but Trump seemed to picture swashbuckling Jack Sparrows stumbling across the beaches. And he didn't want anyone from that country allowed into ours.

Elaine held firm. The acting secretary had an ace up her sleeve. She laid it on the table as Trump rattled off nationalities he wanted to block from entering America.

If the president rejected the independent assessment of the agencies, she said, our lawyers predicted the courts would strike down whatever arbitrary list he came up with. That got Trump's attention. He dreaded judges. They could proclaim the final word against him. They could make him into a *loser.* After a long debate and the president's realization that he was boxed in, Trump very begrudgingly approved the plan.

An equally angry White House punted much of the rollout to DHS, directing me speak to news outlets as a "senior administration official" to describe the changes. I told reporters the measures were certainly "tough" on the listed countries but thankfully more "tailored" than before. What may have started in Trump's mind as a Muslim ban no longer was one. He'd been outmaneuvered. Containment was working.

Elaine went further when speaking to Congress, deliberately contradicting Trump's vision of a sweeping blockade.

"This has *nothing* to do with race or religion, and our goal is *not* to block people from visiting the United States," she declared. "America has a proud history as a beacon of hope to freedom-loving people from around the world who want to visit our country or become a part of our enduring democratic republic." I heard from an irritated Stephen Miller afterward. He wanted to know who had approved this language. Who had written Elaine's pro-immigrant remarks? I had.

Any sense of victory was fleeting. My anxiety swelled during a bloody October. The first day of the month, a Las Vegas gunman murdered more than sixty festival-goers, indiscriminately firing into a crowd from an upper floor of a hotel on the strip. And on Halloween, an ISIS-inspired terrorist mowed down a dozen civilians with a white pickup truck in New York City. We scrambled to elevate security levels around the country to prevent copycat terrorist attacks.

On top of that, I was on hair-trigger alert about another looming danger, worse than any I'd dealt with in government. . . .

Meanwhile, home life was on pause. Anabel and I had gotten en-

gaged, but she spent most nights at home alone. I was usually in the
office until late, often close to midnight. At the same time, my siblings
were frustrated that I was unable to help with an alcoholic family member who'd relapsed. Once after a daytime bender, she'd been found
floating unconscious in a hot tub and nearly died as paramedics rushed
her in an ambulance to the hospital. I wired money to help pay for
rehab, but I could barely find time to address my own issues. I sprained
my wrist one day and found out months later that it was broken. I had
worked through the pain because there wasn't time to make doctor's
appointments. Every other week, I canceled therapy to free up calendar
space for work.

"So when are you leaving?" Courtney rephrased the question.

"As soon as the new secretary is confirmed," I told her, shifting un-
comfortably on the therapist's couch. Trump had recently nominated
Kirstjen Nielsen, who had gone with John Kelly to the White House. She
was poised for confirmation in a few short weeks.

Courtney looked skeptical of the answer, and she reminded me of a
piece of advice she'd raised early on.

"If you don't take time for yourself, Miles, your body will do it for
you," she said, "when it's least convenient."

Our session was cut short. My phones (one personal, two for work)
were silenced during therapy, so I tapped them intermittently to see if
there was anything urgent. That day several missed calls glared disap-
provingly from the lock screen, so I looked at my emails. *Fuck.*

I told her I had to go.

En route back to the department, I called the switchboard to get
the acting secretary on the phone. They couldn't reach her. She was un-
derground in the SCIF, and they told me they were not at liberty to say
anything over an open line (an unclassified call). But I was pretty certain I knew what was going on, based on the flurry of news alerts on my
phones. I tempted fate by speeding up Embassy Row on a street dotted
by cop cars.

At headquarters, I found Elaine sitting in the secure conference
room. In front of her, the story was retold by bright-orange cover sheets

blaring the words TOP SECRET. Scattered papers with grainy satellite photos were spread out across the table.

North Korea had launched an intercontinental ballistic missile, or ICBM. The acting secretary had tried to find me before heading into the SCIF to monitor the situation. The powerful Hwasong-15 was the reclusive regime's first projectile that could hit anywhere in the world, including right here in Washington, D.C. The president had tracked the launch, too, and later called Elaine, who was busy making sure the U.S. homeland wasn't the missile's final destination.

In an ongoing contest of brinksmanship, North Korean leader Kim Jong Un kept firing rogue missiles, while Trump responded by firing off rogue tweets. In the national security world, anything having to do with nuclear weapons is handled with extreme sensitivity—well planned, carefully scripted—yet we didn't know what Trump might say at any given moment. One day, he threatened North Korea "with fire, fury and frankly power the likes of which this world has never seen before." He almost seemed to welcome a nuclear conflict, which terrified us.

Defense Secretary Mattis had cornered me one day on his way out of a contentious meeting in the White House Situation Room.

"You all need to prepare like we're going to war," he warned. Mattis was serious. DHS should assume the homeland was in mortal danger.

The president had mused to advisors like John Kelly that he badly wanted to strike North Korea with a nuclear weapon. He wasn't coyly playing the role of "madman" in order to call North Korea's bluff. He was actually prepared to take America into a deadly apocalyptic conflict, history's first two-sided nuclear war.

We convened every top leader in DHS to discuss the brewing crisis. Experts walked through various scenarios of a nuclear strike on the U.S. homeland, dusted off response plans, and outlined best-case scenarios which nevertheless sounded horrifically grim. I cannot provide the details, but I walked out of those meetings genuinely worried about the safety of the country. In my view, the department was unprepared for the type of nuclear conflict Trump might foment.

"Fix it," I was told. I didn't know where to begin. The situation was becoming so serious that states such as Hawaii had reinstated their public alert systems for nuclear attacks for the first time since the Cold War. (A few months later, Hawaii accidentally sent out a public warning that a missile was inbound, sending residents fleeing for their lives.)

As I arrived from my truncated therapy appointment, I was told about the missile launch. Thankfully, early reports indicated that the North Korean test had failed. The missile's re-entry vehicle broke apart and smashed into the ocean off the coast of Japan.

When I found Elaine, she was fighting back tears in the secure conference room.

"It's so broken," she confided from her chair at the head of the table. "This isn't why I came back into government."

I realized that the acting secretary wasn't talking about the ICBM launch.

"Ma'am," I asked, "what happened?"

She told me that Trump had called. Although a nuclear-capable missile had just ripped through the skies, the president's mind was on the border. He wanted DHS to "deport them all," Elaine recounted.

The White House was pressuring her to end something called "temporary protected status." The program allowed migrants from disaster-stricken countries to stay in America until conditions improved enough for them to go home. Trump wanted to kick these people out of the country. Under the law, DHS—and therefore, Elaine—was responsible for managing the program.

Honduras was one of the countries. More than fifty-seven thousand Hondurans lived in the United States under the program after a series of disasters had rocked their home country. They worked in the United States and had raised their families here while conditions remained bleak back home.

The president was itching to deport them. Elaine disagreed. Her eyes welled up as we talked about how much of a distraction it was, including from the threat that was symbolized by the classified papers on the table in front of us.

"I don't know how much longer I can do this," Elaine confided. "When do I leave?"

"When saying no is no longer enough," I told her. That was the internal mantra at DHS under Trump—a redline for deciding when to pull out our draft resignation letters, if we had them.

Elaine decided to extend protections for some migrant groups. Trump and his aides were angered by her recalcitrance. But in her mind, the decision bought more time to figure out a permanent solution, perhaps with the help of Congress.

Meanwhile, the temperature actually went down on North Korea. I was relieved when the president seemed to move toward the idea of negotiating with the hermit kingdom and its erratic leader. In any other administration, I would be opposed to talks with Pyongyang, but Trump badly needed an off-ramp before he got us into a war. The president smirked at the thought of his own chaotic nature.

"I won't rule out direct talks with Kim Jong Un, I just won't," he told attendees at an event a few months later. "As far as the risk of dealing with a madman is concerned, that's his problem, not mine."

"You helped create this monster."

Arriving guests beamed as they entered the ballroom at the White House Correspondents' Dinner, appearing relieved by an effervescent Saturday night. It was April 28, 2018. At first glance, you wouldn't have known the socialites were under siege—or that they weren't all on the same side. Men wore near-identical tuxedos, separated only by tailoring quality. Fitted suits denoted veterans of the annual gala, while loose ones gave away first-timers who'd rented their attire. Women sparkled in sequins as they walked the freshly laid red carpet, in defiance of the saying that Washington, D.C., was just "Hollywood for ugly people."

They weren't actually at ease, though. Beneath faces of makeup and the musk of cross-pollinating cologne, many attendees were at war with one another, battling it out in the press; a handful were recovering from the public humiliation of recently being fired; some nursed the calloused wounds of daily abuse; and others were striving to contain the chaos that was overtaking the nation's capital. That night, I thought I was in the latter camp.

My collar was tight as I entered the ballroom, as if choked by an invisible hand. A few extra pounds in the job were enough to push me to the tuxedo shirt's limits. An ABC News reporter named Katherine spotted me from the table where I was slated to dine with employees from the news outlet.

"Hello, my friend!" She rose and hailed my arrival with a hug. "Have you met Jake Tapper before?" She introduced me to the CNN reporter as he was cutting through the crowd.

Tapper was one of the night's honorees. In January 2017, he had dropped a massive news story about how the intelligence community had briefed President-Elect Trump that Russia claimed to have compromising information on him. The story was followed by an FBI investigation into Russian election interference, infuriating the incoming president and unleashing political mayhem that still engulfed the city.

"Jake, Miles works in the administration," Katherine explained. "He just became the deputy chief of staff at DHS." Tapper's broad smile receded almost imperceptibly.

The CNN anchor was in the category of dinner guests who were "at war." Trump had labeled Tapper's network "the FAKE NEWS media" and "the enemy of the American people." The veteran D.C. reporter countered that the Trump administration's behavior toward the press was "un-American" and a betrayal of "checks and balances and accountability."

He shook my hand politely and turned his attention to another guest. I could tell he had mentally lumped me in with the rest of the MAGA people. There wasn't an opportunity to protest.

I needed a drink. Wine bottles dotted the table, but I excused myself to seek something stronger. I was several weeks into a demanding new role at DHS and searching for faster decompression.

After Kirstjen Nielsen was sworn in as secretary of homeland security, she had beseeched me to stay for a few additional months. Once again, I slid my departure timeline to the right. I agreed to serve as the department's deputy chief of staff, taking over for Elizabeth Neumann, who stepped away to become the DHS assistant secretary handling counterterrorism issues. Chad Wolf was promoted to chief of staff.

Elizabeth and I had a farewell wine night before I moved into her office, and she left me a few bottles. "You'll need it," she said, knowing how difficult the role was. I ended up stocking the filing cabinet with whiskey, tequila, and mescal instead.

In theory, it was my post-9/11 dream job. I was charged with leading DHS strategy on everything from stopping mass shootings to preventing cyber warfare. This is why I had come to Washington. In reality, though, Donald Trump's immigration obsession and his bad-idea bonfires sucked up most of the oxygen, making it almost impossible to run the country's third-largest department.

Trump phoned one morning while I was briefing the secretary on a national security threat.

"Kiiiirstjen," he said in his distinctive New York accent. "I can't believe what I am seeing at the border." The president was rankled by footage of migrants crossing into the United States and wanted to talk about creative options for blocking them.

He had an idea: "a big, deep moat."

She muted the line. "Did he just say what I think he said?"

"I want you to figure out how deep you can dig it, okay Kirstjen?" Trump proposed filling the moat with "snakes and alligators" to eat people alive if they fell into it. "How much would this cost, honey?"

She unmuted. "We'll look into it, Mr. President." He kept pressing the point until she assured him again we'd get back to the White House.

He wasn't joking, and we weren't laughing anymore. The call derailed the morning as DHS cobbled together a back-of-the-envelope estimate for digging a border-long ditch and filling it with snakes and alligators. Telling Trump it was a ridiculous idea wouldn't stop him. He needed to see a huge price tag to let something go, so we told him a two-thousand-mile reptile-filled moat would cost tens of billions of dollars. Trump dropped the psychotic suggestion.

We established a daycare routine with the president, alternating in shift-work-like fashion. The secretary and Chad fielded the ceaseless demands from the Oval Office on border security and immigration. I usually ran point on the non-immigration issues, but everything I was working on kept getting pushed to the back burner.

I shared my exasperation with someone who felt the same way, Hannah Hummelberg. The twenty-something policy advisor had joined the DHS front office early that year after serving as an aide to Senate majority leader Mitch McConnell. Hannah shepherded decisions on the thorniest topics that landed on the secretary's desk—terrorism, election security, counterintelligence. Like me, she found that the issues weren't getting the attention they deserved.

We had bigger problems. And they were emanating from the Oval Office. Hannah and I ended most days reviewing intel reports in the SCIF, where I told her about the bizarre conversations we'd had with the president.

"Zero—*ZERO!*" Trump roared one day.

He went on a tangent, asking why America was letting in tens of thousands of refugees each year. The president didn't want to accept any more. Period. The demand was appalling, for sure, but his comments were also bewildering because no one had brought up refugees. In fact, the meeting wasn't about immigration at all. He'd brought the topic up out of nowhere, like a dementia patient with a synaptic misfire.

"It was some pretty crazy shit," I told Hannah, wondering aloud about Trump's mental health.

"You think he's sick?" she quizzed me.

"Without a doubt," I told her. Medically, I wasn't qualified to make the assessment. I just meant it as a layperson. And I was relieved that John Kelly was keeping a watchful eye over the West Wing.

In the bar line at the Correspondents' Dinner, I wasn't eager to socialize. The ballroom was packed like a rush-hour subway car, and my anxiety was peaking. For some reason crowds seemed to be something of a trigger, causing me to feel claustrophobic.

I asked for a beer and a double Jack on the rocks, knowing I wouldn't have to face Courtney's judgment. Months ago, I had canceled my counseling sessions amid the work onslaught. I couldn't miss ICBM launches for talk therapy.

A familiar face appeared on my way back to the table. Tom Bossert towered above the crowd, helpless in avoiding stares as he made his way past curious attendees. It was his first public appearance since getting sacked as the White House homeland security advisor weeks earlier.

Trump was becoming a sniper, steadily picking off the Adults whose loyalty he questioned—economic advisor Gary Cohn, Secretary of State Rex Tillerson, Acting FBI Director Andrew McCabe, National Security Advisor H. R. McMaster—and, most recently, Tom. The firings were one reason Kirstjen didn't want the White House to nominate anyone to become the DHS deputy secretary; if we had a Senate-confirmed deputy, it would make it easier for the president to fire her, too. By law, that person would become an automatic replacement.

Tom caught my eye and came over.

"How are you, buddy?" he asked, preempting the same question.

"Eh, you know," I shrugged.

We talked only briefly. I asked Tom what he was planning to do next. Out of government, I half expected him, Tillerson, and McMaster to go on offense against Trump, yet they'd all remained conspicuously silent. I told him we were still trying to fight the good fight.

"I'll be out there rooting for you guys," he said cheerfully.

I didn't know whether he meant he'd be cheering for the Trump administration or the people trying to keep it from burning down. Tom patted me on the shoulder before making his way into the sea of suits and dresses. I saw him later in the evening laughing alongside Sean Spicer and Reince Priebus, two men who'd also been thoroughly humiliated on the way out of the White House. Inexplicably, they continued to be Trump's cheerleaders.

Once the dinner started, I returned to my table. Normally, the highlight of the evening was a self-deprecating speech from the president. Trump skipped the event that night, the first chief executive to do so in nearly four decades. He was too thin-skinned to attend a dinner where he'd be the butt of all the jokes.

The president was represented by Press Secretary Sarah Huckabee Sanders, as well as White House advisor Kellyanne Conway. Having two women take his place was notable, I thought, given Trump's undisguised sexism. When we were with him, Kirstjen did her best to ignore the president's inappropriate behavior. He called her "sweetie" and "honey," and critiqued her makeup and outfits.

"Trust me," the secretary whispered, seeing my face after a crass comment from Trump, "this is not a healthy workplace for women." Kellyanne referred to Trump as a "misogynistic bully" following a meeting during which he berated several female leaders in the administration.

Sarah Sanders was subjected to it as well, whether she knew it or not. During a meeting in the Oval Office, the president thought he saw the brunette press secretary waiting in the anteroom outside the Oval.

"Come in here, Sarah!" he shouted.

"It's just me, sir," a young woman—one of Trump's personal assistants—poked her head in the door. "Sarah is not here."

"Whoops," Trump responded. "I was going to say, 'Man, Sarah, you've lost a lot of weight!'"

Everyone in the room sat in awkward silence.

Worst of all were stories about the president's lewd comments about his own family members. Aides said he talked about Ivanka Trump's breasts, her backside, and what it might be like to have sex with her, remarks that once led John Kelly to remind the president that Ivanka was his daughter. Afterward, Kelly retold the story to me in visible disgust. Trump, he said, was "a very, very evil man."

As the lights dimmed at the Correspondents' Dinner, comedian Michelle Wolf took to the podium as the night's entertainment. She wasted no time roasting the administration.

"I did have a lot of jokes about cabinet members," she informed the crowd, "but I had to scrap all of those because everyone has been fired."

So Wolf turned to Trump's surrogates in the room.

"There's Kellyanne Conway. Man, she has the perfect last name for what she does. *Con-way,*" the comedian emphasized to laughs. "It's like if my name was 'Michelle Jokes Frizzy Hair Small Tits.' You guys have got to stop putting Kellyanne on your shows. All she does is lie. If you don't give her a platform, she has nowhere to lie."

Then it was on to Sarah.

"I actually really like Sarah. I think she's very resourceful. She burns facts, and then she uses that ash to create a perfect smokey eye. Like maybe she's born with it, maybe it's lies. It's probably lies."

Poised in a royal-blue dress, Sarah kept a steady gaze on the comedian, trying not to react.

Ivanka wasn't spared either. "She was supposed to be an advocate for women," Wolf remarked, "but it turns out she's about as helpful to women as an empty box of tampons. She's done nothing to satisfy women. So, I guess, like father, like daughter."

I watched one of Trump's communications aides, Mercy Schlapp, walk out in protest. But Wolf saved her harshest for last by mocking all the dinner attendees, collectively.

"You guys are obsessed with Trump. Did you used to date him? Because you pretend like you hate him, but I think you love him. I think what no one in this room wants to admit is that Trump has helped all of you. . . . He's helped you sell your papers and your books and your TV. *You helped create this monster,*" she emphasized. "If you're going to profit off of Trump, you should at least give him some money, because he doesn't have any!"

Afterward, Wolf's set was widely panned as disrespectful toward the prominent women in the administration. Attendees consoled Conway and Sanders, chiding the comedian for being too crass. The critiques were thick with irony, given who the women worked for.

Something else made guests feel uncomfortable, though no one admitted it during the after party. The lewd jokes didn't make us squirm. It was the truthful ones, like the bit at the end. People in the room who despised the president nevertheless relied on him.

One of them was Rod Rosenstein, the deputy attorney general. I briefly got sandwiched into a conversation with him after the speeches ended. He was the highest-ranking official overseeing the Russia investigation, and Trump regularly lambasted him in public and private. Yet

I listened with surprise as Rosenstein assured dinner guests that any suggestion of turmoil between the White House and the Justice Department was completely overblown.

I knew he felt differently. The deputy attorney general saw Trump as a danger and perhaps already a criminal. Rosenstein had discussed the idea of wearing a wire in the Oval Office, as well as the possibility of invoking "the Twenty-Fifth." Codified in 1967, the Twenty-Fifth Amendment to the Constitution outlines a process for the vice president and the heads of the fifteen executive departments to declare the president—by simple majority vote—unfit for office and to strip the president of his or her powers.

As recently as a week before the Correspondents' Dinner, Kirstjen and I had met and talked about the "forbidden" provision. John Kelly had done an informal whip count. A number of cabinet members were prepared to take the vote in an extreme scenario, but no one thought it was a viable option at the moment. Trump would call it a coup. His supporters would violently take to the streets, and Congress would probably overturn the determination anyway.

Rosenstein had canvassed administration colleagues about the possibility, too. That's why I was perplexed to hear him at the dinner, casually downplaying concerns about the president. The Adults who despised Trump still seemed to be choked by his vise-like grip. In fact, a year later, Rosenstein would write the president a flattering departure letter—thanking Trump for the honor of a lifetime, praising the administration's policies, and glowingly recalling the president's "courtesy and humor."

The woman I was searching for in the crowd popped into the conversation from behind me.

"Hello, friends." Kirstjen greeted us wearing an ocean-blue dress. "How about that speech? Whew." She let out a hearty laugh, breaking the tension.

"Good to see you, Madam Secretary," I said. "Come with me to get a drink?" She agreed. As Kirstjen and I wound our way through the crowd to get cocktails, I made an observation.

An undertone of edginess had permeated the room at the beginning of the night. Insular camps avoided one another. Yet eventually, with more libations, the camps had blended and conversations swelled into a back-slapping cacophony across the ballroom. All of these people were the same. The sparkle of the dinner guests masked the craven artificiality that had brought them together—a desire to be something they were not. These were the lab-grown diamonds of American politics.

When we had our drinks in hand, Kirstjen toasted the end of an exhausting month. She offered up hope that the coming summer wouldn't be so manic, and she asked me about the family member who'd been struggling with alcoholism.

"She's fine now," I lied.

"Let me know if you need to take some time," Kirstjen offered sincerely.

I hadn't been able to make it back home. There was no such thing as taking time off in the administration. The crises followed you no matter where you went.

Kirstjen hadn't fully expected the crushing workload either. She wanted to be the government's cybersecurity chief, not the head of DHS and certainly not an immigration official. Border security wasn't her forte. My colleague Gene Hamilton chose to quit after Kirstjen's nomination, knowing she wasn't a hardline immigration policy expert, and he went to the Justice Department to work for Jeff Sessions, who eagerly championed Trump's strict border policies.

Kirstjen's background and hard-nosed style were a relief to many at DHS. She brought a sense of order amid the disarray and instituted rigorous policy processes. A trained lawyer, she was also a stickler for following government guidelines.

Places like DHS were the "Wild West" of the bureaucracy. Some of Trump's initial DHS appointees—known as the "landing team"—saw themselves as antigovernment vigilantes, and a few even tried to bring their guns into work in violation of federal law. To them, there were no rules. They could do whatever they wanted because *they* were members of the president's gang. Then Kirstjen came in. She was like a sheriff walking into a lawless town to restore order, at least at first. ("No," she told a Senate-confirmed Trump leader, "you cannot bring a fucking gun into the office.")

Guests at the Correspondents' Dinner approached Kirstjen as we sipped drinks, eager to offer a kind word (and to brush shoulders with someone important enough to be trailed by security agents). The secretary was relaxed and boisterous, perhaps for the last time in the role. In the weeks to come, she would be forced to walk the tightrope between "containment" and "complicity" like no one else in the Trump administration.

It began two weeks later, when the president soured on her.

★ ★ ★

"If I lose re-election, it's because of you!" Trump spat at Kirstjen in front of the entire cabinet.

He was sick of her saying no. *No*, you can't seal the border. *No*, you can't deport anybody you want. *No*, you can't gas and electrocute migrants. The insubordination was intolerable, so Trump effectively put Jeff Sessions in charge of immigration and embraced the attorney general's plan to prosecute everyone who crossed the border illegally.

Kirstjen threatened to quit. She drafted her resignation letter that day and was prepared to submit it, until the vice president and John Kelly talked her down. She was vehemently opposed to the Sessions policy and pleaded with the White House to shelve it, worried the immigration system would buckle under the pressure of "100 percent enforcement."

DHS border agency chiefs sent her a draft memo seeking approval to execute the Justice Department plans, known as "zero tolerance." I hadn't been involved in the deliberations up to that point, but I offered my two cents anyway: don't sign it. The concept seemed poorly crafted, and some officials signaled that it was impossible to arrest all undocumented immigrants at the border without overwhelming already crowded detention facilities. However, Kirstjen didn't think she could overrule the attorney general without Trump's backing, which she didn't have. Career immigration officials assured her that the border prosecutions wouldn't result in a catastrophe.

The debate caused intense internal friction. Someone sent the draft memo to the *Washington Post* in an apparent attempt to call attention to the brewing controversy. Over dinner at a downtown restaurant in May, Kirstjen asked me pointedly if I had leaked the memo. Several border officials knew that I was opposed to the Sessions policy, and one of them told her I had spilled the draft document to the press to create a public uproar and limit her options. It was true that I thought the Justice Department plan appeared incredibly stupid and clearly needed more discussion to be made feasible, but I didn't leak the document. I knew little about immigration and assumed the concept would die, like other misguided Trump border ideas. I told her it wasn't me. In hindsight, I wish I *had* been the person who leaked the memo and sounded the public alarm. Kirstjen didn't know who to trust because it seemed like people on both sides of the debate were going behind her back.

And they were.

Kirstjen was called to the White House for a surprise meeting on the subject. After a contentious discussion, Trump's aides asked for a show of hands on whether to move forward with "zero tolerance," which eventually became known as "family separation" at the U.S. southern border. Kirstjen was reportedly the only one to vote no. She was outgunned by Jeff Sessions and his immigration team at DOJ, which—ironically—was being led by our former colleague Gene Hamilton.

With that, the most immoral policy of the Trump era went into effect. A slow-moving train wreck, the preventable humanitarian disaster took weeks to become a full-blown national crisis. By the time it did, there was no mistaking the fact that the government policy had resulted in migrant families separated for days, weeks, months, and—in some cases—forever. There were no excuses. It never should have happened.

The White House went into panic mode as the public outcry grew. Trump demanded Kirstjen take to the podium to defend it, even though it wasn't her policy to defend. John Kelly and DHS chief of staff Chad Wolf, who were with her that day, told her not to. Stephen Miller and Sarah Sanders pressured her to speak.

"We can't have Sessions do it," Sarah insisted. "He sounds like a fucking idiot."

Kirstjen relented. In doing so, one of the few people who had fought inside the administration to delay family separation wound up becoming the face of it. Morale in the DHS front office plummeted.

The secretary returned from the White House shell-shocked from the briefing. While she spoke, the press had played audio of crying children being ripped from the arms of their parents. Afterward Kirstjen was furious, protesting that DHS agencies weren't telling her how bad the situation on the ground really was.

She raged from her office, "This is fucked!"

That day she resolved to get Trump to shut down the program immediately, or to leave. Stephen Miller didn't want Trump to back down. But by reaching out to people around the president—including family members—the secretary persuaded Trump to "pause" the policy or the courts would do it for him. Again, fear of judges came in handy. Trump conceded.

The secretary called from the White House to let staff know the news. She asked for my help. So, working with department lawyers, I codrafted an executive order that overruled the DOJ policy and effectively ended family separation.

But the damage was already done. The debacle was "a sickening display of bad judgment" and "a seminal moment of Trumpism gone too far," I later wrote in a warning to voters about how it could happen again. "Trump's character rubs off on people who came into government to do what is right. Before long, they find themselves supporting and defending policies they never imagined they would."

I was confronted with a stark reality that I'd avoided up to this point. Saying no was no longer enough.

Weeks before all of that, drunken Washington elites celebrated at the downtown Hilton as if nothing were amiss in the nation's capital. Kirstjen bid me an early farewell as she tried to exit the Correspondents' Dinner without being noticed, disappearing with her Secret Service detail before midnight.

The rest of us partied the night away, not knowing it was the last time Trump officials would mingle with the press at the annual gala.

The president heard he'd been mocked. He later issued an order forbidding staff from attending the dinner in the future.

I joined an after-after party with my ABC News hosts inside the nearby Mayflower Hotel. We found a corner in the gold-trimmed bar. Despite plenty of drinks, my anxiety lingered, and the containment techniques weren't working. I took a Xanax.

Thirty minutes later, I melted into a leather chair. With a few more cocktails, everyone was synthetically disposed to speak their minds. The overworked journalists talked about how much the town had changed. We swapped stories about White House mishaps and what we'd do when this was all over. Whether you were working in it, covering it, or just following it on social media, you longed for the day when the Trump administration finally faded away.

"This is the worst assignment I've ever had in my fucking life." I can't remember who said it. For all of us, journalists and government employees alike, the statement was true. We drank until the misery became revelry, turning the night into a fogged-glass blur.

When the bar lights came on in the early morning hours, I wasn't quite ready to accept the truth: it was time to go.

PART II

When I first met Andrew McCabe, he didn't seem like the political type. In fact, there was no telling what his partisan leanings were in mid-2015, when he briefed me and my colleagues on the particulars of a recent terrorist plot targeting Washington, D.C. The suspect was an ISIS-inspired radical—a "homegrown terrorist," McCabe specified—and had used the terror group's instructions to pull together a detailed plan to attack the U.S. Capitol Building. He sought to detonate bombs around the facility and kill as many lawmakers as possible, purchasing semi-automatic rifles and ammunition to carry out the attack.

The suspect had been ready to move forward. What he didn't know was that he was under round-the-clock FBI surveillance. The Washington Field Office (WFO) where McCabe was chief would never have let him get close to the Capitol.

"He didn't stand a chance," the seasoned FBI veteran explained.

The suspect was arrested, convicted, and later sentenced to several decades in prison. McCabe was pulling near all-nighters to help disrupt attacks like this. But it was the plots that weren't on his radar that kept him awake.

He briefed us on a sweltering day in June 2015 at the WFO headquarters, near D.C.'s Chinatown neighborhood. I was working on Capitol Hill at the time, leading a bipartisan counterterrorism task force with a dozen members of Congress. We were reassured that McCabe was on the job. He was one of the most trusted officials in the Bureau and had handled sensitive cases—from massive organized crime to Chinese espionage on U.S. soil—under presidents of both parties. When the ISIS terror threat surged, FBI leaders put him in charge at WFO, where the best of the best investigate the worst of the worst.

The members of Congress who were there with me that day thanked McCabe. His team's work to protect the U.S. Capitol could have saved their lives, they said. He humbly deflected the praise. It was the only briefing I've ever been in where congressional representatives clapped at the end.

He didn't know it at the time, but some of these legislators would eventually turn against McCabe. After he left WFO, he became FBI deputy director, then acting director when Jim Comey was dismissed. ("You could have knocked me down with a finger," he told me of his shock when he learned Comey was fired.) He had never imagined political interference at the Bureau—an institution regarded for its investigative autonomy—and certainly not from a president.

Then he found himself on Trump's enemies list. McCabe was instrumental in convincing DOJ leaders to appoint an independent special counsel to lead the Russia investigation so that the White House couldn't interfere with efforts to get to the bottom of whether Moscow had somehow infiltrated Trump's inner circle. The president was incensed. He accused Andy McCabe of being a Democratic mole inside

DOJ and attacked the FBI leader on Twitter with regularity. Trump even singled out McCabe's wife, drawing spurious connections between her personal political activities and her husband's job.

"We were under incredible pressure from the most powerful man in the country," he reflected about his time in Trump's DOJ. "He installed people who made it clear to us they were there to do what he wanted."

We reconnected before the 2020 election. McCabe was out of government and feared that if Trump won a second term, the White House would try to use DOJ, the FBI, and the justice system to prosecute the president's rivals.

"Could they succeed?" I asked.

"Everyone at the Bureau—from deputy director down to the front desk—is there to uphold the Constitution and protect the American people." But he added a caveat. "I guess you could try replacing them, too."

His words were prescient. After Trump's loss, GOP leaders started talking about detonating the FBI, and they haven't stopped. Critics include MAGA-aligned members of Congress, such as Representatives Scott Perry and Barry Loudermilk. Both men served on the counterterrorism panel that applauded Andrew McCabe and the FBI in June 2015 for possibly saving their lives.

THE NEXT TRUMP WILL MANIPULATE THE JUSTICE SYSTEM TO COVER UP CORRUPTION, PUNISH POLITICAL ENEMIES, AND RESHAPE U.S. COURTS.

The justice system doesn't reside in a single branch of government. Although the judicial branch was designed to interpret the laws independently, it relies on the other two branches to function. The legislative branch confirms federal judges, while the executive branch is charged with investigating and prosecuting crimes in front of those judges. Additionally, the investigative functions within the executive branch have traditionally been firewalled from the White House to prevent political tampering.

Alone, the judiciary is the weakest of the three branches. As Alexander Hamilton wrote, "it can never attack with success either of the other two." It merely interprets the laws and cannot rewrite them or enforce its own edicts. The Founders feared what might happen if the separation of powers within the justice system was erased.

"Liberty can have nothing to fear from the judiciary alone," Hamilton explained, "but would have everything to fear from its union with either of the other departments. . . . It is in continual jeopardy of being overpowered, awed, or influenced by its co-ordinate branches."

A president who can investigate, prosecute, and serve as his own judge is not a president at all, but a despot. Donald Trump worked assiduously to break down the barriers between the presidency and the justice system, fiddling with every part of it along the way for personal benefit. He planned to go further in a second term, and his political movement is poised to perpetuate those tendencies, putting another democratic guardrail at risk.

MAGA forces will tip the scales of justice in their favor, starting with investigative agencies.

Another far-right president will enter office prepared to assert full control of the FBI, and maybe even get rid of it entirely. Movement firebrands like Steve Bannon have long complained about the "weaponization of the FBI," and influential former Trump officials have spread the idea that the Bureau is "corrupt" and "politically motivated." The ex-president himself has promoted articles blasting the agency as "the Fascist Bureau of Investigation" and derided agents as "vicious monsters."

The message has gone mainstream. Republican legislators are planning widespread probes into the Bureau, proposing to investigate the investigators. (As of this writing, Republicans in the House of Representatives have already launched a "Select Subcommittee on the Weaponization of the Federal Government" to do exactly that.).

"NOBODY trusts the FBI & DOJ anymore," Congressman Ronny Jackson tweeted, capturing the sentiment of his MAGA colleagues. "They've morphed into a political organization that's hellbent on intimidating & scaring law-abiding conservatives." Once-moderate Republicans like Florida senator Rick Scott have joined in, equating the Bureau to "the gestapo" in Nazi Germany.

"I think the FBI has gotten heavily, severely off track since 9/11," Texas congressman Chip Roy told news outlet *Politico*. The Judiciary Committee member, who helps oversee the FBI, said Congress needed to do a "deep dive" into the agency to make sure it isn't "witch-hunting Americans."

Some want to take more drastic measures. Representative Marjorie Taylor Greene has called for "defunding the FBI," while her colleague Paul Gosar released a blunter statement: "We must destroy the FBI. We must save America." GOP senator Ted Cruz made a similar proposition.

"It is horrific the abuse of power at the FBI, and it's wrong," Cruz told a supporter after an event in Georgia. "There needs to be a complete house cleaning that happens at the FBI."

This isn't the first time the FBI feared a "house cleaning." Early in Donald Trump's presidency, top agents worried the White House might take over the building. Literally.

The day FBI director James Comey was fired, one of the Bureau's counterintelligence chiefs, Peter Strzok, was nervous. He heard the bad news about his boss's dismissal while working at the FBI's headquarters, the Hoover Building. From his fourth-floor office, Strzok gazed down Pennsylvania Avenue and could just barely make out the White House fence line. Strzok was concerned that Trump and his team might dispatch operatives to come down the street and rummage through the facility.

"What happens if U.S. Secret Service agents—or some other agency, or a team of presidential lawyers—come into our offices to seize all of our files?" he wondered after the director was sacked.

The notion would have sounded absurd the day before. After Comey's firing, it seemed like a potential reality. Strzok and his counterparts knew the damage that could be done if the White House scooped up or destroyed the Bureau's investigative files, such as those related to the Russia investigation, the president, and his allies.

That evening, agents scrambled to stash sensitive documents. They came up with an improvised filing system to make sure unauthorized personnel couldn't locate documents related to important investigations. FBI employees spent hours meticulously scanning case files into a digital format that couldn't be keyword searched and stored the files in disparate locations—"in layers," Strzok said—while safeguarding hard copies.

The incident echoed the past. Agents investigating President Richard Nixon during the Watergate scandal stashed case files, too. They reportedly rented safety deposit boxes at nearby banks and stored documents away from the Hoover Building out of fear that the president's henchmen might try to enter FBI headquarters to seize the documents. As Strzok recounted, no one from the Trump White House ended up storming the building the night Comey was sacked, or at any time after.

But both stories foreshadow what could happen in the future. Given the level of conservative animosity toward the agency today, it is not a stretch to imagine the Next Trump mounting a hostile takeover of the FBI. While he or she is unlikely to have the Bureau ransacked, it's reasonable to assume a MAGA White House will install loyalists at the Justice Department and the Bureau who will influence the government's investigative priorities in ways favorable to the president.

"Agents aren't just going to start persecuting people or round folks up unconstitutionally," Strzok clarified. "But you could easily create investigative priorities that would dramatically shift what people are doing."

For instance, a Trump-like future president could order DOJ and the FBI to focus on something like immigration enforcement, all the while shifting resources away from public corruption, financial crimes, or counterintelligence investigations. That would be well within his or her authority, might not appear entirely corrupt, and could have the effect of redirecting the Bureau's attention away from wrongdoing in the executive branch.

"You could radically re-engineer . . . our whole investigative and law enforcement posture," Strzok noted.

It already happened in the Trump administration. I saw it firsthand. The White House wanted to steer the attention of agencies like DHS and the FBI away from domestic terrorism. The president's advisors believed that violent extremist groups such as the Proud Boys and the Oath Keepers were supporters, not suspects. In the draft of the administration's national counterterrorism strategy, they intentionally deleted most of the language I wrote about combating domestic violent extremists. The final document made scant reference to the threat and casually lumped neo-Nazi groups in with animal rights activists and environmental extremists.

"There was zero appetite for addressing domestic terrorism," Matt Castelli recalled. He served for two years in the Trump White House as a director on the NSC. Castelli believed Trump didn't want MAGA supporters to get investigated. "There was no space or oxygen for [discussing] a domestic terrorism strategy," Castelli said.

The administration allowed the danger to metastasize. How else do you explain why DHS and the FBI failed to detect a domestic terrorism plot to storm the U.S. Capitol on January 6, 2021—an organized, nationwide conspiracy that involved planners and armed rioters from nearly all fifty states? A former FBI agent told me that his superiors were more attuned to left-wing vandalism in Portland and racial justice protests than MAGA operatives plotting to violently advance Trump's "Stop the Steal" goals. They didn't want to get caught in the political crossfire, and as a result, they failed to connect the dots.

We are still facing the consequences. "It used to be in the dark corner of the internet that domestic terrorists conspired, but now it's happening on our TV screens and coming out of the mouths of political leaders," Castelli lamented, citing MAGA rhetoric and conspiracy theories that have directly emboldened white supremacist groups and antigovernment militias.

Pressure from another MAGA administration might cause the FBI to become even more risk averse.

"There would be a great deal of danger of the Bureau reverting into a protective political crouch that makes them vulnerable to accusations of . . . reluctance," explained former FBI agent Brian Murphy, who was an intelligence official during the Trump administration. "Organizations try to survive. But they can go too much 'into the turtle [shell]' that they become ineffective."

Who will benefit from that?

"Corrupt politicians and foreign adversaries," Murphy noted.

If all else fails, supporters of the Next Trump will be ready to physically intimidate government investigators. They've perfected the pattern. Days after Donald Trump's home was searched by federal authorities on August 8, 2022, users on right-wing online forums demanded retaliation.

A Trump supporter responded to the call. The former U.S. Navy veteran attempted to breach the FBI field office in Cincinnati, Ohio, with an AR-15 rifle and a nail gun. He was killed in a standoff with law enforcement. A social media account allegedly left behind by the perpetrator told pro-Trump followers to arm themselves and prepare for combat.

"Kill the FBI on sight," one post read, "and be ready to take down other active enemies of the people and those who try to prevent you from doing it."

Another MAGA president will try to use the justice system to prosecute rivals.

After his presidency, Trump sued former rival Hillary Clinton, alleging a "malicious conspiracy" to undermine him with damaging claims about Russian interference in the 2016 election. The case was thrown out by a federal judge, who declared that Trump was a "prolific and sophisticated litigant who is repeatedly using the courts to seek revenge on political adversaries." The judge blasted the ex-president and his lawyer for undertaking what amounted to "strategic abuse of the judicial process." Trump was fined almost a million dollars for the frivolous lawsuit.

Back in power, Trump and his allies will be less worried about conscientious judges. They'll have the full weight of the U.S. Department of Justice to wield against enemies. And they'll have the know-how to do it efficiently this time.

"We were fortunate that Trump was not particularly competent and didn't know how government worked because it slowed him down," Bob Shanks shared with me, reflecting on Trump's tenure. He was a top lawyer in the State Department during the administration and previously served at DOJ. "[Trump] wasted several years trying to figure out how to coerce the government to do what he wanted, and by the end he figured out how to do it." Shanks said a future MAGA administration would learn from these lessons in order to manipulate the justice system from the outset.

Other former Trump lawyers share the worry.

"Generally speaking, Trump and his ilk will be unconstrained and untethered," former DHS general counsel John Mitnick said. "What little restraint was exercised in terms of respecting the rule of law [under Trump], it will all be gone."

A future White House might use a threat like terrorism as a pretext for investigating political rivals. Tom Warrick sees this as a possibility. He was one of the U.S. government's leading counterterrorism officials during the Trump years and witnessed officials misuse investigative tools.

"The effort to say there was an Antifa terrorist threat was really the creation of a phantom menace," Warrick explained, noting that the loosely organized anarchists didn't represent much of a real threat. But the narrative of "left-wing terrorists" benefited Trump politically. MAGA leaders took note.

"You will see them cock the weapon and aim it at a new target," he predicted. "I assume we are going to see the invention of domestic terrorist enemies. This is one of the scariest aspects of what a 'Trump Two' would bring into office."

Security searches at the U.S. border are just one example of what they could do. "Hassling people at airports will become a sport—just like hassling people with their tax returns," Warrick said.

Peter Strzok added to the hypothetical: "They could sift through the pocket litter of a Democratic congressman"—police terminology for the personal effects of a target—"or maybe their electronic devices, all in the name of fighting Antifa." Whatever personal information they find could be used to intimidate, threaten, or silence opponents.

The harassment won't end with border searches. It will escalate into sham prosecutions of political rivals. The idea sounds exaggerated, but it's where the Trump presidency was headed. The administration's former DOJ prosecutor in New York, Geoffrey Berman, documented a range of "overtly political" demands inside the Justice Department, including orders to go after opponents of the president, such as former Democratic senator and secretary of state John Kerry.

"Throughout my tenure as U.S. attorney," Berman wrote in his memoirs, "Trump's Justice Department kept demanding that I use my office to aid them politically, and I kept declining—in ways just tactful enough to keep me from being fired."

Trump's legal advisors will return for a MAGA redux. One told me that "sue the blue" will be watchwords when the movement retakes the executive branch. Prosecutors will prioritize cases against Democratic states, cities, and municipalities; left-leaning companies; liberal causes and organizations; and progressive politicians, while setting aside investigations into the far-right equivalents. They will attempt to tie up these people and institutions with costly litigation to force them to settle and to shut up, or else.

To understand how this will happen, multiple former officials pointed me toward the special-counsel power. Appointing "independent" prosecutors is how a Trump-like future leader will bring charges against rivals, while maintaining the appearance of legitimacy. Under federal regulations, the attorney general is authorized to appoint a special counsel whenever he or she "determines that a criminal investigation of a person or matter is warranted" and when the probe might create a conflict of interest for DOJ. The president can direct his attorney general to exercise this power and appoint whoever he or she wants. A corrupt prosecutor could torment the president's enemies and keep judicial probes open for years.

"If you watch someone long enough, you'll catch them breaking the law—whether it's jaywalking or reckless driving," a former Trump official explained, outlining the scenario.

Donald Trump already wrote the playbook. After he railed for years against the "Russia hoax" and an intelligence community he claimed was out to get him, he got his revenge. Attorney General Bill Barr appointed a special counsel to look into the origins of the Russia investigation. Though the review found little to support the president's paranoid claims, it kept intelligence leaders on edge and mired former Obama administration officials—whom Trump detested—in legal proceedings for years.

In his final days in office, Trump attempted to take the concept to the next level. He debated naming one of his lawyers, Sidney Powell, as a special counsel to investigate "voter fraud" in the 2020 election as part of a scheme to overturn the results. Powell later recounted how Trump asked White House lawyer Pat Cipollone whether he had the authority to appoint Powell to the post. Cipollone told the president he did.

"Okay, you know, I'm naming her that and I'm giving her security clearance," Trump responded. A worried Cipollone buried the idea by not doing the necessary paperwork to appoint Powell.

A smarter MAGA president will succeed where Trump failed. He or she will rely on an army of special counsels—appointed with seemingly legitimate orders Bubble Wrapped in legalese, but whose real mission will be prosecutions of political adversaries. The Next Trump might assign a special counsel to, let's say, conduct leak investigations into government employees who have released unauthorized information. This might be a cover to probe the private lives of whistle-blowers who've spoken out against the White House.

People who defected from the Trump administration joke darkly about being sent to the terrorist prison in Guantánamo Bay, Cuba, (known as "Gitmo") under a MAGA successor. They have good reason. Trump once proposed that we transport illegal immigrants to the detention facility, which is home to the 9/11 attack plotters, in order to send a message to would-be border crossers. He was talked out of it—not because it was wrong but because the jail was too small for large numbers of inmates. If America elects another leader like Trump, we could see high-profile political prisoners shipped off to Gitmo instead. And books like this will be written from prison cells, if at all.

The White House will attempt to get rid of noncompliant judges, or simply ignore them altogether.

The permanence of judges is what gives them power and neutrality. In the words of the Code of Conduct for U.S. Judges, lifetime appointments allow them to be free from "partisan interests, public clamor, or fear of criticism," and focus on being faithful to the law. These federal employees can still be removed for misconduct. As the Founders wrote, the courts were designed to be "composed of judges holding their offices during *good behavior*" (emphasis added), so they outlined a process for Congress to impeach corrupt judges. Scarcely more than a dozen have been removed this way.

They *cannot* be fired by the White House. To the architects of the Constitution, no one was a bigger threat to a judge's independence than the president.

Under the pseudonym Publius, Alexander Hamilton explained why: "By being often associated with the Executive, they might be induced to embark too far in the political views of that magistrate and thus a dangerous combination might by degrees be cemented between the Executive and Judiciary Departments. . . . It is peculiarly dangerous to place them in a situation to be either corrupted or influenced by the Executive."

Donald Trump wanted to narrow the separation between himself and the robed men and women who could determine his fate. His primary means of influencing judges was bullying on social media. He developed a pattern of verbal abuse against federal judges who ruled against him—"totally biased," "incompetent," "so-called judge," "putting the country in danger," "mind is shot," "misconduct," "witch hunt," and so on—to stir public animosity. The missives got more ominous over time.

"It would be great if the 9th Circuit was indeed an 'independent judiciary,'" Trump wrote in November 2018, assailing a federal appeals court that struck down one of his immigration policies. He said the judges were "making our Country unsafe," demanding they back off and let his people "DO THEIR JOB!"

"If not," the president wrote ominously, "there will be only bedlam, chaos, injury and death."

GOP leaders have echoed Trump's rancor, contributing to dwindling public confidence in the justice system, and worse. Physical intimidation of judges is on the rise. U.S. law enforcement agencies continue to issue warnings about the danger to judges from crowd-sourced calls for violence, including after a Wisconsin judge was assassinated and a man was arrested for plotting to murder a U.S. Supreme Court justice. The judge who approved a search warrant against Donald Trump saw his own home address re-posted across right-wing websites and received a slew of death threats.

The intimidation works. A state GOP official shared a story with me about a judge who punted a case in 2021, partly out of fear of ruling against MAGA plaintiffs. The judge chose an obscure procedural route to avoid making a decision. It would be a danger to democracy for federal judges to do the same with their rulings.

The Next Trump will perpetuate hostility toward courts. Or he or she will simply try to remove judges, as Trump wanted to.

I vividly remember one such Oval Office meeting. The sky was dark outside, as a half dozen of us sat on the couches in front of the Resolute desk, listening to Trump complain that the courts were making him look weak politically. They were striking down his orders left and right. No one was giving him good ideas to fix the problem, he said.

"We need to get rid of the judges," the president declared, pounding a fist on the desk. He was particularly angry at the Ninth Circuit Court of Appeals for reversing his decisions. "They are ruining this."

"Yes, sir, a country without judges would help," Stephen Miller piped in without a hint of sarcasm.

Trump didn't seem to notice. "They are tearing the country apart. We don't win any cases. We lose all of these cases. The only cases I've won as president are on Stormy Daniels and the weak-ass travel ban. That's it!"

The president knew he lacked the MAGA supermajority in Congress needed to impeach federal judges. So he demanded that White House staff write a bill and send it to Congress to address the problem in a different way. He wanted to break up and rejigger courts, especially in left-leaning regions.

GOP leaders weren't averse to the idea. In fact, several of the president's congressional allies introduced bills to split up courts that ruled against Trump policies, including the Ninth Circuit, which they called the "Nutty Ninth." It was naked judicial gerrymandering. Although the legislation didn't pass, another MAGA president will work hard to get the votes, whether it's to impeach perceived left-leaning justices or eliminate the courts where they sit.

Jon Burks, former chief of staff to GOP House Speaker Paul Ryan, forecast another potential tactic: indifference. The Next Trump might just ignore judicial orders, sparking "war in the justice system."

"Everything will end up in the courts," he said. "Then we will quickly end up in the Lincoln-and-the-Writ scenario."

Burks was referring to the Civil War, when Supreme Court Chief Justice Roger Taney challenged President Abraham Lincoln's wartime suspension of habeas corpus. The suspension was designed to give military commanders the ability to silence dissenters and rebels. Taney ruled it was illegal. Lincoln ignored him, knowing the chief justice had no ability to enforce the order.

MAGA diehards like to invoke U.S. President Andrew Jackson for similar reasons. Jackson responded defiantly when the Supreme Court and Justice John Marshall struck down one of his controversial decisions.

"John Marshall has made his decision," Jackson allegedly responded. "Now let him enforce it."

In the Oval Office, Trump prominently displayed Andrew Jackson's portrait.

"It's important that people know what happens when a career government servant stumbles into the cross hairs of a president who wants to destroy you—who has no concern for the rule of law or the welfare of our democracy or for the institutions," Andy McCabe told me about his experience trying to preserve the integrity of the investigative process, while facing a president determined to corrupt it.

He was attacked relentlessly by a White House that accused him of treason and raised questions about his personal life. Over time, the FBI executive got tired of the abuse and announced plans to retire in March 2018, when he would qualify for his pension. Trump pressured DOJ to get rid of McCabe first, expressing faux shock on social media that the man would be allowed to leave government with full benefits.

"He was racing me to my retirement," McCabe recalled.

Two days before his scheduled departure, McCabe was summoned by Attorney General Jeff Sessions. He was fired on the spot and lost his pension benefits. Trump celebrated the news on Twitter, but it didn't stop there. McCabe was threatened with prosecution for allegedly misleading the FBI about his contacts with the media regarding an old news story on the Clinton investigation.

"My kids were terrified their father was going to get thrown in jail," he said. "Of course they were. It's the president and the Department of Justice that are doing this. Who can stop them?"

While DOJ never pursued a case, the threat hung over McCabe's family for two years. Not until Trump left office did he get restitution. He sued the Justice Department for wrongful termination and won. Still, the damage was done. Trump's crusade against investigators and judges set a precedent within the Republican Party for manipulating the justice system, as long as it's in their favor.

Looking forward, the system can't be expected to defend itself. We must rely on the legislative branch to fortify this guardrail. Among other measures, Congress should consider: imposing stricter limits on contact between DOJ and the White House; strengthening employment protections against political interference for federal law-enforcement agents; bolstering DOJ's top watchdog to be able to identify and expose corruption; and revisiting expired laws around the independence of special counsels.

Unfortunately, if a MAGA agitator retakes the White House, the legislative branch will be in the cross hairs, too.

Chapter 4

THE ASSEMBLY

When occasions present themselves, in which the interests of the people are at variance with their inclinations, it is the duty of the persons whom they have appointed to be the guardians of those interests, to withstand the temporary delusion, in order to give them time and opportunity for more cool and sedate reflection. Instances might be cited in which a conduct of this kind has saved the people from very fatal consequences of their own mistakes.

—ALEXANDER HAMILTON, FEDERALIST NO. 71, 1788

PART I

Our weary team crossed the blacktop in Las Vegas and boarded Coast Guard One. The private Gulfstream jet had purportedly belonged to Oprah Winfrey before it was purchased by DHS as the primary plane for executive leaders. Flying on it hardly felt glamorous, because it was often bound for hot spots, and not of the vacation kind. We spent most of August 2018 hurtling between disasters and comforting Americans in places destroyed by hurricanes, wildfires, and now—at the very end of the month—volcanic eruptions.

The ultimate destination was Australia. Our core leadership team at DHS was headed to meet with leaders from the "Five Eyes" intelligence alliance, the group of Western governments that share sensitive threat data, and Attorney General Jeff Sessions was slated to join us. But first we had a stopover in Hawaii. The island's Kīlauea volcano had recently buried several communities, destroyed hundreds of homes, and forever changed thousands of lives. We'd stop there on the way to Australia and on the way back.

As the pilots fired up CG-1's engines, a military aide handed me the latest forecast. Another disaster was inbound. Hurricane Lane— a Category 5 storm—was bearing down on Hawaii. We'd have to make a "go, no-go" decision partway over the Pacific about whether to continue onward. Past a certain point, there wouldn't be enough fuel to turn around, even if the landing looked dicey. I asked for hourly updates.

"He wants to raise the flags back up."

That August had begun with a trip to Puerto Rico and the U.S. Virgin Islands. Kirstjen and I flew down to assess the damage a year after hurricanes had ravaged the islands. Trump was furious that billions of dollars were being spent on recovery, so we thought it was important to remind the president why aid was desperately needed and to show solidarity with the people.

After Hurricane Maria originally hit in 2017, Trump was more focused on fighting with island leaders than on life-saving emergency response. The president wanted to withhold money to the territory. He said it was "dirty and the people were poor," and he pitched then DHS acting secretary Elaine Duke on selling Puerto Rico to another country or swapping it for somewhere nicer. Specifically, he proposed trading it for Greenland.

When news broke about Trump's "swap," the White House denied it. The president hadn't said any such thing, aides claimed; if he did, it was "a joke." Then Trump made his communications team look foolish by openly discussing the idea of acquiring Greenland from its host nation, Denmark. When the Danish prime minister later called the proposal "absurd," Trump said she was being "nasty" and canceled his trip to the country.

Meanwhile—back in Puerto Rico, a U.S. territory that the president was actually responsible for—the wreckage was still staggering in August 2018, a year after it had been hit. The secretary and I toured a school that had been shredded by Hurricane Maria but looked like it had been bombed the day prior. Windows were blown out, debris filled the hallways, and the gymnasium roof was half-gone, exposing a gray sky as aluminum panels dangled from the rafters. Students were taking classes inside cramped trailers while rebuilding was under way, which might take years.

We called Trump at the end of the day on August 3.

"I'm sick of all the money being spent down there," he grumbled before Kirstjen could get a word in. "Pull it back."

The president disliked San Juan's mayor, Carmen Yulín Cruz, who had criticized his mismanagement of the crisis. The Democrat was ungrateful for the aid, he said. To Trump, the island was a left-leaning bastion that didn't support him, and he wanted to punish these anti-Trumpers by withholding aid.

Kirstjen told him there wasn't a choice. Congress had approved the recovery dollars for Puerto Rico, and the president couldn't just hoard the funds. Left unsaid was the starker reality: DHS wasn't going to withhold relief because a Puerto Rican mayor was mean to Trump.

He pressed us about specific grants that he knew hadn't gone out the door yet. Trump wanted to know if we could at least slow down the disbursements. Kirstjen told him unconvincingly that we'd look into it. I changed the subject.

"Mr. President," I jumped in, "can we ask you about the drone issue?"

"What issue?" he responded, easily distracted.

I refreshed his memory. DHS was worried about a spike in threats from weaponized drones. We didn't have the legal authority to protect the public. Specifically, we needed Congress to update wiretapping laws to allow us to disable an armed drone electronically, whether it was speeding toward an airport or a crowded Super Bowl stadium. Our "ask" was simple.

"Sir," the secretary chimed in, "it would be helpful if you tweeted in support of the legislation. It's already drafted. We just need the bill to pass and—"

He cut her off. "Sweetie, just shoot 'em out of the sky. Okay, honey? Shoot 'em out of the damn sky."

"That's the problem, Mr. President," I clarified, explaining that we needed to intercept drones electronically. Some could fly in excess of 100 mph, too fast to shoot down with a gun. Trump talked over me, uninterested in the details.

"No, no, no, just shoot 'em down."

We gave up. Even the distraction proved counterproductive.

No more than two weeks passed before the president was at it again, looking for ways to mix politics with disaster response. The secretary flew to California in mid-August in response to the Carr Fire, the sixth most destructive wildfire in state history, and briefed the president on the damage and the urgent need for a federal response.

Trump didn't see tragedy. He saw revenge. California's governor Jerry Brown was a vocal critic of the president, and Trump wanted him to feel the pain. He told the secretary not to release FEMA aid to the state's wildfire victims. She was taken aback and pretended the conversation hadn't happened.

The president wouldn't relent. When FEMA updated him again, he went on a harangue about how much he hated California Democrats like Jerry Brown and said not to release assistance grants. Afterward, I called the FEMA administrator and told him not to take the president's venting as a direct order. If the White House sent a written directive, then we'd have a problem, but until then, it was just the ravings of an angry man. When Trump later refused to approve a disaster declaration for California—a decision only a president can make—we enlisted the help of House Majority Leader Kevin McCarthy to change Trump's mind.

"Why the fuck did it take me to do this?" McCarthy complained to Kirstjen and me on a phone call. "What's his problem?"

I'd given up on answering the question because Trump wasn't fixable. That much was clear. Knowing that our efforts to manage the man were faltering, the real dilemma was what to do next. Before the series of disaster response trips in August, I'd had drinks on a rainy night with a group of close friends, many of whom I hadn't seen in months because of the 24/7 nature of my job. The gathering at a downtown D.C. bar was supposed to be relaxing. It wasn't. A woman in our group whom I'd known for ten years lashed out, asking why I voted for Donald Trump.

"I didn't," I told her. "I actually opposed his election."

"So why did you go in to serve him?"

"I didn't go in to serve him. I went in to serve you," I told her irritably, listing off the ways DHS protected the country.

"Oh, like ripping kids at the border away from their moms?"

The comment set me off. I told her I wasn't in charge of immigration at DHS, opposed the policy so directly that hard-liners accused me of tipping off the media, and cowrote the executive order to end it for good.

"If you're blaming someone for the Trump presidency," I pointed out, "there are sixty-three million fucking people ahead of me. They voted for him. I didn't. At least I'm helping clean up."

"How's that working out?"

"He's more unstable than you know. So sometimes pretty damn well."

"If he's so crazy, I don't know why you'd work there."

"*Because* he's crazy. Do you want MAGA people running things?"

"I'd prefer Republicans grow a backbone. Why haven't you said something, or better yet, quit?"

Until that summer, I had been sure of my answer. We blocked a dozen bad ideas a day, but Trump was striking back. Family separation was the most horrifying example.

My friend wouldn't let up. She said anyone who worked in the Trump administration was an enabler. At one point, she hassled the bartender and told him to cut me off.

"Don't serve him. He works for a fucking criminal," she said, seething.

"I'm not putting up with this shit." I left money on the bar and walked out, forgetting my umbrella. I didn't want to go back. I walked a half mile in the downpour to my car, her words seared into my head.

Days after my friend's lecture, the president of the United States demanded we cut off disaster aid to victims in Democratic localities. Would we stop him? Or would he overrule us? Maybe I was asking the wrong questions.

★ ★ ★

At the end of August, on the flight to Hawaii, we talked about the gloomy atmosphere inside the executive branch. The secretary, Chad, and I sat in the forward cabin of CG-1. We'd just gotten word from Chief Kelly that something was afoot that could "break the administration." Chad leaned back in his seat. Over his shoulder, he asked a Secret Service agent and the advance team to pull together a contingency plan, just in case we needed to turn the plane around and head back to Washington.

Midair, we got a hint of what might go down. The attorney general's team informed us that Jeff Sessions would no longer be joining us at our final destination in Australia. He was clearly worried he might be fired, imminently. We had suspected it might happen. The president had already asked John Kelly multiple times if he'd go run DOJ. If I'm being honest, I have to say I wanted Sessions to get sacked. I assumed Republicans would panic if the president fired the attorney general for not bending to his will. They might try harder to contain him after that.

A military aide interrupted to ask for the go, no-go decision. Hurricane Lane had been downgraded to a tropical storm off the coast of Hawaii. We were well on our way over the Pacific and could take a gamble that the storm would pass in time for us to land safely. Or we could turn around. I had no interest in going back to Washington.

"Let's proceed," I told him.

Then we got darker news. A press staffer came to the front of the cabin to tell us that U.S. senator John McCain had passed away, losing his long fight with brain cancer. The war veteran's death wasn't unexpected, but the news hit everyone hard, especially me. McCain was one of the first elected leaders I met as a young page on Capitol Hill, and he was one of the last I still respected. The Arizona senator was a fearless voice within the Republican Party, willing to defy the MAGA wing.

As we got closer to Hawaii, I told Kirstjen and Chad I wanted to take a nap, lowering my baseball cap over my face. In truth, I needed a moment. I felt very alone.

I didn't get time to dwell on the feeling, because as it turned out, staying the course was a mistake. CG-1 hit serious turbulence. The updated forecast showed we wouldn't dodge the downgraded hurricane. We were flying right into it.

★　★　★

One phone wasn't enough to rouse me. But two of my devices rang in alternating fashion, performing slow pirouettes on the nightstand. I squinted at the glowing screens.

I was exhausted. After a very rough landing in Hawaii (the storm rattled the private jet like a cranky toddler with a toy), the tropical storm had grounded us for several days. Some of the volcano victims we met became flood victims, too. We shuttled between moldy and partly submerged hotels, unable to sleep. When it was safe to proceed, we took another long flight and finally made it to Australia for the Five Eyes meeting. At our hotel on the country's Gold Coast, I thought I'd finally have a chance to rest.

Then buzzing woke me up. Both of my phones were ringing.

The phone number caught my eye: (202) 456-1414. The White House switchboard. I answered. Trump's deputy chief of staff, Zach Fuentes, wasted no time in telling me POTUS was pissed off.

"Did you all lower the flags?" Fuentes asked.

"I don't know what you're talking about," I responded, explaining to him that we were halfway around the world.

"In honor of John McCain—the flags are at half-staff across the country. Did you guys give that order?" He and John Kelly needed an answer, fast.

DHS typically notified federal buildings to lower their flags in periods of national mourning. I told him it was such a standard procedure that it rarely came to me for approval. I could check.

"I'm just letting you know the president is really mad," Fuentes warned. "He wants to raise the flags back up."

He and Kelly didn't need to say anything else. Trump hated John McCain. The president clearly didn't want Americans showing respect for the man. I made a few phone calls and rang back.

"Yes, it was us," I confirmed. "DHS issued the order." If the president was directing us to send the flags back up, I said, the answer would be no.

I was told to hang tight. Zach and Chief Kelly told me they were obviously pushing back against the president and only wanted us to be aware, in case he called.

Eighteen months into the Trump presidency, there were better reasons to snap. But this struck a nerve. After hanging up, I sat on the bed suppressing rage. Amid everything else that was happening, Trump was dancing on my hero's grave.

Fuck that.

I went over to the hotel room desk. In a T-shirt and boxers, I opened my iPad and started writing. It started off as a journal entry.

Donald Trump is immoral. His leadership style is impetuous, adversarial, petty, ineffective. His behavior is erratic, antidemocratic. His own Cabinet is frightened, so much so that officials have considered invoking the Twenty Fifth Amendment. . . .

The President is working against GOP principles. Pushing back against half-baked, ill-informed, and rash decisions is not the work of a nefarious "Deep State." We're a "Steady State" trying to steer the Administration right until—one way or another—it's over. . . .

This is about more than Trump and what he's doing to the presidency. It's about what he's doing to us. He's dividing us, destroying us. We can't let him. We need to heed John McCain's words and put country over party, before it's too late.

As the nighttime glow of the city was replaced by daylight, the journal entry flowed into a longer essay. A sudden thought hit me. Before I could talk myself out of it, I sent an encrypted message to a contact at *The New York Times.*

Would the paper be interested in an opinion piece? I attached the document. At the end, I signed it with a pseudonym: *Publius.* Then I waited.

"Who is Lodestar?"

Heading into the fall of 2018, Congress remained a partial check on the president, even if his most prominent GOP critic was dead. Donald Trump was scared to lose the House and Senate in the 2018 midterm elections. So he tried to show a minimum level of restraint—whether it was holding back on firing the attorney general, on slashing refugee admissions to *zero*, on pulling U.S. troops out of terror hot spots, on cutting assistance to disaster victims, and so on—just enough to make sure *he* didn't get blamed for costing the GOP its majority.

But his temperance was tested when it came to Russia.

Trump couldn't stand it when agency leaders raised the subject. The president assumed the words "Russian interference" were code for people who questioned the legitimacy of his election. He rejected our proposals to punish Moscow after 2016, opting instead for a tepid response (he sent a few dozen of Putin's diplomats back home, when he should have shuttered their entire embassy and imposed crippling sanctions, if not more than that). When we detected signs that the Kremlin was planning to meddle in the 2018 midterms, Trump was dismissive. He didn't want to hear it, and he certainly didn't propose doing anything about the threat.

We refused to sit on our hands. I helped create a "ghost NSC," away from the White House, charged with developing a response even if Trump wanted to look the other way. Chris Krebs, our cybersecurity chief, ran the show. He knew that taking a forward-leaning posture against Russia could get him fired, and he didn't care. We convened meetings with intelligence agencies and the FBI to hatch a plan to protect our electoral system against Putin—including sophisticated threat monitoring, new digital defenses, 24/7 support to poll workers around the country, and non-public measures.

But we still needed someone to tell the Russians: "Back off." The Kremlin wouldn't be deterred unless they expected severe consequences for hacking our democracy again. So in a previously planned speech to eighty foreign ambassadors, I proposed that Secretary Nielsen do it. She agreed. Kirstjen stood in front of the diplomats in a room across the street from the White House and spelled out the consequences for meddling in American elections, directing her attention to the Russian envoy seated in front of her.

The speech made headlines. *The New York Times* called it "an unusually stern warning" and "among the harshest threats of retaliation by a member of President Trump's cabinet." Vladimir Putin's ambassador was so livid that he walked out of the gathering. I got an angry call from the White House press office afterward. They demanded that from now on Kirstjen submit her speeches for review by the president's team before she opened her mouth in public.

"Technically, the president is the only one that can give her that order," I responded, recalling John Kelly's advice about the chain of command. "If the president has time to review her speeches, he can let her know directly."

Trump never called.

DHS planned a press conference at the White House to drive home the warning to Moscow before the 2018 midterm elections. Kirstjen was joined by FBI Director Chris Wray, Director of National Intelligence Dan Coats, and NSA Director Paul Nakasone.

I entered the White House briefing room knowing we were about to poke two bears. Putin *and* Trump. I sat in a fold-out seat adjacent to the podium, as the national security chiefs blasted Russia for "pervasive" election meddling. Coats said the Kremlin was trying to "weaken and divide the U.S."; Kirstjen warned "our democracy itself is in the cross hairs"; and Nakasone pointedly stated that the NSA was "prepared to conduct operations" against any country that dared to interfere in the vote.

Putin was on notice. And Trump was enraged. The president called Kirstjen and me afterward and said he thought it was a mistake. "Terrible . . . terrible . . . *terrible*," he repeated, telling us the press conference was a disaster. Why would we be so rude to his friend Vladimir?

"I think it went fine," the secretary told Trump coolly.

The president was trapped into doing the right thing, or at least not blocking it. If he told us to stand down, the outcry from Congress and the public would be enormous. His top security advisors had just told America how serious the threat was. Trump clearly wanted us to forget Russia, but for the moment, he knew he couldn't deactivate U.S. election defenses.

The White House was fretful going into September. CNN predicted that for Trump the period would be "a hugely consequential chapter in his turbulent presidency" and "might lay the foundations for the nation's ideological course for years." Behind the scenes, the president was behaving erratically at the start of the ten-week sprint to the midterm elections, unable to focus on his job.

And I was about to pull back the curtain.

Within hours of when I submitted my opinion piece from Australia, *The New York Times* confirmed they would accept it. They wanted to publish a dissenting voice from the inside of the Trump presidency. I saw the essay as a straightforward statement of fact: *The president is unstable, which is why Adults around him are asserting themselves.* It became something else entirely.

The newspaper put in place extraordinary measures to protect my identity. In an encrypted call before it was published, opinion editor Jim Dao explained the steps they were taking, from securing their communications to limiting the number of individuals involved. The only people who knew were a handful of staff at the paper—not my colleagues, not my family, not even Anabel at first.

There was a catch. Jim said the *Times* didn't accept pseudonyms. I hoped to publish the essay as Publius, the pen name used by several of the Founding Fathers to promote ratification of the Constitution. I wasn't comparing myself to them, but I used the literary device for the same reason they had. I wanted the public to focus on *the message*, not *the messenger.* In a world of snap judgments and online mobs, readers would have to pay attention to the point, and Trump would be unable to distract attention by quarreling with its author.

The paper chose "Anonymous" instead, describing the writer the same way the White House did when they put me on background calls with reporters, as "a senior official in the Trump administration."

On September 5, 2018, it hit Washington like an earthquake. The secretary and Chad were traveling, and I was alone in a DHS office a few blocks away from the White House. I got a burst of news alerts on my phone about a "bombshell" op-ed from someone within the administration. I opened the piece, which was headlined, "I AM PART OF THE RESISTANCE INSIDE THE TRUMP ADMINISTRATION." In the quiet of the office, I re-read some of the opening lines:

> *The president continues to act in a manner that is detrimental to the health of our republic. That is why many Trump appointees have vowed to do what we can to preserve our democratic institutions while thwarting Mr. Trump's more misguided impulses until he is out of office. The root of the problem is the president's amorality. Anyone who works with him knows he is not moored to any discernible first principles that guide his decision making.*

The piece cited foreign policy as an example of a "two-track presidency." Trump wanted to placate America's adversaries, like Russian President Vladimir Putin, as long as their manipulation of U.S. affairs was helpful to him personally. His advisors opposed such appeasement and kept the administration on the rails. These Adults weren't a "Deep State," I wrote, but a "Steady State."

It didn't take long to feel the aftershock from the Oval Office.

"TREASON?" the president tweeted, as the piece went viral. Within hours, it was one of the most read articles of the year.

Trump demanded the newspaper hand over the "GUTLESS" author for unspecified "national security purposes." He threatened to prosecute whoever had written the piece. Then he told reporters he wanted the Justice Department to investigate the *Times* itself, in addition to the unidentified writer. In a rare rebuke, former president Barack Obama condemned the White House for trying to "pressure the Attorney General or the FBI" to punish political opponents.

Trump seemed ignorant of the irony. I'd written a piece about the president's abuses of power. In response, he sought to abuse his power to root out a dissenter and punish speech protected by the First Amendment.

The president's explosive response led the newspaper to increase security at its New York headquarters, fearing potential retaliation from MAGA supporters.

White House press secretary Sarah Huckabee Sanders urged Trump backers to harass the *Times*, tweeting out a message with a private phone number for the opinion editors. "If you want to know who this gutless loser is, call the opinion desk of the failing NYT at"—I've redacted the number—"and ask them. They are the only ones complicit in this deceitful act. We stand united together and fully support our President Donald J. Trump."

The paper also upped its cybersecurity protections. As Jim Dao shared with me, employees began encrypting their messages daily. Some staff were even wary of having conversations in the iconic building's glass conference rooms facing the street, worried that sophisticated listening devices might be pointed at the windows to gather information about the unnamed author.

Amateur sleuths tried to use textual analysis to identify the writer, homing in on the word "lodestar."

"We may no longer have Senator McCain," the piece read, "but we will always have his example—a lodestar for restoring honor to public life and our national dialogue. Mr. Trump may fear such honorable men, but we should revere them."

"WHO IS LODESTAR?" headlines blared. Vice President Mike Pence used the word frequently, making him an early suspect. But there were so many people at senior levels in the Trump administration who journalists suspected harbored negative views of the president that it was tough to narrow the field.

I started getting text messages from reporters at *The Washington Post*, CNN, NBC, and elsewhere. "Is it you?" "Any ideas?" They sent the same messages to everyone. I brushed off the inquiries.

Debate erupted over the merits of exposing wrongdoing anonymously. Most critics didn't embraced Trump's view—that the opinion piece was sedition, punishable by death—but many were unsatisfied with trusting *The New York Times* that the author was a credible source. They wanted the person to be named so that *they* could evaluate his or her claims themselves.

The Government Accountability Project, a whistle-blower organization, presented a contrary view. "Some commentators insist the only honorable course is for the anonymous whistleblower to expose him or herself, and resign," the organization wrote. "It is essential that anonymous whistleblowers do not quit and give up. By doing so, they can continue to describe what is actually going on within the White House, decline to carry out illegal orders, or stop actions that pose threats to national security."

I agreed with both perspectives. I wanted to stay in the shadows long enough to finish critical work at DHS, chiefly making sure the midterm elections were secure. Then I felt it was important to quit and come forward, I told myself. In a city of spilled secrets, I assumed Anonymous would be outed and fired anyway, before I had the chance to do all of that, so I prepared a simple backup statement: *I am the author. And I stand by every word. Signed, Miles Taylor.*

In the meantime, the administration's internal inquisition began. The president was consumed by it, quizzing everyone around him about who they thought it was. He also tasked the Justice Department with finding the offender.

Not long after publication, a White House number called my mobile phone. I took a deep breath and answered.

"Miles," a gravelly voice intoned, "I hate to ask you to do this."

It was John Kelly. *Wow, that was fast.* I waited for the inevitable—the request for my resignation letter.

"Can Kirstjen send a note to POTUS confirming she's not the anonymous author?"

In his rage, Trump wanted every cabinet secretary to write him a personal note promising they hadn't written the op-ed. I couldn't help but let out a laugh. Kelly admitted the search was a farce. Everyone knew the piece was accurate, so there was no point in finding the writer. We were all culprits. I wrote a note on Kirstjen's behalf, signed it in her name, and sent it off to the Oval Office.

For a moment I worried the guessing game was all anyone cared about, which would have defeated the purpose. Fortunately, the essay also provoked a more serious conversation. Former secretary of state John Kerry called the revelation about the cabinet discussing the Twenty-Fifth Amendment "a moment of enormous consequence to our country." Republican senator Bob Corker confessed that the piece reflected the deep misgivings his GOP colleagues shared about Trump, which needed to be known.

"This is what all of us have understood to be the situation from Day One," Corker revealed to reporters. "That's why I think all of us encourage the good people around the President to stay."

The term "resistance" was controversial. In the essay, I was referring to officials who pushed back against irresponsible, immoral, and illegal demands. *Not* people reversing the lawful orders of a commander in chief. Still, there was a risk that Trump would spin it differently. *The Atlantic*'s David Frum argued it would cause the president to "grow more defiant, more reckless, more anti-constitutional, and more dangerous." Years later, former White House communications director Stephanie Grisham validated the point.

"His paranoia has always been crazy," she told me about Trump, "but I think that his level of paranoia started to go bonkers when that op-ed dropped."

"The second burning of the White House"

Anabel could sense something was weighing on me. She still didn't know about the piece. I wanted to protect her and my family from carrying the secret burden.

Maintaining discretion wasn't necessarily the hard part. After years in the national security community, I was trained to keep secrets. This was no different. I needed to keep the circle small, avoid creating a physical or digital trail, and make sure those who knew kept the knowledge compartmented.

A deeper enigma troubled me. I had a secret within a secret, so to speak, and no one to talk to about it. The problem was more personal and consequential than hitting "send" on an uncredited op-ed. I wasn't ready to tell anyone yet because I was hardly ready to admit it to myself. So I buried the secret internally.

A few days after the essay was published, I came home drained. Anabel suggested an evening without phones and laptops. We made a fire and settled in to watch a late-night movie.

Then the secure phone chirped upstairs in the guest bedroom. I went to answer it. The caller was Kirstjen.

"The president just called," the secretary said. "He wants to fire David Glawe, effective immediately."

Glawe was the DHS spy chief. Earlier that day, we had dispatched him to brief the House Intelligence Committee about the midterm elections and the threat from Russia. Trump got word of the meeting.

"He doesn't want anyone talking to Congress about the 'Russia hoax,'" Kirstjen relayed. "He wants to shut down Russia work. I'm going to hold him off as long as I can."

The next morning, Kirstjen and I canceled meetings and went to the White House to intercept General Kelly. We armed him with arguments to talk Trump out of firing Glawe. Losing our top intelligence officer would be a huge setback in U.S. efforts to protect the elections. Also, it could imperil Trump with the special counsel investigation by creating more evidence that Trump was trying to cover up Moscow's meddling. Did he want to wreck his presidency?

"I've got it," Kelly told us. He went into the Oval Office and talked the president down.

In late September, Trump took another tack. He told foreign diplomats and reporters at a United Nations gathering that *China* was the adversary interfering in the elections to hurt him. Trump said nothing about Russia—the bigger threat to the election—surely hoping Putin would try to help him again by boosting Republicans.

As we soon learned, the Russia saga was only the prelude. Trump's eruption over the southern border was to be his symphony.

★ ★ ★

News reports in October claimed several thousand migrants were headed in a caravan toward the United States. The president reacted to the group as if it were a foreign army slowly marching on U.S. territory, rather than what it was—a loosely organized group of civilians, mostly women and children. Amid the situation, Trump tested the White House and DHS like never before.

In a series of phone calls, Oval Office meetings, Situation Room discussions, Air Force One flights, and directives, the president made outrageous demands to stop the civilians, which included:

- Shutting off all U.S. financial assistance to countries on the caravan route
- Sealing the entire Southern Border and turning away all the asylum-seekers ("Don't let a single fucking one into the country!")
- Deploying armed soldiers to intimidate and block the migrants
- Launching tear gas at anyone headed toward the border (aides inquired about using new technology—heat-ray devices—to make people in the caravan feel like their skin was on fire)
- Painting the border wall black and adding sharp spikes at the top (so it would scorch the hands of anyone who touched it in the hot sun and impale climbers)
- Shooting migrants to stop them from getting too close (when he was told that using deadly force against unarmed civilians was illegal: "Then shoot them in the legs if you have to!")

Border policy wasn't supposed to be my focus, but the subject consumed the administration as Trump unspooled. White House lawyers rejected the majority of the president's demands, though I wasn't sure they'd be able to keep him at bay much longer. Panicked press aides inquired about whether TV outlets could stop airing footage of migrants rushing the border because it was whipping Trump into a frenzy.

"This is getting really fucked up," I told Kirstjen and Chief Kelly after another round of bad ideas during an October meeting in the Oval Office.

"I know," the secretary replied. "That's why Mattis is ready to leave. And we have to make a decision about whether we are, too."

"Among us friends, let's be honest," Kelly said. "About a third of the things the president wants us to do are flat-out stupid. Another third would be impossible to implement and wouldn't even solve the problem. And a third of them would be flat-out illegal."

On October 18, the chief went to the Oval and unloaded on Trump, telling the president he simply didn't have the legal authority to do what he wanted to at the border. The best option was to focus on getting Congress to reform our broken immigration system. Trump was unmoved. If his people were going to defy him, he'd empower new ones.

The president tapped his son-in-law to take on immigration. Jared was in charge, Trump said. Kirstjen and I were sitting in Kelly's office when the chief came back from down the hall. I'd never seen him so mad.

"Fuck him," Kelly roared. "I'm done here. I'm leaving, going home, and quitting this job."

He walked into the hallway to tell his Secret Service agents to get his motorcade ready.

"I quit."

Back in the office again for a brief moment—briefcase in hand—Kelly picked up the phone and got Jared on the line.

"POTUS says you've got it figured out. So fuck you. It's on you now, Jared. I'm out." He slammed the phone.

With that, Kelly left the West Wing.

I cleared the secretary's calendar the next day. We convened a group of advisors at a private location outside of Washington to talk about an exit plan. Arriving separately at an empty building in rural Virginia, we dumped our electronic devices in a box in the entryway, unsure whether our phones might be monitored. The administration felt increasingly like an autocracy.

Kirstjen kicked off the conversation. She'd talked to Kelly, and despite storming out of the White House, he hadn't officially made up his mind about resigning. He was leaning that direction and was considering whether to implode the administration by bringing others with him.

"What's our game plan?" Kirstjen asked the group.

I made my position clear. A mass resignation would be a powerful statement about Trump's behavior. It would be impossible for Republicans—and the country—to look away if Trump's top lieutenants left in a blaze of glory. It would be "the second burning of the White House," I noted (the British literally torched the building during the War of 1812).

Others were considering leaving, too. We ran through the names. Defense Secretary Jim Mattis. Intelligence Director Dan Coats. Chairman of the Joint Chiefs Joseph Dunford. Education Secretary Betsy DeVos. Interior Secretary Ryan Zinke. A surprising name came up: First Lady Melania Trump. I didn't press for further details, but one attendee asserted that FLOTUS would actually consider leaving her husband if enough key officials quit.

Not everyone agreed quitting was the right approach. My colleague DHS Chief of Staff Chad Wolf remained largely silent, while a communications aide warned the secretary that Trump would blame us if we quit and caused the GOP to lose control of Congress.

"It's not gonna play out how you think," he asserted. "The president will turn it around and say we cost the party its majority. The base will believe him, not us."

Kirstjen added another wrinkle. Trump aide Stephen Miller had worked up a short list of people to install as DHS leaders. It included far-right extremists who would do whatever the president wanted. At the same time, it was clear our "no's" didn't make a difference anymore. We discussed exit planning until nightfall.

"For the first time, I am actually scared for the country," Kirstjen told me afterward. "The insanity has been loosed."

In the end, I lost the argument. The majority of my colleagues favored waiting until after the midterms, so we didn't inadvertently hurt congressional Republicans in the election. I was dejected. Only weeks after publication, my anonymous missive was already hopelessly outdated. The Adults didn't need to reassert themselves to contain Trump; they needed to quit their jobs and make a statement. But a midnight self-massacre—a mass group resignation from the Trump administration—never happened because the president struck first.

★ ★ ★

Thankfully, the Russians were unsuccessful in disrupting the midterms. But the president destabilized the U.S. political system anyway. Democrats won back the majority in the House of Representatives in a stinging repudiation of Trump's policies, and the day after the election, he vowed a "warlike posture" in dealing with them. And he made grandiose claims about his power. Chad buried his head in his hands as we watched the news conference on television.

"I could fire everybody right now," Trump boasted. Soon he began the task.

First, he sacked Attorney General Jeff Sessions. Then stories broke in the press that Trump was considering axing two other leaders he tussled with frequently, Secretary Nielsen and Director Coats. Kirstjen summoned DHS Acting Deputy Secretary Claire Grady into her office on November 13, along with me and Chad.

"It's very likely you're going to be the secretary of homeland security this week," Kirstjen told Claire. "Let's start planning."

The secretary decided to move me into the role of DHS chief of staff and designate Chad as the head of the Office of Policy. We could provide some amount of continuity if the White House sacked her, though I only expected to take on the role temporarily. If I wasn't fired with her soon, I needed to leave on my own terms.

Not long after, John Kelly discovered that the president was searching for his replacement, too. On December 8, Trump casually told reporters that General Kelly would be leaving for good—announcing the departure as suddenly as the general's shock hiring the year before. The chief told Kirstjen he had managed to buy her a little more time to insulate DHS against an anticipated onslaught. Kelly wasn't sure how long, but his warning couldn't have been clearer: batten down the hatches because Trump is feeling unconstrained.

On December 18 and 19, I witnessed it.

Sun streamed into the Oval Office as I entered in the early afternoon of the eighteenth with Kirstjen, notionally to talk to Trump about a surge in mass shootings. The president didn't care about the issue, or at least didn't seem eager to do anything about it. Before we could open our mouths, he set a new agenda.

He wanted to talk about the border. Congress was considering an end-of-year deal to fund the federal government, and the president decided he wanted to use the negotiations as leverage to get money for his border wall. He would shut down the government over the issue. In fact, Trump pledged to do something more extreme.

"I want to close the border," Trump told us, his eyes widening with excitement. "Let's do it. If [Congress] doesn't give me the money, we shut the whole fucking border."

We reminded him he didn't have the legal authority to seal the entire border and warned that a shutdown could be calamitous. Trump brushed it off. His mood that afternoon said, *I can do whatever the fuck I want.* I went back to DHS headquarters and alerted our lawyers that they needed to be on high alert for any sudden executive orders or directives from the president. Our first heads-up might be his Twitter account.

I was right about the means of attack, just not the target.

The next morning, I was back at the White House. Frozen leaves crunched under my feet like potato chips as I trudged up to the Secret Service booth for another day of uncertainty. I flashed my badge and proceeded through three checkpoints until I was in the West Wing.

As I warmed up in the chief's office, the mood was subdued. John Kelly sat at his desk with National Security Advisor John Bolton across from him. They were politely quarreling with each other over a diplomatic issue related to Mexico, in which I was hoping to broker compromise. The president was still in the residence, late as usual to begin his workday. No one had heard from him.

On the television, CNN announced breaking news. Trump had said that the United States was pulling its forces out of Syria.

"We have defeated ISIS in Syria," he'd tweeted, "my only reason for being there during the Trump Presidency."

Sitting feet from me, Bolton let out a gasp.

"Holy shit," he whispered, before dashing out of the office.

Trump hadn't consulted anyone on the final decision. Not his chief of staff. Not his national security advisor. Not his secretary of defense. He'd just tweeted the withdrawal into existence. Kelly's face struggled to hold back fury at the unplanned announcement.

"People are going to fucking die because of this," he asserted through gritted teeth.

Minutes later General Mattis called Kelly from the Pentagon, flabbergasted. U.S. allies were phoning him, he said, confused about why America was quitting the battle against ISIS without any planning or forewarning. The military brass was in the dark.

Kelly and Mattis speculated that Afghanistan was next, and they were right. Trump soon announced he was also bringing thousands of troops back from that country, overruling his generals and civilian advisors, and surprising the Afghan government. The sudden moves created confusion on the ground in Syria and Afghanistan. American troops realized they might become sitting ducks, targeted by enemy forces keen to seize the advantage against a retreating United States.

Mattis was done. The defense secretary announced he was quitting the administration in the wake of the debacle. This was not the way to run the world's most powerful military. And Kirstjen finally seemed ready to quit, too. She asked me to draft a resignation letter for her to review, citing the precipitous pullouts from Afghanistan and Syria— and the resulting danger to the U.S. homeland—as the rationale. On his way out, Mattis encouraged her to wait a little longer and provide some stability inside the cabinet in case something worse happened.

The Axis of Adults was going up in flames. Before any of them could precipitate a second burning of the White House, Trump had lit the match himself.

A day later, I woke up to an encrypted message from Jim Dao. The *New York Times* editor who published my anonymous essay had sent me a link. It was an article written by Bret Stephens, entitled "Dear Anonymous Inside the Trump Administration." The open letter was addressed to the still-masked author.

"You . . . believed that your efforts to resist Trump were often successful," he wrote. "On foreign policy, you noted, the Administration's policies were far more sober and serious than the President's reckless rhetoric. You were wrong. This week proves it. . . . You must know by now that you are no longer keeping a bad thing from getting worse. All you are doing is disguising how bad it is, thereby helping it to become worse."

Stephens closed with an exhortation.

"Trump will never have trouble surrounding himself with ambitious and unscrupulous flunkies. Do you want that to describe you? Get out while you still can, whoever you are."

PART II

Shortly before that Christmas, I attended the annual Congressional Ball at the White House. Given everything that was happening, I had no interest in spending an evening with Donald Trump. That said, it was one of the final opportunities to say goodbye to John Kelly, a man among the dwindling few in Washington whom I respected.

The State Floor of the White House was gussied up for a holiday celebration, yet the atmosphere was closer to a wake. Kelly had known from the start his days were numbered. But rather than lie on display in a casket this particular evening, the corpse roamed the floor, shaking hands with sullen senators and congresspeople who worried about a White House without him. They weren't comforting John Kelly. He was consoling them.

Before I could get to the chief, I was stopped by a wave of people. The crowd flowed against me, toward the base of the stairs in the grand foyer. I turned. The dour mood lifted as the president emerged beaming in a black tuxedo, cueing an obedient band to play "Hail to the Chief." Trump swaggered down the stairs from the residence, basking in the moment.

Melania Trump, who by some accounts had considered leaving her husband, was on his arm smiling in a dazzling ivory gown. Next to me, a Republican congressman from Virginia, who had lost reelection in the midterms because of Trump, excitedly snapped pictures of the commander in chief on his phone. And in front of us, Vice President Mike Pence—a silent hostage to the president's daily transgressions—applauded his approaching boss. Pence would be remembered for an erect posture and flaccid conscience. He stood proudly next to the chief executive but never stood up to him. He was built to obey.

Trump took to the podium.

"No administration has done more in two years than the Trump administration," he declared triumphantly, scanning the crowd. He seemed to notice that there were far more Republicans than Democrats standing before him.

"We have *a lot* of Democrats here, and I am very happy about that," Trump boasted. "I have *a lot* of friends who are Democrats." He changed his tune about Congress, predicting an "exciting year" of bipartisan deals on everything from infrastructure to healthcare—before urging his guests to relax and explore the White House.

"To me, it's a happy place," he said.

From his demeanor, you wouldn't have known Donald Trump was

preparing for an explosive confrontation with the legislative branch. He was playing nice. But a week later, Trump butted heads with Congress and sparked the longest government shutdown in history—forcing almost a million federal employees to go home or work without pay—just in time for Christmas.

THE NEXT TRUMP WILL BEND CONGRESS TO THE MAGA MOVEMENT'S WILL THROUGH OBSTRUCTION, INSTRUCTION, AND DESTRUCTION.

Article One of the U.S. Constitution comes first in the document for a reason. The section outlines the role of the legislative branch, which the Founders considered to be the most closely connected to the people. They also saw it as a counterweight to a power-hungry chief executive. The legislature can restrain the president on almost every aspect of his or her job by making laws, controlling government funds, approving presidential appointments, and monitoring executive agencies. It should be the toughest guardrail against a wayward president.

That's why the Next Trump will work hard to bypass Congress.

"Article One is pretty well undone," former Republican congressman Reid Ribble told me. In a second MAGA term, he said, "it will be undone entirely."

Ribble doesn't believe it will happen in a sweeping constitutional clash but quietly and gradually. Members of the GOP will grow accustomed to another Trump-like president governing by executive order.

"They will allow [the Next Trump] to become a soft dictator by complying with his legislative circumvention because it's in the service of implementing policies of which they approve," he said. "It slowly normalizes legislative nullification."

"Obstruction" will be used to thwart congressional oversight.

After the 2018 midterms, the White House called a meeting of the chiefs of staff at top agencies. We gathered around an elongated wooden table in the Secretary of War Suite, a connected series of stately rooms that once served as the inner sanctum of American defense. Historic military offensives were planned at the table and profound decisions were made about war and peace. That particular day, the decision was war.

Trump's liaison to the cabinet, Bill McGinley, opened the session.

"Listen up, folks." His deep voice struck the room like a judge's gavel quieting the court. "The Democrats are taking control of the House again soon. We're expecting investigations, subpoenas, the works. Today we'll talk about how to handle it."

The plan—in a nutshell—was obstruction. Though McGinley didn't use the word, the end result was clear. The White House wanted agencies to prepare for battle with Congress and to forcefully reject requests to testify, rebuff demands for internal documents, and defy legislative orders—whatever was needed to protect the president's administration from prying eyes.

The White House promised legal support to every agency represented in the meeting. They were working on a confidential plan to stitch together an administration-wide contingent of attorneys who'd take up legal arms against the blitz of congressional probes. Democrats were expected to launch investigations into everything from Trump's business practices to the politicization of the intelligence community.

"Game on," McGinley asserted.

The president didn't keep the plan secret for very long.

"We're fighting all the subpoenas," he told reporters after the House changed hands. Trump's top lawyer, Pat Cipollone, informed a leading congressional committee that administration officials—including former ones who'd left the government—would not be permitted to cooperate in probes that were "harassing and seeking to embarrass" the president. The White House directed the ex-officials to ignore a slew of subpoenas related to misconduct in the Trump administration.

The Next Trump will do the same. He or she will equip agencies with legal strategies and personnel to prevent Congress from performing its oversight functions and to stop them from unearthing abuses of power. Systematized stonewalling is dangerous for obvious reasons. It makes it hard for the people's representatives to understand what's really happening inside the government and to hold dishonest officials accountable. It also makes it easier to hide nefarious schemes.

In short, obstruction enables misconduct. I use the term "obstruction" here broadly. A future MAGA administration will try to firewall agencies from congressional investigations and, more generally, ignore the legislative body's oversight role whenever and however it pleases. This will be especially true when it comes to the power of the purse.

Money is Congress's most important tool. I spent part of my career as a congressional appropriator, working on the committee that decides how much to spend on government programs, when to cut their budgets, and what strings to attach to the cash. If Congress doesn't trust a president, it can put strict conditions on federal dollars to ensure the money goes where it's supposed to go, or simply cut off funding.

As James Madison wrote in the Federalist Papers, "The power of the purse may, in fact, be regarded as the most complete and effectual weapon with which any constitution can arm the immediate representatives of the people."

Donald Trump didn't care. He moved funds between government accounts to pay for pet projects in ways Congress never intended, such as when he reallocated Pentagon dollars meant to be spent on U.S. troops to be used to build his border wall. He demanded that staff withhold money from programs he didn't like. At first, White House budget officials pushed back, but by the end, they were searching for ways to satisfy his demands.

I remember a meeting in the Oval Office in early 2019 when Trump told Secretary of State Mike Pompeo to cut off assistance to the Northern Triangle countries in Latin America for not cracking down on migration. I knew the move wasn't legal. So did Trump. He was required to spend the money that Congress had allocated to be transferred to our allies in the region. However, in the meeting, White House budget director Russ Vought assured the president he'd make it happen. The aid would be turned off. I walked out of the Oval assuming Russ wasn't serious and that he was just trying to pacify the president.

But in a similar situation later that year, Trump got his way. After

Congress passed a bill to provide military assistance to Ukraine, the White House quietly broke the law by sitting on the funds. The president wanted Ukraine to investigate one of his political rivals, Joe Biden, and he didn't want to disburse the money until they agreed. Internal whistle-blowers exposed this quid-pro-quo plot, leading to Trump's first impeachment.

Don't expect the Next Trump to get impeached for mishandling money. Congress relies on the executive branch to tattle on itself about spending errors and violations. In another MAGA administration, the White House will make it harder for legislators to detect the misuse of federal funds, and it certainly won't report such wrongdoing of its own volition.

Congress's "advice and consent" functions will also be obstructed. It's the job of the U.S. Senate to review and approve nominees for leadership positions across government. Trump was content to circumvent Congress by installing "acting" officials in top posts when it looked like they couldn't get Senate approval, regardless of whether it was legal. In fact, during Trump's last year, the Government Accountability Office concluded that the two highest-ranking people running DHS—the "acting secretary" and "acting deputy secretary"—were serving unlawfully. Because Congress lacked the Republican votes to do anything about it, no one was fired, no one was punished, and the Department continued to be run by two illegitimate appointees until the final days of the administration.

Former Trump officials I spoke to were confident that another MAGA president would do the same. Executive obstruction will become a regular occurrence. Confirmation hearings will be skipped. Subpoenas will be flouted. Spending reviews will be disregarded. And the situation could get much worse.

What happens if the president decides not to answer legislative inquiries about a looming economic depression or a national security crisis? Can Congress function if it's in the dark? Can it force an unwilling president to comply? What happens if an unstable president decides to ignore the law altogether?

Political "instruction" will be used to keep GOP lawmakers under the president's sway.

Congress and the president have a relationship of "opposite and rival" political branches, in James Madison's words. Every president tries to keep their party members in line in the legislature—to "instruct" them on how to vote and what policy positions to take. But during the Trump years, "instruction" looked more like "threatening."

"I don't use the word 'frightening' very often, but it really did frighten me," recalled Scott Rigell, a former Republican congressman from Virginia. Rigell said his House colleagues were consumed with Trumpism, whether they were true believers or just afraid to go against the movement.

When he decided not to endorse the New York businessman's candidacy in 2016, Rigell was ostracized. Republican Party officials in Virginia prepared to kick him out of the GOP, and House colleagues stopped associating with him.

"I've never seen that cult worship in America," he told me.

Former Republican congressman Denver Riggleman had the same experience. As noted earlier, he was sidelined in the House GOP for taking a rare vote against the administration.

"I remember someone came up to me and said, 'You've pissed off the big man. You've really gotta back off,'" he recalled. "My reaction was, 'Fuck off. I [used to] kill terrorists. Get out of my face.'"

Although many Republicans in the House shared his views of the MAGA movement, they held their tongues.

"Half of them agreed with me," he said, "but there was no way they were going to go against the polls and fundraising."

The Next Trump won't have to worry about internal dissenters.

Moderate Republicans have been abandoning the party in droves since the MAGA wing took control. I remember when Paul Ryan was Speaker of the House, he spent hours every week trying to convince rational Republicans not to retire, bringing them into his office to persuade them to stay for "just one more term."

The blood loss was severe. Of the 293 Republicans who were serving in the Senate or House when Donald Trump was inaugurated, close to half were gone four years later. Some lost their races. But most of the turnover was from members of Congress who voluntarily retired, especially moderates fed up with the GOP's direction. Data from *FiveThirtyEight* shows their replacements tended to be further to the right politically.

Charlie Dent was one of them. The Pennsylvania representative had served a dozen years in Congress and was ranked by the *National Journal* as one of the chamber's most moderate Republicans. By 2018, he didn't see a role for centrist conservatives like him in Trump's Washington. He quit the House in frustration.

"What we used to try to do in the House was marginalize the crazies and elevate the rational ones," he told me, explaining that the MAGA GOP is different. "Now the opposite is happening. They are elevating the fringe members—the ones who talk about Jewish space lasers and vaccines that don't work—and are sidelining the Liz Cheneys and Adam Kinzingers, the rational ones."

The remaining independent-minded Republicans are reluctant to hold town halls with their constituents because of how contentious the political environment has gotten. One former Republican congressmen I sat down with shared that, after he spoke out against Trump, MAGA supporters began intimidating his family. (He asked that his name be withheld for personal security reasons.)

Strangers showed up unexpectedly at his wife's office demanding to know where he was. Others confronted him in grocery store parking lots. After a series of combative encounters, he received a word of advice he'd been fearing.

"I got a call from a good friend of mine who said, 'You need to carry,'" the ex-congressman recalled, referring to obtaining a concealed firearm. "Now I carry at all times. I'm carrying a Wilson Combat 45."

He showed me the weapon, holstered in his waistband. His wife and adult children now have concealed carry permits, too.

I asked someone on the other side of the aisle—Democratic congressman Eric Swalwell—why so many MAGA Republicans refused to condemn the hostility. He said they saw it as a performance, not as loaded-gun rhetoric. To them, there was "entertainment value" in "pandering to people who are authoritarian curious."

"I see this with so many of my colleagues who will go at me on Twitter, attack me on Fox News, but then they'll bump into me and be like, 'Hey Swalwell, how ya doing, buddy?'" the Congressman explained. "One of them keeps inviting me to go to dinner."

His GOP counterparts view their jobs like professional wrestling, Swalwell said.

"They think in the ring we're supposed to hit each other over the head with chairs, but backstage we're supposed to know it's fake and the fans just want it. And I think that is really, really corrosive that they view so much of their role . . . as just to entertain the fans and give them what they want."

Legislative "destruction" will be used to remake America in the MAGA image.

I met with a GOP representative, an old friend, for beers at an Irish bar along the Potomac River a year after Trump left office. We hadn't spoken in years. I wanted to gauge his thinking about the direction of the GOP and, frankly, to see why he was staying.

To my surprise, he confessed he was thinking about leaving Congress after his next term. I asked why.

"It's a performance, man," he said, echoing what I'd heard from Swalwell. "It's all about the fucking performance."

He had no interest in showing off on social media by "owning the libs" and using his time in Washington to punish Trump's political rivals, which had become the top focus for the House GOP, despite the fact that Trump was long gone from office. My friend cared about policy.

The conservative was once a rising star in the Republican Party—clean-cut, articulate, well educated, and in command of the issues, from taxes to foreign affairs. He knew those weren't the qualities MAGA leaders were seeking in the coming years. The new rising stars were willing to do dirty work.

"I don't want to take the votes. It's all gonna be political retaliation and impeachments and lock-her-up shit," he vented. In his view, the Speaker's gavel in the U.S. House was becoming a hammer, not used to legislate but to destroy.

Joe Walsh feels remorse for helping create the monster. The former Illinois Republican and firebrand came into Congress as part of a Tea Party wave in the early 2010s. He garnered attention for controversial comments on race, religion, Democrats, and political violence. Before the 2016 election, Walsh famously tweeted: "On November 8th, I'm voting for Trump. On November 9th, if Trump loses, I'm grabbing my musket. You in?"

"I helped seed the ground for Trump by inflaming the base," he admitted to me in an interview.

Walsh was shocked by what he saw during the Trump years. MAGA forces weren't advancing Republican ideals at all, he realized, but promoting a brand of pseudo-authoritarianism. Walsh had a change of heart. He tried to convince fellow Republicans that they'd made a horrible mistake and needed to return to their conservative roots. It was too late.

"I do not see the party changing enough in my lifetime to ever welcome someone like me back," he said.

Walsh predicted that a future GOP Congress would seek to remake America in the image of the Next Trump. What might be called the Two Houses of MAGA (the White House and a right-leaning House of Representatives) would play off each other in dangerous ways and do each other's bidding. Walsh expressed worry that the White House would feed information to partisan congressional committees to smear enemies, with investigative files from the Justice Department, for example, or private tax information from the Internal Revenue Service.

A MAGA congressional majority will use impeachment as a weapon to take out Democratic rivals. This might include impeaching *former* officials, too. Republicans have discussed whether they could initiate proceedings against Democratic cabinet secretaries who've left office. Why? Because a conviction could prevent those officials from holding public office again, including running for president. The move would be a deceptive way to cull the Democratic presidential field, although it would require a supermajority in the U.S. Senate.

The GOP's legislative priorities will represent a sharp break with the past.

When I came to Washington, conservatives were focused on free minds, free markets, and free people. Put another way, Republicans considered themselves supporters of open debate and a competition of ideas, advocates for loosening restrictions on the private sector in order to unleash American innovation, and champions of open trade and democracy, at home and abroad. That's no longer the case.

Leaders in today's Republican Party preach the opposite. The GOP has become more confrontational toward the media (by parroting Trump's attitude that the free press is the "enemy of the people"), more hostile toward private industry (by calling for regulation against U.S. companies that are seen as unsupportive of MAGA cultural views), and more isolationist, protectionist, and antidemocratic when it comes to foreign policy (by pulling back from international commitments, implementing new trade barriers, and celebrating autocratic leaders).

The culture wars will be the primary legislative agenda—"guns, gays, and girls," as one GOP operative told me. All three areas will receive focused attention. In the name of protecting the Second Amendment, MAGA forces will pass legislation to lower restrictions on firearms purchases, lift background checks, and eliminate gun laws. They will legislate on sexual orientation and gender identity, including reversing protections for same-sex marriage. And they will seek to outlaw abortion procedures, including criminal penalties for patients and providers.

Gavin Smith, one of the few openly gay appointees in the Trump administration, said the whiplash shift on LGBTQ+ caught him off guard.

"When the MAGA movement started, Trump was seen as someone who didn't care about gay marriage. He wasn't going to be a threat to the gay community. People breathed a sigh of relief," Smith reflected. Then Trump empowered the far right.

"Now you've seen the GOP take hardcore anti-LGBTQ positions

since his presidency. We've taken twenty steps backward," he lamented. "LGBTQ rights are under threat from the MAGA movement."

In some cases, the Next Trump won't need Congress to wage the culture wars.

A former senior official at the Education Department under Trump said "Don't Say Gay" policies—prohibiting educators from talking about same-sex marriage—could be implemented without legislation. The former aide explained how it could be done: the department has the power to restrict funding from school districts that are on probation.

"They would tell the Office of Civil Rights at the Department of Education that any complaints of 'grooming' automatically open a systemic investigation," he noted, "and put school districts under consent orders."

Knowing this, right-wing figures will try to gin up false allegations. That paves the way for the department to open investigations and withhold education dollars, or attach conditions to them, such as forbidding discussions of same-sex marriage in the classroom.

"It's the 'Don't Say Gay' version of entrapment," the official deadpanned.

★ ★ ★

Of democracy's guardrails, the integrity of the legislature will be among the hardest to defend. Anything Congress does to protect itself can be undone when control changes hands. Only the voters can stop their elected representatives from doing the Next Trump's bidding, and they might not be entirely aware of what's happening. Among the scariest possibilities I heard in my conversations was the one referred to as "secret laws."

In civics classes, American students are taught that all laws are public. A bill becomes a law by getting debated and considered in the open, for everyone to see. That's not entirely true. When key national security bills—such as intelligence authorizations, defense bills, or annual spending packages—are passed, they often include what's called a "classified annex." The long-standing practice allows legislators to write additional instructions to U.S. agencies about programs that shouldn't be disclosed openly, perhaps a new weapon or a spy program.

These annexes are important. Congress has no other way to control the government's secret programs if it can't do so in a safe and secure manner. Yet access to these undisclosed addendums is restricted to lawmakers, select staff, and a limited group of agency officials. While the existence of the practice is not secret, the specific legislative language is rarely (if ever) made public.

In a nightmare scenario, the practice could be used to pass laws that might otherwise get rejected. And few would know about it. In my experience, most members of Congress didn't bother to read the classified annex attached to a bill. Doing so required blocking off precious time on their calendars, traveling to a secure facility, and sitting alone reviewing arcane language that they'd agree with anyway. They trusted staffers to do the job for them.

What if the Next Trump nudged a GOP ally to slip in legislative language that has a nefarious purpose?

A committee staffer could add text to the classified annex that might seem innocuous on the surface. If read differently, it could authorize the president to exercise powers *not* envisioned by Congress. For instance, in the name of election security, the annex might be edited to allow DHS to seize and "audit" voting systems after an enemy cyberattack. The authority could open the door for the president's cronies to scoop up ballots, cast doubt on the election results, and even to surreptitiously change vote tallies.

Operatives around Donald Trump considered something like this after the 2020 election. They misconstrued an executive order that I helped write (EO 13848), as part of their plot. The EO empowered the president to punish countries that meddled in U.S. elections, but MAGA lawyers twisted it to justify the potential seizure of voting machines. Fortunately, they didn't succeed. But what if those powers had been enshrined in a classified annex and preauthorized by Congress? It would have been much easier for the president to abuse those authorities and harder for the public to figure out what was going on.

I should note that I don't see the "secret law" scenario as particularly probable. Democrats, Republicans, and nonpartisan lawyers must review the language of classified annexes ahead of time, before the documents get attached to bills and voted on by the House or Senate. Abusing the practice would be difficult.

But the fact that the idea came up is a red flag. Former members of Congress and their staff are so concerned by the rise of far-right figures in the American political system that they now view routine aspects of the lawmaking process with suspicion. A former official who broached the subject asked me not to take notes, just in case a MAGA majority came looking for him.

"I don't want to get subpoenaed," he explained.

Chapter 5

THE SHIELD

Energy in the Executive is a leading character in the definition of good government. It is essential to the protection of the community against foreign attacks . . . the steady administration of the laws . . . the protection of property . . . [and] the security of liberty against the enterprises and assaults of ambition, of faction, and of anarchy.

—ALEXANDER HAMILTON, FEDERALIST NO. 70, 1788

PART I

March 28, 2019

The large wooden desk had seen thousands of moments like this, moments of decision. It had been in the Oval Office for more than a hundred years, a gift from Britain to the United States fashioned from the timbers of an abandoned naval vessel, the HMS *Resolute*. The desk was a national stage for presidents to pronounce formidable words, a platform for celebrating triumphs, and in certain tumultuous periods, a graveyard of bad decisions.

Seated behind the iconic helm of American power, Trump weighed his options. He squinted his eyes as a bevy of advisors took turns speaking about the issue at hand. On the Resolute desk, his fingers hovered near a red button—prepared to make a fateful decision. The mood was tense as aides argued with each other.

But it became clear by the look on his face that he'd made up his mind. His finger was now on the button. The president pressed it, decisively.

Click.

The door to an anteroom swung open almost instantly, and an attendant strode into the Oval Office, placing an ice-filled glass on the desk and popping open a Diet Coke.

"Does anyone want anything?" the president asked insincerely.

No one was stupid enough to answer. The waiter poured the soda into the tall glass. When it was full, the president waved him away and Trump resumed the heated conversation.

It was late in the day. Donald Trump was growing impatient with the strictures of the office. His team was trying to talk him off a ledge, but he was really ready to jump this time.

I sat on one of two couches in the center of the Oval Office, alongside Mick Mulvaney, the acting chief of staff; Pat Cipollone, the president's lawyer; Kirstjen Nielsen, the embattled homeland security secretary; Mike Pompeo, the secretary of state; Jared Kushner, the president's son-in-law; and, of course, Stephen Miller. The meeting had been scheduled as a quick fifteen-minute sync, but as it approached two hours, Trump meandered between grievances.

At present, his ire was trained on the border and the increase in crossings of undocumented immigrants.

He seethed. "I can't believe we are doing so badly. This is not a strong response. This is *not* General Patton. By now, General Patton would be killing the enemy."

Trump turned to Jared.

"Mexico is full of shit. They are totally full of shit. Stop groveling to them. They are swindling us, Jared." Trump wanted to cut off all assistance to Mexico and the Northern Triangle governments because they were "busing their worst people into our country."

Jared tried to reason with him, clarifying that U.S. funds actually *helped* those governments manage the migrant flows and weed out criminals.

Trump interrupted.

"I don't give a shit. Close the fucking border. Seriously, close it."

The conversation had been months in the making, though no one in the room seemed ready for it. Trump had mused about closing the entire border and now he seemed serious. I sat taking copious notes. I didn't know what I was going to do with them, but as the Trump presidency devolved, "Anonymous" loitered subconsciously. My alter ego wanted me to act.

"Shut it down, okay?"

We were three months into the new year, which had already started off badly in January. The government shutdown dragged from the holidays well into 2019, throwing the Trump administration deeper into turmoil. Everything was on hold. Whether it was DHS operations, Trump's plans to gut his own administration, or—to my frustration—unfulfilled discussions about exit planning, nothing moved forward.

Kirstjen had heeded Defense Secretary Mattis's parting recommendation, much to my chagrin. She remained in office to provide a voice of reason in the cabinet, seeing herself as one of the few who could end the shutdown and reopen the government.

Meanwhile, I was supposed to leave for my wedding in Latin America in January. With everything falling apart, I felt stuck. Anabel had already dealt with a dozen canceled vacations, lost weekends, and my near-total absence, seven days a week. But I was now officially the chief of staff of a massive department with hundreds of thousands of employees, who wouldn't be able to pay their bills if we didn't get Trump to cut a deal with Congress, fast.

In any other administration, someone would have covered for me.

In this one, the bench was thin. I was forced to shorten my absence and punt the honeymoon down the road to an undetermined date. As if that wasn't enough, someone broke into our home before we left.

The intruder picked the locks of two doorways into the Capitol Hill row house, including an iron grate and a thick wooden front door that I found ajar. In the process, the individual somehow disabled the alarm system and the video doorbell, both of which went dark during the incident—blacked out for about five minutes. Even stranger, the inside of the house was undisturbed. Not a single possession was moved, broken, or stolen.

I contacted the police, but I didn't think this was any ordinary burglar. Neither did DHS. The department dispatched security personnel to do a sweep of my house, particularly because of the sensitive communications equipment installed in my residence.

My own reasons for alarm were different. After the unsigned essay was released, I suspected that a foreign intelligence service might try to unmask Anonymous. The fastest way for world leaders to ingratiate themselves with Donald Trump was to flatter him, or attack his enemies. How better to curry the president's favor than to hunt down and expose the dissenter in his midst?

Luckily, nothing in my house tied me to the op-ed. There was no paper trail anywhere, save for a single signed document affirming my authorship, which the *Times* kept in a locked safe at their headquarters. Still, I felt uneasy about home security. We upgraded our alarm system, replaced the deadbolt with a keypad lock, and added more video cameras which ran on batteries even if the power was cut off.

I knew also that I needed to share the truth with Anabel. She didn't know I was the author of the piece. But after the intruder broke in, I felt like I couldn't keep the information from her any longer. Anabel reacted the way I'd expected. While she was no fan of Trump, she knew that vocally opposing him as a nameless internal objector was risky and guaranteed to result in retribution if I revealed myself.

I had bought a gun in the aftermath of the decision to blow the whistle. When I casually asked a military buddy, he advised me to purchase a Sig Sauer P365, the perfect concealed weapon. That's what I did. The thin, lightweight pistol held ten rounds and boasted a tritium night sight that allowed it to be aimed with deadly accuracy even in the dark. I needed a refresher on how to shoot.

An off-duty Secret Service agent (I'll call him Mitch) took me to an outdoor range on a chilly winter afternoon to practice. I'd gone shooting a few times growing up in Indiana, but it had been years since I fired a weapon. You couldn't easily get approval to keep a gun in Washington, D.C. Buying the wrong box of ammunition was proof of my inexperience.

"These are full metal jackets," Mitch explained. The agent emptied my new box of ammo, pointing to the smooth tips. "Round nose. You can use these for practice, but if you really want to stop a bad guy, you want these."

He placed one of his cartridges on the counter. The tip of the projectile was a tiny crater, not a smooth edge.

"These are hollow-point rounds. For home defense."

Mitch did a demonstration.

Twenty or so feet down the firing lane, a paper target was suspended from the track. A 1950s-era bad guy stared back at us in a blazer, pointing a pistol in our direction. We were about to obliterate him.

First, Mitch retrieved a gallon of water from his trunk. He tied it up so that it hung in front of the target. I was confused.

He loaded his pistol with my round-nose ammo and pointed it downrange. He fired. Two small streams of water poured from opposite ends of the jug.

"See? Straight through. Entry wound, exit wound."

Then Mitch reloaded, this time with *his* ammo. He shoved the magazine back into the pistol and racked a round. He fired again. The jug exploded. All that remained was a mangled piece of plastic, dangling on a string of yarn, and behind it the fifties goon was drenched.

"That's hollow-point. If you want to stop somebody in their tracks, this is your buddy."

Mitch explained that the bullet would mushroom inside a target, rather than pass straight through. He warned that if I fired one of the round-nose bullets at a burglar, it might keep going into another room or a nearby house and hit an innocent person.

"Got it," I told him.

The gun weighed a pound-and-a-half and felt good in my hand. My aim was poor at first. Bullet holes dotted the paper target randomly, without any clear pattern. By the end of the afternoon my groupings were tight and on target. We practiced until the tips of my fingers burned with cold. Afterward, we went to a brewery to warm up.

★ ★ ★

On the way home from my truncated January wedding in Latin America, I hoped to find normalcy back at the office. Little had changed while I was away. The government remained shuttered, and the situation at DHS was dire.

We held emergency meetings at the White House. The secretary and I used the looming deadline of missed paychecks to force Trump's hand, raising the visual specter of DHS families standing in food lines—something the president knew would be deeply harmful to his re-election. He finally blinked.

Congress passed a budget without the billions in border funds Trump had demanded. The president had nothing to show for the debacle except for thirty-five days of political wreckage and an exhausted federal workforce.

Up to that point, I thought I'd seen the nation's chief executive unglued. But after he lost the showdown with Congress, his remaining reservations (if any) were gone. In the three months that followed, China could have launched a nuclear strike on the United States, and Trump wouldn't have cared. Everything was about the southern border.

The best way to describe the mayhem of that period is merely to recount Trump's words and actions, which proved—once and for all—that quitting the administration was the only appropriate option.

On a January flight down South, the president demanded that we involve him in negotiations with contractors over the border wall.

"Two things matter to me," he said, leaning back in the chair in his Air Force One office. "Price and beauty. I want it to be cheap, and I want it to be fucking beautiful."

It was legally problematic for a president to engage directly in bidding wars with federal contractors. His involvement could ruin the entire selection process. I explained this to Trump, who ignored me, waving his hand for silence so he could unmute a Fox News segment about himself. He smiled back at his own smiling face on the television.

A week or so later, the president called the secretary with a different order. He wanted to "bus and dump" all illegal aliens picked up at the border into Democratic cities. He wanted to punish those localities for protecting undocumented immigrants by trying to stir up mayhem. Trump later told us he wanted to send the worst ones—the "murderers, rapists, and criminals"—into the cities to create even more instability.

I consulted our lawyers, who reached the obvious conclusion that this would probably be illegal for any number of reasons. I put several of Trump's aides on an email and told them our position. None of them responded.

The next week, Trump called again to submit more instructions about the design of the border wall (which had long since been designed). In a rambling conversation, he told us to paint the wall "matte black"—he didn't want it shiny—and complained that the contractors building it were "filthy fucking rich, having lunch with each other every week and deciding how they are going to divvy it all up." I wasn't sure what he was talking about.

We muted him for most of the rant. Painting and repainting the border wall was the conversational equivalent of Trump's pre-naptime coloring book. We would let him go and go, until he wore himself out.

On February 19, Kirstjen and I met with the president about a diplomatic issue. During the meeting, he asked yet again about the U.S. aid money being sent to countries in Latin America's Northern Triangle and instructed that the funds be shut off until those nations started arresting more migrants.

Once more, we told him it was unlawful to cancel funds that Congress had already appropriated to be spent. He couldn't veto something that was already signed into law. Trump pretended not to hear the explanation by changing the subject, venting about a comment Lindsey Graham had made on cable news.

Two weeks later, we were summoned by the president to the White House to talk about—what else?—immigration. This time he was mad that DOJ lawyers had resisted his ideas for how to take control of the situation.

"Jeff Sessions is the dumbest human being ever created by God," Trump spat, deriding his former attorney general, whom he blamed in part for the situation.

The president insisted that we use his "magical authorities" to keep more people out of the United States, a reference Trump sometimes made to a loose assortment of emergency presidential powers and special immigration authorities that can only be invoked in extreme circumstances, such as a global health crisis or an armed foreign invasion.

"Mr. President," Kirstjen explained patiently, "you'll get enjoined by the courts if you do that."

"What the fuck happened to the good old days when someone arrived at our borders, and we told them to just get the hell out?" Trump protested, harking back to an era I wasn't familiar with. "The Northern Triangle countries are sending us the worst. They stick their shittiest people in the flows and send them up. These are robbers and rapists, okay?" (I made a mental note. He really did bring up "rape" and "rapists" a lot.)

For the umpteenth time, I chimed in to remind him we didn't have much flexibility beyond working with Congress to close legal loopholes and undertake immigration reform. Trump chafed at the suggestion. He wanted to act unilaterally.

On March 7, we were back in the Oval Office because Trump wanted to continue the conversation on the border wall. This time, the president told us he had received a letter from Senator Kevin Cramer of North Dakota about a company that could build the wall cheaper than anyone else. The firm proposed constructing it with concrete. Trump had called for a concrete wall during the presidential campaign, but he'd begrudgingly changed his mind when border agents said the material was unsuitable.

"I don't care anymore," Trump said. "Let's do concrete."

A Pentagon official in the room from the Army Corps of Engineers reminded the president that the wall design had been finalized a long time ago. The structure was already being built so that law enforcement agents could have visibility to the other side.

"I don't care. Tell them to put cameras on top or drill holes to see through it. I like concrete. Politically, concrete is better for me."

Out of nowhere, Trump complained that ranchers in Texas were being allowed to open doors in the wall to allow their cattle to reach the Rio Grande River.

"No doors. I don't want doors," he said. "How crazy is this? There are doors in the border wall? It's stupid. They can just walk up, open the door, and thousands of [illegals] rush in."

Kirstjen told him that wasn't exactly true. Border Patrol monitored the gates. And there were very few of them.

The president didn't care and said that in order to end the practice for good DHS needed to acquire any land where ranchers had access to the Rio Grande.

"Just buy the land. I know more about land than any other human on Earth. Let's do it, okay? Give the ranchers ladders. They can use ladders to get to the other side, but not doors. You could use small fire trucks. Call the local fire stations, and use the ladders on their trucks to help them get over."

Hold on, I thought. *We're going to tell Texas ranchers not to use the gates, borrow fire trucks instead, lean the ladders against the border wall, walk their cattle up the ladders (and over the other side, somehow?), let the animals drink from the river for a little bit, and then hoist them back over?*

It was so incandescently stupid I couldn't laugh.

"You know why we need this?" Trump continued, pointing to a photo of the border wall on his desk. "Mexico is a *hellhole.* Have I said that yet? Because it is. It's a hellhole, and no one fucking wants that place. Forty thousand murders. Can you believe it? Sheesh."

No one said anything.

On the way out, Trump asked me if he should use the word "apprehended" or "captured" when talking about migrants arrested at the border.

"Well, apprehended is the appropriate legal and operational term—" I explained before he cut me off.

"Eh, come oooon. No one knows what that means. I want to say 'captured' because it sounds tougher. What do you think?" He polled others.

Vice President Pence, who had stood there quietly for the meeting, spoke up to agree with the president. The secretary sided with me.

"We'll see," Trump retorted. "I like 'capture.' I think we should start using that."

On Saturday, during the president's weekend tweet storm, he posted: "Border Patrol and Law Enforcement has apprehended (captured) large numbers of illegal immigrants at the Border. They won't be coming into the U.S. The Wall is being built and will greatly help us in the future, and now!"

The afternoon of March 15, we returned for another immigration meeting. The Oval Office lights were off.

"Oooh." The president smiled as he entered. "Dark in here. Kind of sexy."

As he settled into his chair behind the desk, Trump told us he wanted to get creative with immigration policy. In particular, he wanted us to revisit the travel ban. He was still fuming that we'd convinced him to pare it back, and thought the latest iteration was "too watered down."

"We just need more countries," Trump insisted. "We need to ban more countries, okay?"

There was a process, I told him. The Supreme Court had only upheld the limited travel restrictions because they were designed by career officials after an impartial review based on intelligence community threat assessments, not politics. We needed to defer to the experts.

Stephen Miller corrected me, noting that the president had the ultimate say and could overrule his agencies. Trump preferred Miller's analysis.

"Imagine the headlines!" the president mused. "*'Trump's Newest Travel Ban'*—it will be beautiful." He told us to come up with a bigger list of countries.

I dutifully documented the order in my notebook, along with a doodle of a man (me) jumping off of a three-dimensional box.

The president went back to his greatest hits—"a big, big border wall!" "cut off the cash!" "screw the Mexicans!"—and we sat there listening to the diatribe that had begun to sound like a Broadway sing-a-long from hell. We left without any clear direction about what was happening next.

Two days later, on March 19, he did the song and dance for us again. The Oval Office meeting was supposed to be about combating opioid addiction, but we didn't spend more than a few minutes talking about the millions of Americans suffering from the drug epidemic. Why would we do that, when we could use the valuable time to talk about immigration again?

Trump steered the briefing to his favorite subject. He ran through his list of cruelly imaginative immigration policies once more. This time there was a tangent to the already tangential conversation, as he paused to pay homage to the MyPillow CEO.

"This guy, you've seen him? He's unbelievable! The pillow guy. He buys all the airtime, it's so brilliant. He's also a Trump supporter, you know."

The pattern continued until the end of the month. Meetings. Phone calls. Late-night tweets. More meetings. Trump's border obsession was consuming him—and as a consequence—consuming us.

The month concluded with a volcanic tirade in the Oval Office on March 28, 2019, which brought the situation to a head. The president went from steaming hot to full eruption over the crisis at the southern border. DHS was standing in his way, he said, and he was sick of it. Why was the department stonewalling all of his requests?

The president told us to reinstitute his family separation policy.

Trump was angry that we'd persuaded him the year before to shut down DOJ's disastrous zero-tolerance program. Disaster is what he wanted.

"Now we just get these women coming in with seven children saying, 'Oh, my husband he left me.'" The president had briefly switched into a high-pitched Mexican accent. "They are useless. They don't do anything for our country. At least if they came in with a husband we could put him in the fields to pick corn or something."

If we didn't do something fast, he'd look politically weak. Immigration was his signature issue, he said.

"Close the border, and they'll kiss our asses!" Trump barked at Kirstjen, who remained silent.

"These countries are horrible," he fussed, referring to Latin American nations. "They are—I've used a term before, you know the term." He was alluding to his controversial "shithole countries" comment without saying it, although he'd used "hellhole" days prior.

Trump complained that the troops he'd sent to the border were ineffective. They needed to use deadly force.

"But we can't do that," he said ruefully as an afterthought, recalling that the Pentagon had told him to stop talking about "shooting migrants." Trump scanned the room and stopped at me.

"What the fuck are you doing?" he asked.

"Excuse me, sir?" I replied.

"You're taking notes! I don't want any fucking notes. Stop taking notes."

I slowly closed my legal pad and sat there, hands folded on top. Trump's admonishment was two years too late. I had paper notes and mental notes he couldn't touch. I just didn't know what to do with them yet.

He moved on to poll numbers.

"I'm at 55 percent, this is crazy."

He was corrected by a communications staffer who joined the meeting late. Rasmussen said 49 percent today, she updated him.

No, no, he assured her, the real numbers are higher.

Then he was back on the border.

"Man, we are fucking this up, you guys," he fumed. He said his friend Kim Jong Un knew how to do it better at the Korean DMZ.

"Have you seen his border? Guns. Tanks. Barbed wire. Land mines. Am I right? Hard-ass. Look at North Korea—*that* is border security."

Trump turned again to Kirstjen and Mike Pompeo, who were seated opposite each other in armchairs in front of the desk.

"Close the border, I mean it. Do it immediately."

Kirstjen was deflated. "Mr. President, we've been over this. Closing the whole border is impractical and possibly illegal."

"Fine, do one port," he shot back. "Let's just close one land crossing. It's really bad in Texas. Do El Paso and tell them we are closing it in twenty-four hours."

The communications aide interjected. For political purposes, it would be better to seal a crossing into California. Texas loved Trump, and the Democrats in California hated him. The president thought it was a great idea.

"You're right. I don't want to hurt Texas."

Meanwhile, a staffer entered to let the president know his helicopter was waiting. Trump was slated to speak to a rally in Michigan. I turned to Mick Mulvaney and Jared Kushner on the couch, as the room was overtaken by pockets of conversation.

"We can't do this for partisan reasons," I said. "We'll get killed for it." Jared agreed. Despite his flaws, the young real estate scion was one of the few reliable checks on his father-in-law, when no one else could be.

"Mr. President," Jared jumped in, "closing a port will *not* stop the migrant flows. They can just go around the port. It won't stop the actual flows. It will just hurt U.S. businesses and tourism."

"Jared, I don't care. That's not the point! The point is it will make Mexico hurt. It will make California hurt. Kirstjen, announce it. Tomorrow at noon." After that, he said, the plan could be scaled to the entire southern border.

Pompeo and others nodded in agreement. Kirstjen knew it was pointless to protest, though Trump seemed to anticipate an objection.

"*That's it!* No more excuses. Shut it down, okay? You heard me, noon tomorrow." With that, a red-faced Trump stood up and walked out the door to the Rose Garden, stalking off in a huff to Marine One.

Neither Kirstjen nor I said anything on the way out of the West Wing. We were slated to fly to Europe in a few days to meet with allies about cyber threats. Given the president's blowup, I feared Kirstjen would scrap the entire trip and prove my point: that Trump's insatiable border fetish was preventing us from doing our day jobs.

As we exited the side door to the West Wing, dark purple clouds were pressed against a pink sky. Rush-hour traffic hummed in the distance beyond the compound walls.

"Madam Secretary," I implored her, "we're losing here."

"I know," she replied, getting into the waiting SUV. "Let's talk this weekend." An agent closed the door, and she was whisked through the White House gates and out of view.

The situation was enough to drive anyone to drink. It certainly did that to me. I went out for a cocktail near the White House and ended up having a lot of them, which was becoming the norm. I browned out at the bar, so a colleague drove me home.

I stumbled upstairs to put myself to bed in the guest room, where I was staying frequently. I didn't want to disturb a sleeping Anabel down the hallway. In the morning, I would quietly slip out for work before sunrise—and do it all again.

"April Fools"

The firm knock at the door wasn't housekeeping. I opened it, coming face-to-face with one of the secretary's military aides, Nick.

"Chief, I'm sorry to bother you. The president was trying to get in touch with the secretary last night. I thought you should know."

It was April 1, 8 a.m. in London and 2 a.m. in Washington.

"Did you tell the switchboard we're overseas?" I asked.

"Yessir. I told them she was asleep and that we'd have the secretary call back when it was morning, D.C. time."

In the lobby, I updated Kirstjen. She was as anxious as I was to hear that Trump had called overnight. We piled into our car, flanked by British police officers on motorcycles. The armored convoy snaked through the streets of London toward the U.S. Embassy, lights and sirens clearing the way.

The secretary's decision to go forward with the trip had been a small act of defiance—a signal that DHS had other work to do besides monitoring the border—but the decision was about to be tested. By leaving the country, we were calling Trump's bluff about sealing the border. To go forward, he needed us. And he knew it.

After a morning of preparatory meetings before visits to the Home Office and UK Parliament, we broke for lunch, dining at a chic restaurant nearby. The military aide's phone rang just as we ordered our entrees. POTUS was awake and wanted to talk. Secret Service agents cleared a quiet area in the basement of the restaurant for us to take the call.

"Good morning, Mr. President," Kirstjen said, forcing a cheerful tone.

"What the *fuck* are you doing in Europe?" Trump demanded, his voice audible from her ear. "The border is fucking melting down, and you're on vacation?"

"Sir, it's not a vacation. There's serious—"

"No, Kirstjen. *This* is your job. Get the fuck back here right now. I want to see you on TV at the fucking border, do you understand?"

The secretary tried to calm him, but Trump wasn't having it. He reiterated the demand—"get your ass to the border"—and abruptly ended the call.

I broke the silence.

"Let him fire us. Seriously. This is more important."

"He seems like he's going to do something erratic," she responded.

"So what?"

I made my most forceful case yet. Whether or not we tried to prevent another crisis, Trump was well beyond being contained. The best move we had was to sacrifice ourselves. If we tempted him to fire us for doing our jobs, we could call more attention to the president's perilous mismanagement of the government.

Kirstjen and I were at loggerheads, but I knew I'd lost the dispute before the secretary made up her mind.

"Let's call the vice president," she said, "and we'll see what he thinks."

If it was about Donald Trump, Mike Pence wouldn't present a contrary point of view or alternatives. When we called him, his advice was unsurprising. If the president wanted us to come home, the vice president said, we should come home. It was "April Fools Day," and fittingly the White House was making a mockery of us.

★ ★ ★

Through inch-thick glass, I watched orange dust clouds envelope our line of Chevy Suburbans. The motorcade roared through the desert as if it were fleeing an attack. In a sense, it was speeding toward one. The president was flying to the border to meet us. Donald Trump wanted to ensure that his Homeland Security team knew that we served at *his* pleasure, and apparently it wasn't enough to make us do an embarrassing about-face and return from Europe. He wanted to send the message personally.

The White House had leaked the humiliating news. I saw a Fox News Alert on the television behind the secretary's head on the plane ride back.

"BACK TO THE BORDER," the headline read. And below it: "HOMELAND SECURITY SECRETARY CUTS SHORT TRIP TO EUROPE."

While we were en route back across the Atlantic, I got a frantic text message from a senior official at the U.S. Embassy in Mexico. The envoy had seen Trump's public threat to seal the border, and our team in Mexico City was caught off guard. It was the first they'd heard of it. We hadn't briefed the U.S. diplomats because we intended to bury Trump's stupid idea before it came to fruition. Clearly we were failing. The embassy warned that the move would severely rupture relations with our southern neighbor, as Trump's self-imposed deadline loomed.

Anabel was surprised to see me come home. I warned her it wouldn't be for long, as I barely had time to switch clothes and shower before leaving the house again. Coast Guard One was refueled and ready to hit the skies within hours. I returned to Reagan National Airport, this time bound for the American Southwest on what felt like a suicide mission.

Kirstjen organized a phone call of the whole cabinet to seek help from other agencies. The appeal was little more than a performance because none of them could fix the underlying problem—the president. I was beyond ready to quit, but for anyone to pay attention, the secretary herself needed to resign.

This trip needed to be the final one.

On the ground in Arizona, I asked the Secret Service to floor it. We needed time to get organized before the president arrived. Our next stop was Yuma, where we would hold meetings and calls before driving an hour away over the state line to join the president in Calexico, California. The last thing we needed was an unsupervised Trump wandering the facilities, giving errant directives to DHS agents.

We were going fast. The armored SUV creaked and moaned painfully as the motorcade tore across the uneven dirt road. Outside the only sign of life was a multitude of camouflage-green saguaros standing motionless on the desert floor. The cacti were like soldiers who've just realized the war is lost, their spindly arms surrendering to the sun. I considered them through the window.

Up front, the dust-crusted windshield was getting harder to see through, so our driver turned on the wipers. Just then, we struck a sizable rut, launching us from our seats. Neither Kirstjen nor I had seat belts on and—for a moment—she seemed to float in midair. She was small enough that her head only grazed the ceiling before coming back down. I was thrust into the roof of the vehicle and thrown to the floor, as the car came to a halt.

The detail leader whipped around from the front seat.

"Is everyone all right?"

"Yes, but can we slow the hell down?" Kirstjen responded, visibly annoyed. She turned to me. "Are you okay?"

"Yeah, yeah, I'm fine," I offered, pulling myself back into the bucket seat and scooping up papers that had flown from my briefing book. The car started rolling again. I buckled my seat belt and knew immediately that I had a concussion—nauseous, disoriented, dizzy.

We reached a border patrol facility and were escorted to a conference room that had been converted into a miniature command post for us. No one was there yet, and silence was a welcome sound. I excused myself to the restroom and vomited, crouching on the floor in a daze. I don't know how long I was kneeling there when one of the agents, Mike McCool, entered.

"Hey, the secretary needs you. The president is on the line," Mike said, noticing I was doubled over. "You all right?"

I steadied myself and nodded. I brushed past the man with a football player's frame, whom I should have asked for help, and hobbled back to the conference room.

The scene was no longer tranquil. A familiar voice—like an indignant drunk with a working-class Queens accent—filled the room on speakerphone. Despite the pounding headache, I reflexively grabbed a pen and paper and sat down.

"Kirstjen, did you watch Lou Dobbs the other night, like I asked you?" Trump quizzed her.

"Yes, Mr. President. I told you I did."

"Well then why the hell aren't we doing what Kris Kobach said?" He was referring to the controversial GOP Kansas secretary of state, whose anti-immigrant views were often touted during the program. We had heard credible rumors that Trump was considering replacing Kirstjen with Kobach. "He's got ideas for securing the border."

"Most of what he said is out of our lane—like taxing the money people send back to their home countries, the remittances," Kirstjen told him.

Trump wanted to find a way to keep migrants from sending money back to relatives abroad. The move would be a way to punish them and their families and discourage others from coming to the United States to work. We didn't think it was possible, and it might not be lawful.

"Those goddamn remittances. Every time I ask [Steve] Mnuchin about this, he's got another excuse. 'We can't do this, we can't do that.' What good is he? I thought we had the right guy at Treasury. But now I don't know. Maybe not so much. What do you think—personnel mistake?"

The question was actually a veiled threat, as if we were personnel mistakes, too. He shifted gears to illegal border crossings.

"The numbers are too high, Kirstjen. They are too high. You're not doing your job."

"Mr. President I am doing everything possible. We have tried *every* option, but it's the law—"

"I don't want excuses. That's what you always give me. Just do it, okay? How many times have I told you to *stop them*?"

"Sir, with respect, I've said it a million times, and so have you. It's the laws. I cannot legally stop them. The laws prevent me from detaining and removing people who claim asylum."

"What do you need?"

"I need Congress to fix loopholes in the law that are exploited by the traffickers. It's the same loopholes we've been talking about for years." Nielsen listed off the ways the immigration system was broken, but she was cut off again.

"Why are we still talking about it? Why haven't you given Congress the bill, Kirstjen?"

"We've written text to reform the immigration system, Mr. President. But it's been stuck in *your* White House. No one seems to think this is an emergency."

He exploded at the comment. There was chatter in the background, and we realized other people were in the room with Trump. He was clearly in the Oval Office and, thankfully, not yet in the skies headed our direction.

"Goddamnit! Stephen, tell them to get that bill done today. Send the fucking bill to Congress today, you understand? It needs to fix the loopholes. And we need to get rid of asylum. Just get rid of it. We are full, and no one should be able to claim asylum."

The background cross-chat around Trump grew louder. The secretary rolled her eyes. Getting "rid" of asylum—which allowed people to seek humanitarian protection in the United States—was *not* part of the draft bill, nor was what Trump said next.

"And it needs to get rid of the fucking immigration judges. There should not be any judges at all. These guys are unionized, when the fuck did that happen?"

"Many years ago, sir," Kirstjen said.

"All right, well just do it. Get the bill sent. I just need you to do your job."

"Mr. President, I'm doing everything within my power—everything—to respond to this emergency. I've sent requests over and over to the White House for help, and I don't get anything. You need to order other departments to assist."

"Oh, so now it's on me? You're saying it's on *me*, Kirstjen, the President of the United States?"

"Sir, I have asked your staff for more space to hold migrants, a supplemental appropriation to Congress to build bigger and more humane facilities, legislation to fix the loopholes, a single person to be in charge at the White House—"

"Space? Kirstjen I told you to tell DOD to build some goddamn tents!"

"Sir, I am not the Defense Department. I cannot order them what to do. You are the commander in chief."

"So now it's my fault? I have 100—130—140 fucking things I'm supposed to do. I've got North Korea. China. You should just do your job!"

"What do you want me to do that I am not already doing? Tell me, Mr. President. Tell me what I am legally allowed to do that I'm not doing."

"Keep them out. That's your job."

"Sir, I just, I just don't know what you want. You have said it yourself so many times that our hands are tied because of the loopholes and the court decisions. I can't just keep everyone out. I can't break the law."

"Why are you telling me all this shit now?"

"I have been telling you for *months* what problems we have. Months. And your staff every single day. Stephen, have you told DOD what we need? Have *you* made these asks on behalf of the president?"

Trump started yelling at the people seated around him.

"Sir," the secretary interjected. "SIR! I even had to call your cabinet together myself this week because the White House is so disorganized—"

Trump hung up.

"*Fuck!*" Kirstjen threw her cell phone, which hit the floor and slid to a halt across the room.

We sat for a long time, saying nothing. I avoided eye contact and answered emails. This wasn't the time to say, *I told you so.* I hoped it was glaringly obvious that this man couldn't be fixed. He couldn't be managed. He certainly couldn't be convinced to do the right thing. The time spent trying to put bad ideas back into the box was over. Whether she was thinking the same or not, I didn't know.

"Okay, let's go," she sighed and walked across the room to pick up her phone.

There was a small silver lining to the day. Trump concluded that a diplomatic crisis was risky for him, politically. So, without telling Kirstjen, he decided to back down off the threat to close the U.S.-Mexico border. An aide handed me a copy of *USA Today* on the way to meet Air Force One. A modestly reassuring headline on the front page—"TRUMP TO KEEP BORDER OPEN"—was tempered by my knowledge of the man. The president surely had another heedless idea up his sleeve.

When Trump landed on April 5, our cars merged with his motorcade en route to a public event with border patrol agents. The room was packed with reporters, sweltering under the hot glare of TV lights. They weren't interested in the scripted roundtable discussion. Everyone was waiting to see what would happen with Trump's on-again, off-again border threat. Would he seal the roads? Would he halt cross-border trade and travel?

A rush of anxiety hit me in the crowded room. My hands got sweaty, and I felt the now-familiar darkening in my peripheral vision. I sought refuge backstage.

Moving past Secret Service agents, I got to the green-room area. The president was mingling with the border agents. And Kirstjen was looking on from a distance, warily.

"We are full," Trump told a border official. "Tell the judges we are completely full—'the bins are full'—and we can't let anyone else in."

Oh no. He was back on it. The president was pressuring agents to seal the border.

"Just say, 'Sorry, Judge, I can't do it. We don't have the room.'"

He was telling them to ignore federal judges and deport people anyway, even if they had a right to be in the United States. I strained to hear what the agents were saying to the president. A Customs and Border Protection leader tried explaining to him why that would be unlawful.

"Seriously, keep them all out," Trump countered. "Don't let anymore in. If you go to jail for it, I'll pardon you."

The president left the holding area and went onstage. I was bewildered. *Had I heard that right?*

Trump offered a presidential pardon in exchange for an illegal act. When the roundtable was done, I went straight to the CBP official to confirm the president's wording. I also wanted to make sure that no agents were planning to follow the order. Yes, the man recounted, that's what Trump said. The two of us met the secretary back in the motorcade.

"Wait, are you serious? What the actual fuck," she muttered. "What exactly did he say?"

The CBP chief recounted the episode.

"We need to document this," I responded, composing an email to the department's lawyers with a real-time summary and a question. *Did the president just break the law?*

The secretary got a notification from one of her Secret Service agents. She was being summoned to Stagecoach, the nickname for the president's limousine. Kirstjen disappeared for a few minutes and then returned to the car. She said nothing when she got back in, and we started moving to the next location. I got a text from her in the seat in front of me—something she didn't want to say out loud.

"This is far and away the most abusive relationship I've ever had or ever will have," she wrote.

Trump had excoriated her in his limo once more for not shutting down the border, making no reference to the fact that he'd decided to stand down on the threat himself. It felt like the film *Groundhog Day*, where Bill Murray keeps reliving the same events over, and over, and over. But Trump wasn't fooling us with his unpredictable mood swings and flip-flopping. *We* were the idiots for enduring it.

I paid little attention at the final stop. Standing in front of his border wall, Trump backslapped law enforcement officers. He posed for photos and did a self-congratulatory interview with Fox News to tout the wall, during which he declared that "the country is full," presumably laying the predicate for his border agents to lie to federal judges about being unable to process any more immigrants.

My head was elsewhere. I stood on the sidelines and drafted two resignation letters on my cell phone, making sure no one was peering over my shoulder. One was for me and the other was for Kirstjen, though she hadn't officially asked for it. In my mind, Trump had given us a gift—a reason to resign and shine a light inside his haunted house of a presidency.

This was all about to end. The ride back to the airport had the feeling of finality. For months, we'd watched Trump cross our supposed redlines. If a pardon offer to break the law wasn't enough to justify quitting, then we deserved the label assigned to Trump officials who stayed too long: enablers.

A day after the border trip, Kirstjen went to the White House. She told Trump she was unable to do what he wanted. She couldn't violate federal statutes to repel what he termed an "invasion" at the southern border. There was no permanent fix if the president didn't want to pursue immigration reform through Congress.

He fired her on the spot. The news leaked before she even left the White House. And not long after, another story rocked Washington.

Media outlets revealed that the president had proposed a pardons-for-lawbreaking scheme to his DHS lieutenants. A vengeful Trump denied it and launched a wider purge, ridding DHS of officials who were seen as insufficiently MAGA. The White House removed the acting deputy secretary, the heads of multiple immigration agencies, the director of the Secret Service, and eventually the DHS general counsel, who had provided the legal basis for resisting most of the president's outlandish ideas.

The alliance of officials who had come in to run DHS was broken. John Kelly was gone. Kirstjen Nielsen had been fired. Chris Krebs and Elizabeth Neumann had burrowed into the bureaucracy, where they hoped to protect important operations from Trump's whims. Gene Hamilton had decided to join the Justice Department and lean into the MAGA agenda. And Chad Wolf remained on the DHS leadership team. At the time, I didn't understand why.

I remained for a few weeks to provide the thinnest sinew of an orderly transition. Members of Congress panicked that DHS was falling apart and that Trump's firings had decapitated the nation's domestic security apparatus. But there was no sense in putting back together what the president wanted to break. I submitted my resignation letter to the temporary DHS secretary, Kevin McAleenan, a border official who Trump hoped would be a hard-liner.

"Mr. Secretary," I wrote, "the American people are depending on you to do what is right."

The entreaty was meaningless. Right and wrong were lost in the fog of war that was the Trump administration. Morality is an extravagance for people huddled in trenches, bracing for the next attack. Survival is the only necessity.

I felt clarity return on that April border trip. Maybe it was from the shock of what I'd witnessed—or just the throbbing concussion headache that was like a siren in my mind. But as Air Force One took off in the glinting sunlight, I knew what I had to do. One way or another, I would help burn Donald Trump's presidency to the fucking ground.

PART II

Inside the White House complex, an instruction manual is hidden in a secure location for use only in national emergencies. Few people know where it is, and even fewer people are allowed to access it. The "Dooms-day Book" contains the president's break-glass options for keeping the country running in situations ranging from global nuclear war to an armed foreign invasion of the United States.

The options are known by an anodyne name—PEADs—or "pres-idential emergency action documents." Recently declassified records suggest that the PEADs allow the president to invoke extraordinary powers. The records hint at draft authorizations to enable the White House to unilaterally detain "dangerous persons," censor the news media, flip an internet "kill switch," take over social media, and sus-pend Americans from traveling. These might be the type of actions a president would take if the nation's capital was destroyed, enemy forces were hunting down U.S. leaders, or the survival of U.S. democracy was in doubt.

Mark Harvey was once the keeper of the book. He served on the NSC during the Trump administration and referred to the manual as "the Mad Libs for the most extreme measures of government." While Harvey wouldn't confirm or deny the PEAD contents, his job was "to advise whether to pull out that book and go through these extraordi-nary decisions," which he said could be implemented by the nation's chief executive "with the stroke of a pen." He was always on hair-trigger alert.

When Donald Trump was in office, senior aides like Harvey were concerned about protecting access to the PEAD documents. Inexpe-rienced MAGA types roamed the White House halls daily, and NSC experts knew that, in the wrong hands, the special powers could be dangerous. Would someone suggest that Trump try to use the docu-ments for non-emergency situations? Would they try to manufacture a crisis so that he could invoke presidential emergency actions?

The nightmare nearly came true. In Trump's final year in office, the White House sought to put a loyalist into one of the jobs with access to the Doomsday Book. According to sources, that person was Christina Bobb. The Trump staffer—who later became a reporter for the MAGA-friendly One America News Network (OANN) and served as a personal attorney to the ex-president at Mar-a-Lago—was seen by the White House as a diehard Trump supporter. They wanted her on the NSC.

"I worked every person I knew to make sure that Christina Bobb didn't get assigned to the National Security Council," explained an individual closely involved with the situation, noting that the woman was dangerously unqualified. Career officials believed that Bobb was the type of ideologue who might misuse the sensitive NSC perch. "We were a hair's width away from her taking the role," the former official remarked.

Bobb was later involved in Trump's efforts to overturn the 2020 election. Former NSC staffers believe the coup plot would have been dramatically heightened if someone like Bobb had been given access to the Doomsday Book. Indeed, the president and his lawyers might have tried to use the orders to justify seizing Americans' ballots, nationalizing social media companies like Twitter, or rounding up the political opposition.

A former White House lawyer familiar with the situation confirmed that Trump was in the dark. The president didn't have full knowledge of his emergency authorities, and no one who was "in the know" wanted to brief him. If Trump had been made aware of the full extent of the powers he possessed, the person said, the result would have been catastrophic. The near-miss highlights democratic vulnerabilities that, until now, have rarely been discussed.

THE NEXT TRUMP WILL WEAPONIZE THE NATION'S DOMESTIC SECURITY APPARATUS TO WAGE POLITICAL WARFARE.

DHS is the largest federal law enforcement agency in America—the front of the "shield" that is the nation's domestic security architecture. The MAGA movement is keen to exploit that shield in ways that will betray the agency's post-9/11 purpose and threaten the foundations of our republic. I beseech you to trust me. I've lived it.

The homeland defense system should be a formidable guardrail defending American institutions. As Alexander Hamilton wrote, the security powers of the executive branch are crucial for "the protection of the community against foreign attacks . . . the steady administration of the laws . . . the protection of property . . . [and] the security of liberty against the enterprises and assaults of ambition, of faction, and of anarchy." But that's if we have a trustworthy commander in chief.

If we elect another hyper-populist president, the shield will be turned into a political weapon. DHS will be used to bludgeon those who want to become Americans. And if Donald Trump's past designs are any indicator, the department will be used to enforce the law through political favoritism and to welcome the "assaults of ambition, of faction, and of anarchy" in the anti-MAGA enclaves of the country.

In the eyes of aspiring immigrants, America will go from Ronald Reagan's "shining city on a hill" to a fortified bunker in a mountain.

In the second year of the Trump administration, the president visited a counter-drug operation in Florida. The interagency outpost, jointly overseen by DHS and the Defense Department, was responsible for monitoring the flow of narcotics into the United States, as well as other illicit traffic coming up through the Southern Hemisphere. I helped organize the trip to the command center with the hope of focusing Trump's attention on the surge of fentanyl into the country—and cracking down on the criminal networks responsible for smuggling the drug.

Trump stared in wonderment at the array of TV screens on the wall. Small blips showed where suspected traffickers were moving. He was briefed on all the ways we could track the cartel mules and the maritime forces on standby to intercept the drugs. Unsurprisingly, Trump was more interested in how this vast enterprise could be used to capture illegal immigrants. So were his staff members.

On the flight back to Washington, D.C., Trump advisor Stephen Miller took a seat next to me to float an idea. Across from us at a small table sat the commandant of the Coast Guard, Admiral Paul Zukunft.

"Admiral, the military has aerial drones, correct?" Stephen inquired.

"Yes," Zukunft replied.

"And some of those drones are equipped with missiles, correct?"

"Sure," the commandant answered, clearly wondering where the line of questioning was going.

"And when a boat full of migrants is in international waters, they aren't protected by the U.S. Constitution, right?"

"Technically, no, but I'm not sure what you're getting at."

"Tell me why, then, can't we use a Predator drone to obliterate that boat?"

Admiral Zukunft looked nonplussed. "Because, Stephen, it would be against international law."

Miller pushed back. The United States launched airstrikes on terrorists in disputed areas all the time, he said, or retaliated against pirates commandeering ships off the coast of Somalia.

The Coast Guard chief calmly explained the difference. America attacked enemy forces when they were armed and posed an imminent threat. Seafaring migrants were generally unarmed civilians.

They went back and forth on the topic for a few minutes. Stephen wasn't interested in the moral conflict of drone-bombing migrants. He wanted to know whether anyone could stop America from doing it.

"Admiral," he said to the military chief nearly thirty years his senior, "I don't think you understand the limitations of international law."

In actuality, the retiring admiral didn't understand the White House's limitations, or lack thereof. International law meant nothing to the MAGA crowd. According to former Defense Secretary Mark Esper, when officials were watching a live feed of a raid against the leader of ISIS, Stephen Miller reportedly proposed beheading the militant, dipping his head in pig's blood as an affront to Muslims, and parading it around as a warning. Esper says he had to tell the Trump aide that such an action would be a war crime. (Miller denied that the episode occurred.)

The no-holds-barred attitude applied to the border more than anything. Aides would go to whatever lengths were necessary to fulfill Trump's pledge to secure the territorial line with Mexico. That included a willingness to explore lethal drone strikes against innocent civilians.

The border symbolizes the wider aims of the MAGA movement. In order to make America great again, adherents believe Washington must curb the influx of foreigners who are ruining America. Everything

MAGA leaders reject about the existing order—the "globalist" promotion of free trade, the "establishment" story of America as a nation of immigrants, the "woke elites" whose internationalist views are destroying Western culture—is embodied by the situation at the border.

Politics aside, the crisis is real. The United States is unable to control the flow of people and contraband across its territory, which has reached unprecedented levels. Drugs and dangerous individuals infiltrate America easily because of inadequate security, creating a volatile situation for border communities and the wider country.

But the situation is also unfair to migrants seeking a better life. America's porous border has incentivized a spike in human trafficking, cartel activity, and violence, which makes the journey dangerous for these would-be Americans. When they arrive, a broken immigration system forces them into years of uncertainty in the shadows before they're given a final answer about whether or not they can stay here.

Polls show a majority of Americans support tougher border security *and* immigration reform. Whether it's a path to citizenship for undocumented immigrants living in the United States or a faster process for aspiring Americans to become citizens, the solution is uncomplicated in theory. In practice, political polarization has put a legislative solution well out of reach for every recent U.S. president who tried.

Donald Trump saw only one side of this equation: security. To him, this was the primary mission of DHS—deporting undocumented immigrants, punishing those who made it to the border, and making it harder for any others to follow their path. Everything else was secondary or irrelevant. He conveyed this to DHS leaders in some form or fashion weekly.

Kristen Marquardt, who served as a Trump-appointed counterterrorism leader at DHS, compared the president's obsession with the border to the strong desert winds she experienced as a CIA officer overseas.

"You know those 'shamals' in the Middle East—those sandstorms that block out the sun? That's what immigration did to the Department of Homeland Security during the Trump administration," she explained. "There was no light, no air, no room for anything else."

Another far-right president would create the same environment, with potentially dire consequences. I raised the possibility with an advisor who was appointed by Trump to manage national security programs. She saw what happened to DHS under her former boss. "If MAGA comes back," the woman told me, "the department created to stop 9/11 will be willfully closing its eyes to the next big attack, cyber breach, you name it."

First, the White House will make life miserable for undocumented immigrants living in the United States. Stephen Miller once bragged to me that he had a "locked drawer of executive orders" on immigration that were intended for a "shock-and-awe blitz" when Trump got re-elected. The Next Trump will unlock the drawer.

"Right off the bat, [they] would completely ignore the thirty-year court decision that it's a constitutional requirement to supply education, regardless of immigration status," predicted Josh Venable, Trump's former Education Department chief of staff. The idea was a "cockroach that wouldn't die," he said.

In summer 2018, Venable was with Education Secretary Betsy DeVos in the Netherlands on a work trip when they got a call from the White House. It was Stephen Miller. The Trump aide demanded that department leaders figure out how to cut off money to states that allowed undocumented immigrants to enroll in public schools. DeVos and her team had already told the White House it wasn't legal.

"Just find a way to do it," Miller told her. "Are you afraid of getting sued, Betsy?"

Miller was apparently fine with breaking the law.

"Their plan was ignore it, get sued, and litigate it up to the Supreme Court," Venable recalled.

Like this, there are dozens of levers the White House could pull to make daily life harder for undocumented immigrants. None would be as powerful as the threat of mass deportation.

The Next Trump will almost certainly break with long-standing U.S. policy of prioritizing the deportation of *criminal aliens* by ordering a widespread roundup of innocent immigrants and their families, regardless of whether they've committed crimes. Trump realized Immigration and Customs Enforcement (ICE) didn't have sufficient resources to do this. According to former ICE officials, his successor may use presidential powers to "deputize" other agencies to assist with deportation operations.

Many of the anti-immigrant policies eyed by MAGA forces would be difficult to unravel.

"It will be rule-making warfare from Day One," a current CBP official told me, referring to the process of codifying new policies into permanent U.S. immigration rules. "You can't just turn those off overnight. It takes years to undo them."

Second, the White House will turn migrants into political pawns. MAGA acolytes in Florida and Texas are already doing this by implementing "bus and dump" programs of the kind we once told Trump were illegal. The Next Trump will use federal resources to ship migrants from the border to Democratic cities across the United States in order to overwhelm social services and local law enforcement as a form of political punishment.

The White House will also make an example out of recent arrivals. Expect a return of Trump's family separation policies, this time on steroids. Before adopting Jeff Sessions's zero-tolerance program, MAGA officials originally wanted to pull apart every child from their parents at the border, not just those who slipped between ports of entry illegally. They won't hold back next time, and the message will be unmistakable: show up with a kid, and you may never see him or her again.

Third, the Next Trump will go on offense. Americans should expect the resurrection of zombie policies involving destructive force against innocent civilians. This might include the regular use of tear gas to repel arriving migrants, the deployment of heat-ray technology to make asylum-seekers feel like their skin is on fire, or shoot-to-kill orders for anyone who rushes the U.S. border—all in the name of deterrence.

They might even be treated as terrorists. Trump contemplated the possibility. In a phone call with DHS leaders, the president once raised the idea that asylum-seekers should be declared "unlawful enemy combatants" against the United States. In the past, the same classification was given to terrorist suspects the U.S. military targeted for lethal strikes. White House staff also talked about naming migrant smuggling networks as "foreign terrorist organizations," the legal designation that is applied to ISIS and al Qaeda.

You would be right to pause here and ask, *Is any of this really possible?* The fact is, the Trump administration already laid the groundwork. Proposals involving armed drones, troop deployments, "unlawful enemy combatant" designations, and the use of the prison at Guantánamo Bay were not arbitrary. The White House wanted to turn the nation's lethal security forces against immigration violators.

Militia groups will be a worry, too. President Trump was eager to permit roaming bands of armed citizens to help him enforce immigration law. While he never approved an official policy allowing it to happen, a future leader could conceivably use presidential powers to enable private militias to drive away incoming migrants. Elected MAGA leaders in border states have proposed similar initiatives. And it's frightening to think what vigilantes might be able to get away with, while the government conveniently looks the other way.

To American citizens I say: the government of the Next Trump could treat you as friend or foe, based on your political leanings.

Trump imparted a lesson to his MAGA apprentices. He learned it in the business world.

"When you threaten to sue somebody, they don't do anything," Trump told a group of staff gathered in the Oval Office one afternoon. "They say 'Pshhhh!'"

He waved his hand in the air theatrically.

"And they keep doing what they want. But when you *sue* them, they go 'Ooooh!' and they settle. It's as easy as that."

Twice I heard him share the tip. The message was self-explanatory. Words don't work; if you want someone to do something, you need influence over them. The Trump philosophy of leverage has infused the entirety of the Republican Party. MAGA leaders regularly propose using the levers of government to coerce or punish political enemies on the left, and they are keen to institute a system of selective protection in the United States.

Imagine a burglar enters your home. You call 911. The police answer and tell you that before dispatching the nearest squad car, they have to check your voter registration. Republicans get priority. Democrats have to wait.

Now picture this on a national scale. Under the Next Trump, DHS might automatically respond to emergencies in red states but hold out on blue states unless they capitulate to White House demands. This was how Trump wanted to handle the disbursement of disaster aid to everywhere from Puerto Rico to California.

The possibilities for corruption are limitless. DHS spends billions of dollars every year in federal grants to states for cyber defense, protecting soft targets, breaking up drug networks, and more. DHS has wide discretion to adjust how the money is allocated. During my tenure, we resisted political pressure to manipulate the formulas to favor certain regions over others, but a new MAGA team won't be so reticent.

Elected leaders should conduct an end-to-end review of DHS with an eye toward insulating the department from this kind of political abuse. No agency is fully immune to presidential misconduct. Yet with such a long roster of White House appointees, "the shield" of American government is particularly susceptible to it. In particular, Congress should put career officials in charge at key agencies for multiyear terms, spanning presidential administrations, and should pass legislation to rein in domestic security powers.

"Politicization of the department is a huge, huge concern," explained Tom Warrick, who served at DHS under Trump. "There are so many things DHS can and should do, and if it does these things in a partisan way, it loses the trust of the American people."

Warrick cited Portland as an example. In 2020, anti-racism protests in the city grew unruly when activists clashed with police. The Trump administration intervened against the wishes of state and local officials, deploying federal authorities to quell the nighttime rallies, which in turn became more contentious. DHS sent agents of the Border Patrol Tactical Unit, known as BORTAC, into the city as part of the response.

The images went viral. Armed men in helmets with long guns, bul-

letproof vests, dark camouflage, gas masks, and night vision goggles pa-
trolled Portland's streets in the dark—in some cases without any clear
indicator of who they worked for.

"These guys are the Delta Force for keeping terrorists out of the
United States," Warrick noted. "You can't turn them into a junior gestapo. You don't want people who look like they are working on the
Death Star roaming the streets of the United States. But that was a con-
scious decision by the Trump administration—to send a message."

The move set the stage for future abuses of power.

"It was seen as a one-off, but if Portland becomes the norm—
especially if you have BORTAC . . . going after U.S. civilians like you
did in Portland, you will have a department that is rightly no longer
trusted."

Mark Harvey, who protected the Doomsday Book at the White
House during the Trump administration, echoed Warrick's assessment.
He speculated that the Next Trump could use DHS forces in perverse
ways across other areas, such as federal elections.

"It would be the inverse of election security. They would militarize
the elections process," Harvey said. "They would have sheriffs that agree
with them, reservists, potentially even active duty soldiers standing
outside of polling places. They would do anything possible to intimidate
their political opponents from casting a ballot."

He and I spoke before the 2022 midterm elections. When the
vote rolled around, reports surfaced about armed men in Kevlar vests
(self-described "ballot watchers") monitoring polling places in states
like Arizona. Voters said the MAGA-aligned private citizens were trying to intimidate them, and some took the complaints to federal court.

If the Next Trump deploys DHS forces as ballot watchers, there won't
be any such recourse. All of it will be done under the guise of preventing
fraud in the elections and providing security for the voting public. In reality, the goal will be to terrify the political opposition. The playbook has
been around for many, many decades—in foreign dictatorships.

Chapter 6

THE SWORD

The Executive not only dispenses the honors, but holds the sword of the community.

—ALEXANDER HAMILTON, FEDERALIST NO. 78, 1788

PART I

Red flashes refracted off the parked cars as we sped through the night . . . we were going fast . . . above, a blurry figure huddled over me partially obscuring a glaring white light . . . a needle prick . . . my chest was tight, my left arm was numb.

Doom crashed over me in waves, leaving a muted loneliness in the void each time it receded. This was the final feeling. The unrepeatable experience of a billion souls before me.

"Hang on, my man," the figure urged, "almost there."

"We're ready to protect you."

Just before departing the Trump administration in spring 2019, I outlined a plan. I wanted to convince one of the president's ex-advisors or cabinet secretaries—someone well known—to join me in writing the case for Trump's defeat. We could reveal firsthand experiences of the rogue commander in chief's misconduct. If Donald Trump's own appointees didn't support his reelection in the 2020 cycle, surely it would give air cover for Republican voters to defect, too, and create an opening for someone to challenge the president in the GOP primary.

None of the "Adults" would do it. I conferred with dozens of former Trump officials over coffee, at lunch, and by phone to assess whether they would come forward. Everyone declined. They wanted to move on with their lives or expressed hesitation about provoking Trump's ire. He was famously vindictive and would no doubt threaten them with personal and professional retaliation. Others explained (unconvincingly) that it was inappropriate.

Former Defense Secretary Jim Mattis told people he felt a *devoir de réserve*—French for "duty of silence"—about his time serving the president. I was surprised. Behind closed doors, Mattis stridently voiced alarm, once referring to Trump as a "threat to the very fabric of our republic."

I felt abandoned. The gray-haired wise men, who were so disturbed by Trump's behavior that they discussed presidential removal procedures, were disinterested in telling the American people the truth. Was it really more important to keep their mouths shut out of "duty" to the president than to keep democracy from imploding? To me, the justifications felt like convenience masquerading as principle.

There was a backup option. And I knew it would draw attention.

Days before I quit, *The New York Times* wrote an article about two of Washington's best-known book agents, Keith Urbahn and Matt Latimer. The pair had helped produce jaw-dropping national bestsellers about American politics. When asked who their dream author was inside the current administration, Latimer told the paper that they were eager to meet "the anonymous senior Trump official" who wrote a scathing essay about the president.

I sought out the men weeks later. When I arrived at their offices along the cobblestone streets of Alexandria, Virginia, they were expecting me to tell them about a former colleague who wanted to produce a memoir. After we signed nondisclosure agreements, I asked the book agents to remove their electronic devices from the room. They raised eyebrows but complied.

I proceeded to tell them everything. I revealed myself as Anonymous and launched into my turbulent experience in the Trump administration. I told them about the notes I'd taken regarding Trump's behavior while in office. Before I could give either Keith or Matt a chance to vocalize their shock, I laid out my request.

"I want to write a book—not for money, or fame, or score settling. It's about who the president really is and why we can't repeat the mistake we made in 2016. I need your help."

I proposed donating the royalties and directing my fire entirely at Donald Trump, rather than penning another self-important D.C. tell-all about scuffles between staffers trying to get ahead.

"Are you sure about that?" Keith asked.

"About not writing it as a tell-all?"

"No, about the money. You could fetch a million dollars, maybe several million, for the book."

"Yeah. I've thought about it. I want to give the bulk of the royalties to charity, so no one can say it was about the money."

"Anonymous" would write the tome. Not "Miles Taylor." I assumed the moniker would draw greater attention to the substance than if I did it in my own name. Unmasking myself at this juncture would lead to a losing battle with Trump. That was my thinking anyway. He had the biggest profile in the world, while I had almost no public visibility whatsoever. Subconsciously, another reason—the real reason—held me back, but I ignored it for the time being.

Keith and Matt eagerly accepted the proposal, and we went to work.

Two problems stood in the way. First, I needed to prove to a publisher that I was who I claimed to be. No one would amplify my message to millions of Americans without being certain I wasn't pretending to be the masked New York Times writer. Second, we needed to keep the project secret, which would get harder with more people in the mix.

The solution to the first problem was inside a vault, collecting dust.

A piece of paper with my signature was the sole document affirming my authorship of the op-ed, and it was under lock and key at the *New York Times* headquarters. No other record existed.

"You're going to need to get that," Keith told me.

So I drove to New York City on a bathwater summer day to see friends. That was the cover story. The precautions were less paranoia and more practical necessity. Sure, I didn't have any reason to think I was being followed (yet), but I had every reason to believe people were seeking Anonymous. To find him—to find *me*—a smart and committed sleuth would surveil the only person who could confirm my identity. The man I was going to see. The middle man.

I parked on the Upper East Side near the Carlyle. The art-deco hotel was where I was scheduled to have lunch with a former Oxford classmate. Beforehand, I diverted by taxi to a coffee shop a mile away along Central Park. I was early on purpose.

Inside I snagged a table and eyed the entrance, scanning incoming patrons who might seem unusual. I ordered avocado toast. Nothing was out of the ordinary when my guest appeared in the doorway.

Jim Dao, the *New York Times* opinion editor, had a trim frame and sunglasses. He knew the purpose of the visit, which is why he had suggested a spot far away from the paper's headquarters. We greeted each other with a hug like old friends, though we'd only met in person once.

We made small talk for a while. Jim talked about his family and a recent biking mishap. He was an avid cyclist. When my food arrived, he casually slipped an envelope under my plate. I pretended to ignore it and told him about summer travel plans.

Jim couldn't resist asking what was next, so he lowered his voice.

"So what does the timing look like?" he asked.

"No later than a year before the election," I told him. It was already July 2019. I wanted to release the book in November, twelve months before America would decide Trump's fate.

"That's going to be a really tight deadline for a partner," he said, referring to a book publisher. Four months was a lightning-fast turnaround time in the publishing world.

"And for me," I replied.

We chatted a bit longer before I paid. As I got up to leave for my cover lunch, Jim nodded back to my plate.

"Don't forget that."

He wasn't talking about the toast that I'd barely touched. The envelope was still under my plate. I'd nearly forgotten it.

I thanked Jim with a forced laugh, knowing that if a waiter had picked up the document, the tiny slipup could have exposed everything. (Little did I know, the plan would be compromised in far more serious ways in the months to come.)

On the way back to the Carlyle, I placed a call to Keith from an iPhone bought solely for the purpose of communicating with my agents.

"I've got the paper," I confirmed. "Time for phase two."

The next problem was trickier. We needed to keep the circle of co-conspirators as small as possible, and I wasn't sure a publisher could pull it off. Hachette Books was eager to explore the project, but first they insisted on sending representatives to Washington to verify the author's identity, in person. Keith told them they could only send one designee.

The emissary turned out to be my eventual editor, Sean Desmond. A seasoned manager of major book projects, he was George W. Bush's editor for the presidential memoir *Decision Points*. My agents proposed gathering in the living room at my house rather than their offices, but after the January break-in, I was leery of even breathing the word "Anonymous" in my home.

They rented a conference room in an office building near Union Station. Sean would arrive by train. I showed up early to scope it out and found that the building was the same place where NBC News was located.

Great, I thought. A lot of NBC reporters knew me and knew my book agents. If they spotted us going to the same place together, it could raise questions.

Fortunately, the lobby was empty. A few floors up, the conference room itself was secluded and spacious, complete with a whiteboard, chairs, conference table, couches, and too many electronic devices for my comfort. I closed the shades and unplugged everything—television, Wi-Fi router, Apple TV, Blu-ray player—before removing the batteries from the remotes. My nerves were heightened like it was a blind date, though this rendezvous was guaranteed to change my life.

There was a knock at the door. I opened it to find Matt escorting Sean.

"Hi, I'm Miles Taylor." I reached out to shake Sean's hand.

"It's good to finally meet you, Miles." His smile was warm and understanding—that of a man who knew he wasn't being asked just to publish someone's book but, for a time, also to protect him.

On their way over, Matt had already revealed to Sean who I was. We sat down, and the bespectacled editor offered a coda to our introductions.

"Miles, I want to tell you a few things," he said. "What you did was brave, in my opinion. I know the decision wasn't easy. We'd be honored to help you take the next step. We're ready to protect you, and I take it as a personal commitment."

For an hour-and-a-half, we talked about what I'd experienced— opposing Trump's candidacy, going into the executive branch, wrestling with a stay-or-go moral dilemma as the administration got worse, and the vexing issue of how to speak out. Under pseudonym, a book-length Trump exposé would be challenging. For example, I wouldn't be able to describe meetings or phone calls with the president in detail if I was one of the few witnesses, without inadvertently revealing myself.

We talked about how we would communicate with each other. For security purposes, we devised a multilayered process for sharing drafts. The system included encrypted messages, air-gapped devices (no internet), fake accounts, rotating passwords, swapped SIM cards, and burner phones. Most of that responsibility would fall to me.

I told Sean there was an aspect to the project that was important to me. The book should be a pointed repudiation of my op-ed. It should dispel the notion that an Axis of Adults was going to save America from Trump.

He asked why.

"I was wrong," I admitted. "A group of unelected bureaucrats was never going to rescue us from this man. Only the voters can do that. Whatever internal resistance there was, Trump has crushed it."

Before I left, I realized I hadn't shown him the *Times* documentation. Sean still needed to confirm my authorship. I retrieved it from my backpack.

"I don't need to see it," Sean told me. "I trust you."

I gave it to him anyway. We shook hands, and I exited the room ahead of Sean and Matt. As I had feared, in the lobby I spotted a journalist who knew me, so I diverted to a glass side door before we bumped into each other.

Back home, I told Anabel it was a done deal. As I'd planned, I needed to carry out the writing project somewhere else to avoid the risks of remaining in Washington. Holing up in our Capitol Hill row house for weeks at a time would draw suspicion from friends, especially since I should be out hunting for a job.

I packed up the car that night and told my extended family I was going on a road trip to decompress. The truth was stowed in the trunk of my car. Inside, a combination-lock metal briefcase held the only proof that I was Anonymous—the hard copy of my original essay and the publishing agreements—as well as a modified iPad (disconnected from the internet, Wi-Fi, and Bluetooth) with the opening pages of a manuscript.

Opening the briefcase once more, I tucked $10,000 in hundred-dollar bills into a zipper pocket. I didn't want credit cards to reveal my location. In the main compartment, I placed a tube of mace and a serrated knife. Just in case.

"Fire racist, xenophobic Trump ally Miles Taylor"

The pen might be mightier than the sword, but when it's used as a weapon, it's just as heavy to wield.

Knowing the book's message could reach millions of people in one form or another, I felt pressure to get it right. I was crafting a takedown of the president of the United States. I was also on a tight deadline. Sean needed the draft manuscript by mid-September. So I had six weeks to write a full-length tome that would either become my magnum opus or, in another scenario, my eulogy.

I chose a writing hideout. Marco Island was a sleepy place on Florida's Gulf Coast and the perfect spot to lie low. That's what I needed to get the job done. Judging by the sparse parking lot, I was one of the few people staying at the condominium complex during the dense humidity of August.

A strict schedule governed my day. Wake up. Run. Outline in my head. Breakfast. Write. Swim laps. Outline. Lunch. Write. Walk. Outline. Dinner. And write some more. I followed the same routine almost every day for a month.

Alcohol was also included. I opened a bottle of Jack Daniel's at night on the balcony to calm my nerves until I could breathe the salt air slowly. A doctor had diagnosed me with post-concussive syndrome after the head injury in April, and one of the lasting effects was that it magnified my pernicious anxiety.

In large groups or crowded restaurants, I'd get hit with it and step away to splash water on my face until the feeling passed. The same would happen while driving on busy highways, forcing me to pull over. Other than a Xanax prescription, alcohol was the only medicine that took the edge off.

After a few glasses of whiskey, I'd head over to a nearby strip mall bar, where I posted up each night. I befriended the staff and a handful of regulars, some of whom were proud Trumpers. A few wore their red caps into the bar, but we didn't talk politics. We swapped drunk stories and island gossip.

One night the bartenders gave me an honorary staff T-shirt. I put on the long-sleeved tee, hopped behind the counter, and went to work selling drinks. They laughed. We closed down with a pitcher full of tips and decided to head to a cheap bar across the island. I took the crew in my car, telling them I was good to drive when I probably wasn't.

When we got there, I lifted the trunk door and popped open the briefcase. I fetched cash from inside the zipper pocket.

"Whoa," one of my passengers exclaimed. She'd probably seen the weapons, too.

"Drinks are on me," I told her with a smile and shut the trunk.

We entered the sticky dive bar and ordered a round of flaming shots. The night evaporated like the torched liquor.

The next morning I woke up with a headache spanning my skull. I opened an eye to scan the nightstand for the usual checklist. *Keys, wallet, phones.* Neither of my devices were there, or in the condo.

Maybe they were in the car. In flip-flops, with a baseball cap on my head, I crossed the lobby downstairs and out to the parking lot. My spot was empty, and I felt a jolt of panic.

Where the fuck was the car?

I thought back to the night before but couldn't piece together what had happened. Tequila shots under the yellow lights of the bar. The rest was spotty. I remembered opening the trunk in front of other people.

Back in the lobby, I rushed to the elevator. The front desk attendant hollered at me.

"Your girlfriend called!"

That was a weird thing to say, I thought.

"Excuse me?" I asked.

"I got it this morning when I came in. 'Anna Bell' called for you. She left a voicemail message."

"Oh, yeah. Thank you. I lost my phone."

"You lose your mind, too? You can't park in the loading zone, sweetie."

The car was on the other side of the building. I wanted to hug her.

"Yes, sorry. I wasn't sure which one was mine."

It was a stupid lie. The unit numbers were spray-painted in each parking spot.

"All right, well just be careful out there. Take care of yourself, and make sure you're watching out for others. Okay?"

"Always," I replied, my cheeks filling with hot shame. She knew I'd driven drunk.

Out in the car, everything was there, untouched. Personal phone. Burner phone. Briefcase. I was relieved, but I lost a day of writing. I was too hungover and consumed by continuous self-flagellation, as my brain fought itself.

How could you be so stupid? This put everything at risk.

My capacity for self-preservation was continuous, too.

Not a big deal. This hasn't happened before. It won't happen again.

All three reassurances were lies. Nevertheless, the incident became a scared-sober cliché for a period of time. I emptied the liquor bottles in the kitchen, and my nightly routine at the bar ceased. I doubled down on writing, afraid of losing more time.

I also became a touch paranoid. Shaken by the potential that I could have exposed the project if the car had been stolen, I started taking extra steps to guard my possessions. I placed tamper tape on the trunk. I also attached it to the condo door when I left, so I'd know if someone entered.

Weeks later at a hotel, I came back from grabbing food to find the tamper tape breached. My iPad had been in the room with the manuscript on it. What if someone had come in and installed malware? The cleaning staff probably missed the "Do Not Disturb" sign, but I wasn't taking any chances. I went to a shopping center, smashed the device against a brick wall outside with my foot, and bought a new one.

Despite the setbacks, I finished the book titled *A Warning* on time. It was an unsparing indictment of Donald Trump with a two-pronged caution: Americans shouldn't reelect the man and, more importantly, we needed to unite to fix our broken republic.

"If we look within ourselves and undertake the arduous task of moral repair, America can restore the soul of its political system," I wrote in the closing paragraph. "We can once again illuminate a pathway for others onto the vaunted plazas of open society. If, however, we shrink from the task, our names will be recorded by history as those who didn't pass the torch but let its light expire."

Through our back channel, I sent the final draft to Sean and Matt. Fate was in control now. I packed up for the journey back home, and on the drive, I got good news.

For months, I'd been unemployed, and with the writing behind me, I needed a job. Somewhere on the road in Georgia, I got a callback about my application to Google—and an offer. They wanted me to be their head of national security relations. The pay was higher than any job I'd had, and after years of a public service salary, I accepted without a second thought.

Google seems like adult Disneyland. A few weeks later, I started work and found that our Washington, D.C., office boasted unlimited gourmet food, nap pods, game rooms, and massages. At orientation in Mountain View, California, they'd showered us with electronics and swag. To boot, the work was interesting, since I was charged with managing the company's relationships with the CIA, FBI, and other national security agencies.

Then I encountered the activist employee base. A few California-based staff heard that the D.C. office had hired a "Trump official" and decided to make a point. With whatever scant information they could find about me online at the time, they determined that I was clearly MAGA—and the mastermind behind Trump's worst policies.

They say a lie travels halfway around the world before the truth gets its pants on. In the tech sector, it travels at fiber-optic speed. All the while, the truth is dead asleep.

Left-leaning press outlets and tech blogs posted about how Google had hired a Trump immigration fanatic. They portrayed me as a champion of the Muslim ban and an architect of family separation, based on thin sourcing and an avalanche of false assumptions. I got a call from a reporter who asked me for a comment about the fact that Google employees were protesting the hiring of a MAGA hard-liner.

If they only knew, I thought.

The CEO, Sundar Pichai, was forced to address my employment at a company-wide town hall. His office called ahead of time to offer support. They knew the stories were the opposite of the truth (I'd helped *dismantle* the Muslim ban and *end* family separation, including repeatedly blocking its reinstatement) and defended me against the misleading broadsides. If I wanted, I was welcome to put out a statement or address my colleagues, they said.

I chose to say nothing. Enough years in Washington had taught me that if you extend a hand to a pitchfork mob, they'll eventually try to take your head. Just as important, I wasn't going to let this be the moment I came out against Trump, disrupting my plans.

But the defiance wasn't easy.

That week I was stranded in California. On the flight out for an event, I had a sinus infection, and my eardrum burst with explosive pain. I was told to stay put until it healed. Alone in a hotel room, I watched the virtual town hall on my laptop, as fellow employees (whom I'd never met) painted me as a bigot. The comments made in the meeting and on public message boards were a gut punch.

"It makes no sense why we would hire someone with clear racial bias into a government-facing role."

"How can we respect Google's DEI values *and* avoid hiring those who dehumanize marginalized groups?"

"As a Muslim, it makes me feel very psychologically unsafe knowing that an active Islamophobe with this track record was hired for Google leadership."

The last one really got me. I'd spent my career thwarting terrorist attacks, including against Muslims, and had been one of the handful of Republicans to actually do something about Trump's anti-Muslim rhetoric. That didn't matter. The narrative was set.

The town hall and the internal chatter were leaked to the media. Without seeking to fact-check any of it, liberal groups pounced, eager to take out an alleged MAGA leader.

"Tell Google to fire racist, xenophobic Trump ally Miles Taylor," read a petition on MoveOn.org. It got 25,941 signatures. I remember because it was a few thousand more than the population of my Indiana hometown.

Democratic congressional leaders from the Black, Hispanic, and Asian-Pacific American caucuses sent letters to Sundar denouncing my hiring. "During his time with DHS," they wrote, "Miles Taylor undoubtedly demonstrated his support for the Trump Administration's immigration policies." The operative word was "undoubtedly." The assumptions were piling up.

I became depressed. I questioned my decision to defy the trolls rather than reply to them. Friends sent supportive text messages, but between the lines I could tell they thought it was getting bad. My reputation was being thoroughly trashed, and as I sat there, I was being caricatured as a mirthful MAGA hatchet man.

I did this to myself.

By wearing a mask, I had created two personas. They were beginning to diverge. The longer that Anonymous kept his visor down trying to act like a savior knight, the more Miles looked like an unspeaking sinner, guilty by his association with the disgraced president. And yet I stayed motionless, not wanting to disrupt Anonymous's well-laid plan to strike back.

A comment from one Google employee gave me a little solace: "Maybe he was acting to minimize the impact of [Trump's] actions, and he was pushed out because of it," the employee said. "That might make me feel better, but it would need significant clarification."

What timing. That same week, news leaked about the forthcoming release of *A Warning*. The book had remained entirely under wraps up to that point. "TRUMP OFFICIAL BEHIND BOMBSHELL OP-ED IS BACK," the top of the CNN homepage blared. "Anonymous" was the number-one trending topic on Trump's favorite social media platform, Twitter, while pre-orders of the book rocketed it to number one on Amazon in hours, despite being a month from release.

The White House went into crisis response. "NEW DRAMA ROCKS WEST WING," one headline read, as President Trump fretted about what Anonymous might say in the lead-up to the 2020 election that could harm his campaign. He renewed his efforts to have the Justice Department smoke out the offender. DOJ lawyers wrote to my publisher and my agents demanding identifying information about the author. Both declined.

Though I should have been energized about the coming fight, my spirits were dragged down by the Google controversy. I started drinking again. A few beers a night became a six-pack in two hours, plus a few whiskeys.

"I'm just blowing off steam," I told Anabel and myself. I was in control, until I wasn't.

On a fall weekend, I went to California to see my little brother, Patrick. He'd been having a hard time in a different way. Recently out of the closet, he was trying to find an LGBTQ group of friends that he fit into in the Bay Area, and it wasn't going the way he'd hoped. We both needed a weekend away, so we ventured to wine country.

Napa Valley is Novocain for a worried mind. At the peak of a vine-wrapped hill, Patrick and I kicked off a warm Saturday by toasting champagne to the sunny plains below. I spared no expense, thinking I might not have my tech salary much longer. We visited the top vineyards, sipping vintage cabernet sauvignon in cavernous cellars and enjoying chilled rosé as the breeze added condensation to our glasses.

I promised Patrick I'd limit my consumption so I could drive. For most of the day, I did. I drank coffee and soda on the drives. But at the end of the night, I decided to splurge on a few fancy bottles at our last stop. With every uncorking, we made new friends, and an evening of libations unfolded into a longer night of debauchery.

"You want some CBD?" Patrick asked me back at our vacation rental. We were properly drunk.

"Sure."

I knew it wasn't CBD. It was pot, but I smoked it anyway. Inhaling deeply, I admired the starry night, exhaling clouds up at the clear sky.

★ ★ ★

When it was time to sleep, I still felt wired and took a Xanax. I turned off the light and got into bed. The sedative still didn't seem to be working so I took another.

After a while, I felt my heartbeat against the mattress. The tempo was high. I looked at my watch and saw it was approaching 200 bpm. When I got up to turn on the light, I collided with the side table and knocked it over. I staggered into Patrick's room and asked him to call 911. My vision was getting blurry.

In the ambulance, I told the EMT I wasn't doing well. Pain seared my tight chest. During a few moments of lucidity, I knew something was really wrong, and I considered that this was where I might die. Pointlessly.

The ride faded to black.

When I regained my senses in the hospital, they'd already done a battery of tests, hooked me up to an IV, and given me an injection used in cardiac emergencies, to slow my heart rate. My vital signs were going back to normal. The doctor came by and told me sternly that I'd over-dosed. Caffeine, alcohol, marijuana, and Xanax—a noxious cocktail of substances at levels that had killed other patients.

Patrick was teary-eyed at my bedside. I was humiliated. I couldn't shake the image of the family member we'd taken to rehab after she nearly drowned in a hot tub, drunk.

"You doing all right?" Patrick asked.

"Not so much," I told him. I was too choked up to talk. He stayed with me for hours until I was discharged.

I sat outside the hospital on a wooden bench, as Patrick ordered a car back to the rental house. The faintest morning light sneaked across the parking lot.

I broke the silence on the ride back with a request that I regret to this day.

"You won't tell anyone, will you?" I asked.

Patrick hesitated. "Are you sure you're going to be all right?"

"Yeah. I've just been under a lot of pressure lately," I told him. "I'm going to cut way back. I just don't want this to become a whole thing."

"Okay, I won't say anything," he promised.

We nixed a final day of winery visits and drove back to San Francisco.

"It sounds exactly like you."

When I quit the Trump administration, I set out to craft an indict-ment of the sitting president by detailing his lack of impulse control and his self-defeating behavior. As I waited for the book to drop, the irony wasn't lost on me that I was facing my own internal arraignment over the skulking influence of destructive tendencies.

Patrick kept his word, and I was in no rush to tell anyone else what had happened in California. I compartmented the episode by resolving that this time—unlike after Marco Island—I would keep myself in check. Too much was at stake to let it happen again, though I had little accountability. I'd long since quit therapy sessions. For several weeks, I lay low, channeling anger at myself into the raw energy needed for the coming fight.

No one in the Republican Party stepped forward to stop Trump. After I left DHS, I undertook a futile effort to help find a GOP senator, representative, or governor willing to challenge him in the presidential primary. One Texas congressman strongly considered it. We met several times for breakfast to discuss the options, but ultimately he backed down when internal polls showed how high the odds were against him.

In my view, Trump administration defectors were the best hope for explaining to Republican voters why they should break from the president. Too few had spoken up. Heading into the general election, I wanted to change that.

The book was my opening shot.

"ANONYMOUS AUTHOR'S 'WARNING' PORTRAYS PRESIDENCY ON THE BRINK," declared the *Drudge Report*, on the eve of the book's release. *Drudge* was one of the websites that aides regularly printed out for Trump to review.

"There is no modern historical parallel," *The Washington Post* wrote.

USA Today told readers that the tome painted "a scathing portrait of a president and administration in chaos," as it knocked Donald Trump Jr.'s book off the bestseller list.

The reaction I cared about in that moment was from the man behind the Resolute desk. And by all accounts, it hit him hard. White House communications director Stephanie Grisham later recounted that the president was as mad as she'd seen him.

"If [the] op-ed took it to one level, the book just blew his stack," she recalled. "He was just nuts about it. It was all he thought about. There we would be in meetings about national security, let's say, and halfway through he would look at anybody, 'Do you know who Anonymous is?'"

Trump ordered Grisham to unload on the author.

"The coward who wrote this book didn't put their name on it because it is nothing but lies," Grisham said in a statement, before doing the rounds on television to make the point more forcefully. "Reporters who choose to write about this farce should have the journalistic integrity to cover the book as what it is—a work of fiction." The book lived up to Trump's fears, as once again Anonymous got people talking about the president's mental state and the rampant culture of corruption in the White House. News outlets speculated that others might come forward, further imperiling Trump's nascent reelection campaign.

I queued in line at a D.C. bookstore to buy my own copy. Later that night, I opened the trunk of my car. I placed the book in the briefcase. Staring at the sparse white cover—with the words "A Warning" and "Anonymous" emblazoned in black—I allowed myself a fleeting moment of fulfillment alone. After the turmoil and angst and self-doubt and anger and newfound resolve, this was my book party. It lasted about a minute. I closed the briefcase, locked it, and shut the trunk.

The heat picked up after that.

Several journalists suspected I might be the author. I'd quit the administration and was known in Washington circles to be privately critical of Trump. On the drive to Thanksgiving with family, I got a call from Michael Shear at *The New York Times*. The opinion and news sections were firewalled from each other at the paper, so Shear had no special knowledge that Anonymous was me.

An anecdote in *A Warning* sounded similar to one I'd told him months earlier. Shear asked me point-blank if I was the author. I denied it, but he laid out his evidence. I laughed it off as a coincidence, perhaps too earnestly.

"Thou doth protest too much," he quipped, nodding to Shakespeare. Without my confirmation, he couldn't find definitive proof.

Around the same time, damning revelations emerged about the president's conduct with respect to Ukraine. Witnesses testified in the House about Trump's efforts to withhold aid to the country unless its leaders investigated one of his political rivals, Joe Biden. I'd warned about his corrupt attempts to threaten foreign governments as a way to get leverage, and now Trump was being impeached for doing exactly that.

The corruption didn't surprise me. What I was struck by was how many people testified against him. Until then, most internal administration critics only gave blind quotes to media. These officials stood up in public, swore to tell the truth with their right hands raised, and detailed the misconduct inside the White House, for the whole country to hear.

Their bravery shattered my assumptions about the need for household names to lead the charge. Hardly anyone knew who Alex Vindman or Marie Yovanovitch were until they testified before Congress in the impeachment trial. Despite having low profiles, they exploded into public view and had a lasting impact on the debate about the president's fitness for office.

Their public criticisms of Trump also put pressure on me. An enigma beckoned again. I was still harboring a "secret within a secret" in the depths beneath my anonymity. Grave-shoveled in my subconscious, I'd buried the real truth of it all from everyone, even those who knew my identity. . . .

Meanwhile, my book agents called with an idea. I hadn't done promotion for the book, leaving the pages to speak for themselves. I had no interest in doing interviews where my face was silhouetted and my voice auto-tuned to disguise me. They proposed doing an "Ask Me Anything" (AMA) on Reddit; I could answer questions in a public chat room under a virtual invisibility cloak, they said.

I agreed. I wanted to lay a marker down, for Trump and for myself. This was the chance to do it.

The night of the AMA, I drove out of Washington and into Virginia. I pulled over next to a public park and turned off the car on an empty, dark street.

In a long overcoat and tie, I got out and grabbed a duffel bag from the back seat. I tossed my electronics under the driver's seat and closed the door. The walk was cold and long. I kept my head down, only looking up occasionally in search of the destination.

A warm yellow light spilled out of a hotel lobby and onto the street. I entered as if I was already a guest and located the stairwell. Up a few floors and down a hallway, I found the appointed room. I knocked three times.

A pause. Then a metallic latch. Keith opened the door with a smile.

"Hello, my friend," he said.

I crossed the threshold, and we hugged. I hadn't seen him since the project started. Matt was standing behind him by a desk with several laptops.

"We're using an old computer of mine," he said, "and a mobile hot spot. Ready to go?"

The session was about to start. I scanned through the questions submitted by the public, looking for one in particular. I didn't see it. So I took them as they came.

Suppose Trump wins the 2020 election. What should we as American people be on the lookout for?

"Anyone should be able to see the chaos has worsened," I replied. "The president has little handle on the day-to-day operations of the federal government. . . . He is hurtling between different controversies and ignoring important matters of state, abusing his power with some regularity, undercutting vital democratic institutions daily, and debasing the national dialogue tweet-by-tweet. We can expect this and much, much more if he is reelected."

[Have] the State Dept. officials testifying made you proud?

"I am proud of all the individuals who have come forward to tell the truth about corrupt behavior in the White House, whether they have chosen to protect their identities as whistle-blowers or to testify before Congress."

Is it possible to undo all the damage Trump has done to our national security?

"If there is a second term, I have doubts about a strong affirmative answer."

★ ★ ★

The Q&A session went on for between thirty and forty-five minutes. I typed the responses with Keith and Matt looking over my shoulder. Finally, I saw it. Someone had asked the question I was waiting for.

Why do you have so little integrity to come out publicly and speak?

I typed out a short, carefully worded response. I had thought about it the whole way over. Time to draw a line in the sand.

"Trump will hear from me, in my own name, before the 2020 election."

I hesitated above the RETURN key. Was I really ready for that?

Click.

After the session ended, Keith and Matt asked the obvious question. How was I going to unmask myself and exactly when in 2020? I told them I didn't know, but that's what I planned to do.

My editor, Sean, was sad to miss our clandestine gathering. He sent a fancy bottle of champagne for us to celebrate. Keith offered to uncork it and also brought along some whiskey and tumbler glasses, hoping we might kick back and chat for a bit.

I eyed the bottle eagerly but declined. I needed to go. I took my duffel to the bathroom and emerged a few minutes later in a winter cap, athletic clothes, and a puffer vest. The business attire was stuffed in the bag.

After a hasty farewell, I was back outside. The streets were still empty. Leaves drifted down the blacktop like tumbleweeds in the cold wind. Back in the car, I warmed up and read the news on my phone. CBS was already carrying the story that Anonymous would step forward against Donald Trump in the coming months.

What they didn't report—what they didn't know—was that Anonymous was full of dread.

★ ★ ★

The start of 2020 cemented the reality that voters were the last, best defense against Trump. The Senate failed to convict him in an impeachment vote, and just as he had been in the aftermath of the Mueller Report (which he falsely claimed "exonerated" him on interfering with the Russia investigation), the president seemed emboldened.

One evening I caught up with my former DHS colleague Hannah. We hadn't seen each other since I quit. We were supposed to be joined by our significant others, but both of them had bailed on us to stay home in the warmth, avoiding the wintry mix outside.

The two of us met up at a Capitol Hill wine bar. I got there first, hesitating about whether to drink but deciding it would look odd not to have a glass. After a few months of cutting back, I felt self-confident that I was in control of my drinking again. Hannah arrived as the merlot was being poured.

She had left the administration to work for a Republican representative and was just as disillusioned as I'd been by House GOP leaders who wouldn't stand up to Trump. We chatted for a while about our partners, work, family.

While I was updating her on post-government life, Hannah pulled something out of her purse. It was a copy of *A Warning*. She set the book on the table in front of us.

"Was this you? It sounds exactly like you," she said matter-of-factly.

"What? Ha!" I was caught off guard and faked a scoff. "Whatever hack wrote that is telling us what we already know."

"You sure?" Hannah knew how much I despised Trump. I noticed the dog-eared pages.

"Yes, I'm sure I didn't write an anonymous book."

"Well if it wasn't you, who do you think it was?"

"I dunno. Who cares. Why write it without your name, when people are testifying openly?" I tried to sound convincing.

"Damn," she sighed. "I thought I had it. The writing was like yours, but only if you were writing for an eighth-grader." She searched my eyes for a tell. I didn't flinch.

We talked for a while longer. She asked about the protests at Google. Everything had settled down, I said, and I quizzed her more about political developments on Capitol Hill to make sure we didn't go back to the prior subject. I ended the drinks early, feeling like Hannah could see right through me.

Not long after, I had another scare.

On February 18, journalists shouted questions to Trump as they often did when he boarded Air Force One. A reporter asked the president if he'd found out who Anonymous was yet.

Trump stopped. This time he didn't wince or move on. He smirked.

"I know who it is," the president boasted. The reporter asked who. Trump paused for effect. "I can't tell you that, but I know who it is."

First Michael Shear. Then Hannah. Now the president claimed to know the truth.

Keith and Matt heard rumblings that the president's aides were going to name a culprit. Trump advisor Peter Navarro led a team charged with smoking out the author, and they wrote a dossier. As I scrambled to prepare for a hasty public revelation, I found out that they'd identified the wrong person.

Navarro's draft report named Trump's deputy national security advisor, Victoria Coates, as the dissenter. The White House debated whether to fire her. Originally, my agents had told reporters that they wouldn't confirm or deny any Anonymous suspects. But when Coates started getting attacked unfairly, they put out a firm rebuttal.

She was *not* the author, they wrote, chiding the amateur sleuths at the White House for putting an innocent person in the cross hairs. I'm embarrassed to say that my first reaction to Coates being misidentified was relief.

I was procrastinating. After the Google uproar had died down, I dithered on my pledge to go public; in fact, I was enjoying a return to obscurity. I was drinking less, putting myself in a better headspace, and finally experiencing much-needed financial security. Unmasking myself would disrupt all of that. Hadn't I already done enough? The temptation to take the easy route was high.

Then people started dying.

PART II

When he was still White House chief of staff, John Kelly rebuked the president one day in the Oval Office when Trump was having another fit about how the drug cartels in Latin America were making him look bad. The president rattled off a list of impossible demands.

"Mr. President, you don't have dictatorial powers to secure the border," Kelly retorted. "Or, if you want, you can just declare war on Mexico, invade, and slaughter everyone."

Kelly was making a graphic but powerful point. Short of exercising his war powers, Trump had to work with Congress to bring the situation under control, through legal changes, funding, and more. That wasn't Trump's takeaway. After Kelly was booted from the White House, the president flirted with the concept of using military force across the border.

Former defense secretary Mark Esper revealed that the president suggested firing missiles into Mexico to annihilate the criminal groups. The proposal sent the military chain of command into a tizzy. A missile strike on the territory of America's neighbor—although it was against cartel operatives—could provoke an armed conflict with the government of Mexico.

In his final year, the president's team asked for plans to deploy 250,000 U.S. troops to the border. The massive mobilization would have rivaled the U.S. operations in Iraq and Afghanistan. Trump was prepared to send soldiers into Mexico to "wage war" against the cartels. Conveniently, the move would have also enabled him to create the buffer zone he fantasized so much about—a militarized, Korea-like DMZ.

If missile launches didn't start a war, invading U.S. troops certainly would have. The Pentagon talked Trump out of military action. But given the rhetoric of the far-right GOP, the next MAGA president might not accept an appeal to reason. He or she might instead raise the sword and take up arms against an ally, indifferent to the consequences.

THE NEXT TRUMP WILL DISRUPT DIPLOMATIC RELATIONS WITH THE WORLD AND WIELD MILITARY FORCE CLOSE TO HOME.

The architects of the American system sought to split the foreign policy powers of the government between two branches. In the Federalist essays, they detailed the necessity of dividing it between the president and Congress: "The qualities elsewhere detailed as indispensable in the management of foreign negotiations, point out the Executive as the most fit agent in those transactions; while the vast importance of the trust, and the operation of treaties as laws, plead strongly for the participation of the whole or a portion of the legislative body in the office of making them."

Yet when it came to military power, they defaulted to the executive branch. The draft Constitution named the president the sole commander in chief. "The propriety of this provision is so evident in itself," they wrote, ". . . that little need be said to explain or enforce it." A blade cannot be swung by multiple people at once. "Of all the cares or concerns of government, the direction of war most peculiarly demands those qualities which distinguish the exercise of power by a single hand."

Practically speaking, both sets of powers have ended up largely in the president's hands. The White House drives the vast majority of all diplomatic and military activities, while the legislative branch occasionally intervenes—usually when it comes to funding. Withholding or supplying money is the main means of control. But presidents of both parties have found ways to shirk Congress's attempts to limit White House control.

The defense community was nervous about Donald Trump well before he was elected. I spoke with one of the officials responsible for planning intelligence briefings for the 2016 presidential candidates. He reported that the briefers conducted drills to prepare for the possibility that the GOP candidate might do something foolish with the defense information he was given.

"We war-gamed potential scenarios about what could happen," the official shared. They considered nixing the briefings, which are traditionally given to both presidential nominees. "What if he started tweeting what he heard? We ran a whole series of machinations up to [the office of the director of national intelligence], including whether to do it or not."

Rather than scrapping the intelligence updates, they ended up scrubbing them.

"The briefings to him and Clinton were fundamentally different," the official explained. "With him, it was like elementary school." More specifically, the briefers presented the information to Trump in such a way that—if he leaked it—the damage to U.S. operations around the world would be minimized.

The fears later proved to be justified. Over the course of four years, Trump recklessly compromised U.S. secrets. He gave sensitive defense information to journalists, shared it with foreign adversaries, and absconded with it to his private residence in Florida after leaving the White House.

On the surface, Trump's mishandling of classified information doesn't seem like something you can ascribe to his movement. That was a personal defect, after all. Every Trump shortcoming isn't imprinted on the wider MAGA coalition, and not all of his characteristics will be shared by the Next Trump.

He has, however, made the GOP downright wrathful toward national security agencies. The distrust runs deep. And Republican leaders have shown newfound scorn toward once-venerated American institutions.

"It's time to end the U.S. intelligence operations against America," MAGA congresswoman Marjorie Taylor Greene tweeted one day in 2022. Far-right outlets cheered.

"Her instincts are very much in line with the liberty conservatives in Middle America who have grown hostile towards the managerial state and DC altogether," a popular right-wing website declared, adding that conservatives should gut untrustworthy defense agencies.

In his final weeks in office, Trump sought radical change. He considered placing political figures in charge of the CIA and sent loyalists into the Pentagon and the intelligence community. A former NSC staffer told me his colleagues were worried that MAGA aides were being dispatched to rummage around in classified programs, to expose "Deep State" conspiracies that didn't exist, and to betray the agency's most closely guarded secrets. He also knew they were setting in motion plans to pull American personnel back from overseas. Indeed, Trump drew up orders to withdraw U.S. troops from various places in Central Asia and Africa.

Anthony Scaramucci summed up why MAGA leaders resent the defense and foreign policy establishment: "They want to take America back to 1890, a walled-off society." As he explained it, the America First approach to international affairs views the past hundred years of U.S. policy—from free trade to democracy promotion—as having harmed Americans, not helped them. The movement's leading figures would "shut down world trade" if they could, Scaramucci explained, and ensure "everything is made in America."

"If the cup costs a penny to make in China, let's make it for twenty-four dollars in America," he quipped. "That's what America First is aiming at, total isolationism, figuratively and literally."

Long-standing U.S. alliances will be diminished or destroyed.

While the White House managed to achieve a number of positive foreign policy victories during the Trump administration with other countries, most successes were owed to the Axis of Adults who pointed the president in the right direction. A savvier successor to Trump will try to dissolve the postwar international system and the Western democratic alliance. Put another way, the next MAGA president will pull the plug on American leadership. This isn't errant speculation. In his first term, Trump's foreign policy goal was retrenchment. He badly wanted to reduce America's overseas footprint, a desire that influenced his conversations with world leaders.

On a regular basis, Trump demanded an end to U.S. commitments abroad. He called for scrapping defense pacts with Japan and South Korea. He called for pulling out of NATO. He called for canceling free trade agreements with an array of friendly governments. He called for yanking U.S. troops out of places they were stationed—Afghanistan, Syria, Somalia, Germany, and beyond. Arguments with his cabinet over these demands slowed Trump down, but his successor won't be cowed.

Whoever assumes the mantle of the MAGA movement will pursue an isolationist foreign policy. The result could be calamitous. Like it or not, U.S. influence and military strength have been the backbone of global stability since the two world wars. Withdrawing from international affairs would make the world less safe for Americans.

Worryingly, isolationist views have infected the wider Republican Party. In the lead-up to Russia's 2022 invasion of Ukraine, for instance, the vast majority of Republicans supported the statement that "we should pay less attention to problems overseas and concentrate on problems here at home," according to an Echelon Insights poll. A mere 30 percent of GOP voters agreed with the statement that "it is best for the future of our country to be active in world affairs."

"My biggest concern would be withdrawing troops from key places abroad, withdrawing from NATO, and abandoning alliances," Donald Trump's former defense secretary Mark Esper told me. "I see growing isolationism because of the MAGA movement." Esper expects another Trump would pull U.S. troops out of strategic positions in Europe, Asia, and Africa entirely.

Chris Harnisch, a top counterterrorism official in Trump's State Department, drew a direct connection to domestic security. He predicted that a populist successor would "bring our troops back from almost everywhere," adding, "You can't fight terrorism this way. You can't pull America back and keep the threat at bay with just drone strikes. So we will pay the price."

It won't stop there. MAGA leaders are not content with America embracing a new isolationism; they want other Western countries to do the same. If there is a pattern in international relations, it's that countries want other nations to look like and act like them. Democracies ally with democracies. Dictators form pacts with other dictators. And all of them hope to see the world remade in their image. Accordingly, Donald Trump and his lieutenants cheered on right-wing nationalist movements in the hope that the MAGA approach to strongman populism would spread worldwide.

"I think strong countries and strong nationalist movements in countries make strong neighbors," Steve Bannon told a European audience before Trump was elected. "That is really the building blocks that built Western Europe and the United States, and I think it's what can see us forward."

If you listen to the intellectual architects of the MAGA movement, openness is the enemy. The postwar focus on free trade, open travel, and political integration have created "the forgotten man." Globalization has left working-class people behind and made Western nations soft. Manufacturing jobs have vanished, stolen away by developing nations. Immigrants have flooded democracies, undoing a white Judeo-Christian culture, and institutions like the European Union have weakened the West.

The myth conveniently ignores crucial facts. In the same period, the West saw an explosion in economic prosperity (GDP per capita soared year over year), unprecedented levels of security (armed conflict among democracies declined), and a surge in political freedom (democracies went from a minority of the world to the majority of nations). Regardless, pro-Trump forces want to turn back the clock. They are urging U.S. allies to embrace anti-immigrant policies and economic protectionism, from Britain and France to Hungary and Italy.

A select group of foreign leaders are eager to see this happen. They want the United States and its allies to retreat, put up their walls, and look inward. Those observers are not our friends.

The world's autocrats will benefit from an isolationist America.

In October 2018, U.S.-based journalist Jamal Khashoggi went into the Saudi Arabian consulate in Istanbul and never came out. According to reports, he was killed and dismembered inside by Saudi operatives at the behest of the country's leader, Mohammed bin Salman, who wanted the dissident silenced.

Following the incident, Donald Trump welcomed reporters into the Oval Office for a conversation. He was under pressure to condemn the brutal killing and sever ties with Saudi Arabia. Down the hall, I was meeting with National Security Advisor John Bolton about an unrelated issue, when there was a knock on the door. It was White House Press Secretary Sarah Sanders.

"Ambassador," she said to Bolton, "I think you should know something."

He ushered her in. Sanders recapped Trump's forty-five-minute interview, during which he begrudgingly acknowledged that Khashoggi had been killed.

Then, she said, the president picked up classified documents on his desk and showed them to the reporters, remarking, "See? Many countries have given us intelligence on this."

There was an audible gasp from Bolton.

"Oh, God," he said under his breath.

"Yeah," Sarah replied, "but he didn't say it was from a specific country on record, just off. You could see pictures but not read any text from where they were sitting."

"Was that part on record?" Bolton asked.

"No," she said.

Bolton asked if there were cameras in the room.

"No," Sarah replied. The national security advisor breathed a sigh of relief.

We were all disturbed by the lapse in protocol and poor protection of classified information. Equally as disturbing was that Trump couldn't quite bring himself to condemn the Saudis.

"It's not a positive, not a positive," he told the reporters about the killing, but then he proceeded to defend the regime. "They've been a very good ally, and they've bought massive amounts of various things and investments in this country, which I appreciate."

In a meeting with the president in the Oval Office months later, Trump expressed his opinion to us in blunter terms.

"I am not going to talk about this anymore," he fumed. "Oil is at fifty dollars a barrel. Do you know how stupid it would be to pick this fight? Oil would go up to one hundred fifty dollars a barrel. Jesus. How fucking stupid would I be?"

He thought the Saudis would retaliate and that higher gas prices would hurt him politically. Trump effectively proposed giving the regime a free pass. He later admitted as much to the press.

Donald Trump's look-the-other-way foreign policy emboldened the world's dictators. By paying less attention to human rights and democracy, Trump broadcast a willingness to tolerate repressive behavior from China, Iran, North Korea, Russia, and other dictatorships.

The attitude will be shared by whoever takes his place.

"The populist MAGA movement has created confusion about who our allies are and who our adversaries are, and that puts America in grave danger," explained Fiona Hill, one of Trump's top former NSC aides. The moral equivalence has "made us weaker in the contest with Russia and with China."

"We had to push through actions sort of by stealth to counter the Russians," Hill explained of her time in the White House under Trump. "Putin had him wrapped around his finger the entire time. . . . He was always kissing Putin's ass. He wanted Putin's adulation."

I asked her what motivated the affection for dictators.

"One of the reasons Trump didn't want to clamp down on autocrats is because he wanted to do the same things as them," she explained. In Hill's view, this reflected broader MAGA ideology. The movement itself is quasi-authoritarian. She pointed to pro-Trump members of Congress who have continued to call for the United States to pull back from supporting Ukraine, a move that would be a permission slip for Putin to pursue his ambitions in Eastern Europe.

Eugene Vindman (brother of Alexander Vindman), served as a top NSC lawyer under Trump. He predicted another MAGA president would allow Russia to absorb neighboring countries, including Belarus and Moldova.

"A country of 140 million becomes a country of over 200 million," he explained, "and a resurgent Russian empire. We'd be in a position where Europe would be far more subject to Russian pressure."

China will also feel empowered to spread its influence. Vindman says Trump or a MAGA successor likely wouldn't protect Taiwan against a Chinese invasion, despite a multi-decade U.S. commitment to defend the island.

Not everyone agrees on this point. A number of Trump's foreign policy aides argue that—despite the MAGA crowd's affinity for autocrats—many of them support a tougher stance against China. However, the fact that there is stark divergence within the movement on this question suggests that Beijing might be able to divide-and-paralyze any U.S. response to Chinese aggression under the administration of the Next Trump.

And what if the sword is turned on America itself?

The U.S. military is one of democracy's last lines of defense, meant to repel foreign aggression. If it's turned inward, it can go from a guardrail of democracy to an existential threat. Just as a future MAGA president is likely to commandeer the domestic security apparatus for political purposes, he or she may also deploy the military to assert control inside U.S. territory.

Until the Trump administration, the proposition had sounded like the plot of a bad fiction novel. But Donald Trump was a few sentences away from making it happen. I was there.

In the run-up to his February 2019 State of the Union Address, Trump saw news about another migrant caravan headed toward the southern border. White House aides informed me the president wanted to invoke the Insurrection Act so he could deploy the U.S. military to forcibly expel the migrants, as if they were a foreign army invading the United States.

Of all the emergency powers a president possesses, this one is best known to the public—and was very much on Trump's mind. It was part of the "magical authorities" he often referenced. The Insurrection Act permits a president to deploy the military inside the United States in order to suppress a rebellion or repel a foreign invasion. If it's invoked, the president can call forth the military to enforce U.S. laws. The statute is the closest thing to "martial law" in our system.

After I got the call on February 4, Kirstjen Nielsen and I rushed to the White House and intercepted Trump in the Map Room.

"This is fucking insane," he protested. "We can't let them in. You have my permission to close the ports—and you need to send them back." He told us to use the military, which I interpreted as a nod to the Insurrection Act that aides had warned me about.

We spent hours trying to get White House staff and the counsel's office to weigh in against Trump's request. If he invoked the Insurrection Act, it would set a dangerous precedent. There was no telling where Trump might use it next.

We went back to the president to assure him that we were working with Mexican authorities to contain the situation. There was no need for extraordinary measures. We bought just enough time to throw him off the idea, while the speech was finalized *without* any reference to the Insurrection Act.

The issue roared back to life the following year amid racial justice protests in U.S. cities. Trump was tempted to use the military to suppress the demonstrations, prompting an unusual reproach from his former defense secretary Jim Mattis in *The Atlantic*. I was heartened to see Mattis finally speak up.

His words captured the gravity of the situation:

> *I swore an oath to support and defend the Constitution. Never did I dream that troops taking that same oath would be ordered under any circumstance to violate the Constitutional rights of their fellow citizens. . . . We must reject any thinking of our cities as a "battlespace" that our uniformed military is called upon to "dominate." . . . It erodes the moral ground that ensures a trusted bond between men and women in uniform and the society they are sworn to protect.*

The Next Trump will have options for how to make the military subservient to his or her whims. One method would be to outsource it. In other words, the Next Trump might hire black-ops personnel as mercenaries.

A former NSC staffer recounted how Trump was transfixed by the prospect of outsourcing warfare to private contractors. Former Blackwater founder Erik Prince reportedly pushed a plan to have contractors take over for U.S. troops overseas, from a five-thousand-man team to help overthrow the Communist regime in Venezuela to privatizing U.S. operations in Afghanistan. Trump was intrigued, and a line of communication was opened to Prince through third parties.

Top NSC advisor Lisa Curtis was alerted to the discussions. She asked one of her deputies to write a memo to the president, explaining why it was a terrible idea to enlist outsiders to do the military's job. The aide scrambled to put together the legal, operational, and moral case for *not* outsourcing core military functions. Fortunately, the proposal died.

"Next time we won't be so lucky," a person familiar with the discussions told me, envisioning a Trump-like future president. "We'll have a military run by mercenaries."

A privatized force. Weaponized for political purposes. Policing U.S. city streets. If that's how the shield and the sword of government are recast, then Tom Warrick's caricature of the Next Trump commanding his own forces doesn't seem so hyperbolic. "A junior gestapo," as he put it, is exactly what it would be.

When I reflect on the nightmare scenario—of an American president hijacking the military for nefarious ends—I like to believe there are safety valves. That's the type of moment when the Twenty-Fifth Amendment gets invoked, isn't it? Surely the president's cabinet would save the day by ejecting him from office if he tried to turn the armed forces against the American people.

But I know better. The Next Trump's cabinet will be stacked with loyalists. If they think about flipping, they'll be watched. Top officials are routinely tracked so they can be whisked away in the event of a crisis. A paranoid president would use those same security measures as a trip wire to determine whether his cabinet was convening—and conspiring—against him.

We can protect our institutions up to a point with obvious remedies. Congress can curtail the two-hundred-year-old law that allows a president to deploy the military on U.S. soil, and legislators should make it harder for the White House to misuse the armed forces. As far as guarding against isolationism, Congress should craft a new Marshall Plan to advance U.S. influence abroad, to protect global trade routes, to defend the territorial integrity of democratic allies, to resist the spread of autocracy, and to prevent meddling in our republic, especially if we want this to be another American century.

★ ★ ★

Up to this point, I've outlined the many plausible ways the Next Trump might dismantle the guardrails of our democracy. He or she will almost certainly do much of the damage piecemeal, a form of low-level democratic vandalism. Other possibilities (such as turning the American military against the citizenry) would catalyze a more drastic civic implosion.

Despite these dangers, I don't think another MAGA presidency will be America's ultimate undoing. At least it won't be the only factor. If our republic fails, the demise will follow the fabled path of other self-defeated democracies throughout world history.

In other words, we'll do it ourselves.

Chapter 7

THE CITIZEN

> . . . [M]en are ambitious, vindictive, and rapacious. To look for a continuation of harmony between a number of independent unconnected sovereignties, situated in the same neighborhood, would be to disregard the uniform course of human events, and to set at defiance the accumulated experience of ages.
>
> —ALEXANDER HAMILTON, FEDERALIST NO. 6, 1787

PART I

The trilling of insects came from all directions, as I set off along the familiar countryside. Back home in Indiana for Independence Day 2020, I was grateful for a reprieve from the pressures of Washington while I thought about what to do next. I took a drive after dark to roam the place I grew up.

In the summer, the humidity carries a syrupy smell from the cornfields in La Porte County. The scent itself feels sticky. I rolled down the car windows hoping for a reminder, but that night it was sulfur. Families lit fireworks at the end of their driveways and kids ran around with

sparklers, sending smoke across the roads and obscuring what was supposed to be a full moon.

I drove by my childhood home. Our family split in two when I was
five, so I had only vague memories of the yellow brick dwelling. A mile
away, there was a dead-end street that led to a smaller house that my
mom moved into, where I remember hiding under the bed from her
drunk boyfriend. After a few years, she got rid of him. No lights were
on when I coasted past my first real workplace, the radio station that I
hoped would set me on the way to meet my heroes.

My wish came true, partly. I wound up face-to-face with my political idols and ended up working for some of them. The thrill wore
off quickly after I saw their flaws in high definition and found myself
regularly disappointed by their indecision. Washington was populated
by children wearing big people clothes who also hid under their beds
from bullies.

On the outskirts of town, I arrived at my destination. The grass
parking lot was situated at the entrance to the county fairgrounds, not
far from the neighborhood where my dad moved after the divorce. The
evening stillness was broken by the sound of distant popping and crack-
ling, as balls of light erupted above the tree line.

I thought about my options. I couldn't decide whether I was being
careful, or whether I was just a coward.

"He's a lowlife."

America was lucky to have avoided "a monumental international crisis"
in the years after Trump took office, I wrote in *A Warning*. "Those of
you tempted to vote to reelect Donald Trump, despite the scandals and
despite credible evidence of wrongdoing, might want to consider what
could happen when that crisis comes."

After the book was published, the emergence of the coronavirus
grimly proved my point. People started dying en masse, and the death
toll eventually included one of my uncles. Trump deserved part of the
blame for the severity. As he politicized the public health response—

mocking mask-wearing and stoking conspiracy theories—Trump's leadership failures raised the stakes for people deciding whether or not to turn on him.

I spoke regularly with my former DHS colleague Olivia Troye. Before I left the administration, she had been detailed from DHS to the White House to be the vice president's homeland security advisor. When the pandemic broke open, she helped lead the staff of the COVID task force at the height of the crisis.

"Miles, you don't understand," she told me during one of our phone calls. "It's so, so much worse than it looks. The president doesn't know what he's doing, and it's costing lives it shouldn't. The whole thing is a clusterfuck."

Meanwhile, *The New York Times* reached out to tell me they'd been receiving suspicious emails from someone pretending to be Anonymous in an apparent phishing scheme designed to get them to expose my identity. Or it was someone subtly threatening to reveal the information themselves. I wasn't sure which.

"Hello, it has been awhile," one of the emails read, sent to *Times* opinion editor Jim Dao. ". . . I am now ready to reveal myself to the American public in the coming days (next week or sometime in August to be precise). Where do we begin? Much has changed for the worse since I wrote the 2018 anonymous resistance op-ed . . .

"Now, I would like to give a final warning to the American public in my own name," the message continued. "I will have my op-ed ready in the coming days. . . . In the meantime, please feel free to reply to this e-mail or give me a call. . . . Your friend, Anonymous, senior Trump official. P.S. Yes, it is me. But if you are skeptical, we can always do background verification by phone, e-mail or by Zoom meeting."

My mind was like a classroom during a test, and the faint click of the ticking clock was maddeningly loud. Time was running out.

Back home in Indiana, I settled on a plan. I couldn't wait any longer to do something, so I decided to step out into the light just before the Republican National Convention in August. Trump would be in the midst of getting renominated for the presidency. A GOP defection—

right as he was about to get coronated again—would throw his campaign off-kilter.

Before doing anything, I wanted to see whether others would join me. I did the rounds once more, arranging meetings with former colleagues who shared my earned disdain of the president. Over coffees and drinks in their backyards, I hinted that I was going to come out against Trump and assessed their willingness to join. The bulk of them demurred or pledged to do something "closer to the election."

There was someone I really wanted to recruit. My former coworker Chad Wolf had risen to become the acting secretary of DHS after I quit. When we worked together, Chad fought to beat back White House policies that we all knew were reckless, which is why I initially cheered on his appointment to the position. I went to see him one evening in early August 2020.

The Virginia night was still sweaty after sundown when I got to Chad's house. Like a lot of people, I'd given up trying to manage my alcohol consumption during the pandemic and showed up with a six-pack of strong IPAs. We cracked open beers and sat in fold-out chairs on his driveway, appreciating how August was a slower month in the nation's capital. I hadn't seen him in probably a year. He looked more energized than I'd expected.

We reminisced as we drank. Chad and I had spent a lot of time together in government. After everyone had gone home, we would be the last two left in the front office, commiserating about how a broken administration was straining our personal lives and our health. We sent each other memes about quitting. I hoped he would still consider it. Trump would be badly weakened in the heat of the campaign if any of his cabinet members resigned in anger.

John Kelly and Kirstjen Nielsen both thought the role of DHS secretary was the most thankless job in Washington. But, as we drank, I could tell Chad was enjoying the trappings of the office. The new headquarters. The private jet. The Secret Service detail sitting inside two black SUVs along the road in front of us.

When the topic of the president came up, Chad was more reserved than usual. He avoided speaking ill of Trump, which was odd. Bashing a fucked-up White House was a cornerstone of our friendship. I asked him about the president's recent deployment of armed DHS agents onto the streets of Portland, since Chad had been caught in the crossfire of the controversial decision.

"The libs are totally freaking out over that," he laughed. "Everything about it is misconstrued."

"It's not a great look. I assume the White House was pressuring you?" I tried to give him an opening to blame the president.

"Nah. It's all overblown. Honestly, I've managed to stay on his good side. It's not as hard as Kirstjen made it look."

Later Chad admitted he'd opted for a less public role in the COVID-19 response, even though DHS was supposed to take the lead during national emergencies.

"It's worked out pretty well," he said, noting that he'd avoided a lot of the criticism Trump was getting over the response. While it might have worked out well for Chad, it didn't for the 200,000 Americans who had been killed by the virus at that point.

"Hey, I've got a TV hit coming up. Wanna come with me before you go?" He was slated to appear on *Justice w/ Judge Jeanine* on Fox News, one of Trump's favorite programs.

"Sure."

I was buzzed as we piled into one of the armed cars. The Secret Service drove us to a nearby parking lot.

"I'll be right back," Chad said. He got out and walked toward an unmarked van.

The door slid open revealing a mini television studio inside, complete with a chair, bright lights, and a fake backdrop of Washington, D.C. The technician helped Chad secure an earpiece and slid the door shut.

I watched from my phone. Judge Jeanine asked him eagerly about the situation in Portland. To me, the militaristic response to the protests seemed Orwellian. Rather than distance himself, Chad offered justifications for the president's crackdown, like a pull-string doll on a loop.

"We are not talking about peaceful protesting. . . . We are talking about violent criminals," he declared. The judge loved it. Recruiting Chad was a lost cause, I concluded.

Back at his house, I think he sensed my unspoken judgment. He assured me he was "holding the line" against Stephen Miller on issues like immigration. That was something, at least. I urged him to keep running interference against the craziest policy ideas.

"Well then, keep killing it," I offered halfheartedly.

After a few more drinks, I told him I wasn't going to stay quiet during the general election campaign. In fact, I was going to speak out against Trump. Chad didn't exactly discourage me, though he seemed concerned about whether I'd criticize him.

"No, no. It won't be about you personally, just the president," I assured him.

"Okay, well . . . if you keep my name out of your mouth, I'll keep yours out of mine."

Chad said he'd consider leaving after the election, but I knew better. If Trump won, he'd stay. Chad wanted the Senate to confirm him permanently, removing the "acting" from his title.

The farewell handshake at the end of the night was our last.

★ ★ ★

Two weeks later, I was ready to come forward. Sort of. *The Washington Post* agreed to publish a piece I'd written, entitled, "AT HOMELAND SECURITY, I SAW FIRSTHAND HOW DANGEROUS TRUMP IS FOR AMERICA."

There was a big caveat. I decided not to disclose that I was Anonymous, at least not yet. The declaration would create a media firestorm and distract from the specific allegations I wanted to level against the president. For the moment, I decided just to be Miles Taylor, not the author of an unsigned op-ed and book.

The Trump years were so filled with moral compromise that the prospect of speaking out in my name made my conscience feel clear again. I didn't want to muddy the waters with multiple personas. The Anonymous "reveal" could come later. However, underneath the reasoning and political calculation, something didn't feel right about coming forward in stages. A voice in my soul issued a warning notice. In my haste, I ignored it.

The draft essay was written as a full-frontal condemnation of the president.

"Like many Americans, I had hoped that Donald Trump, once in office, would soberly accept the burdens of the presidency—foremost among them the duty to keep America safe," I wrote. "But he did not rise to the challenge. Instead, the president has governed by whim, political calculation, and self-interest."

I listed off ways Donald Trump politicized DHS, undermining it with a perverse fixation on immigration. I wrote about his plans to dump illegal immigrants in Democratic cities, to close the border in states where it would help him personally, and to restart a crueler form of family separation.

"It is more than a little ironic that Trump is campaigning for a second term as a law-and-order president," I concluded. "His first term has been dangerously chaotic. Four more years of this are unthinkable."

An organization called Republican Voters Against Trump helped me film a testimonial to be released simultaneously. I announced at the end of the video that I would support Democratic candidate Joe Biden for president, despite being a lifelong conservative. Character was all that mattered in this election. Republicans needed to put the country ahead of their GOP loyalties.

The day the news broke, I was deluged with media requests. An ABC News report announced I was "the highest-ranking former administration official to endorse former vice president Joe Biden," and television cameras popped up on the sidewalk outside the town house where Anabel and I lived. To my surprise, I heard from several of the wary ex-cabinet secretaries I had met with earlier in the summer.

"You said what many people wish they could or had said," one wrote.

"You are awesome. That was wonderful. I'm in!" another texted. I was emboldened. Even Trump-friendly media outlets led with the story.

"FORMER SENIOR TRUMP ADMINISTRATION OFFICIAL BACKS BIDEN," read the headline on Fox News, followed by "FORMER DHS CHIEF OF STAFF CALLS TRUMP 'DANGEROUS' FOR AMERICA."

The president struck back with a well-worn tactic. He pretended we'd never met.

"A former DISGRUNTLED EMPLOYEE named Miles Taylor, who I do not know (never heard of him), said he left & is on the open arms Fake News circuit," he tweeted. "Said to be a real 'stiff'. They will take anyone against us!"

In response, I posted pictures of Trump and me in the Oval Office during briefings, shaking hands, smiling.

The next day Trump attended an event in Yuma, Arizona. Chad Wolf stood next to him, as reporters grilled the president about my claims.

"He said the best things about what we are doing. Unbelievable statements," Trump lied. He claimed I'd been an effusive booster of his administration. "And he left . . . all of a sudden, he's bad-mouthing us. And the reason is the Democrats—or somebody—got to him and said, 'How would you like to speak?' He's a lowlife. Anybody who does this is a lowlife to me."

Chad chimed in.

"What I can tell you is I'm very disappointed in Mr. Taylor," he said. "He was at the department for a number of years . . . [then] left the department praising the administration's policies, procedures—has said nothing since that time. And roughly seventy days from the election, has decided now to start talking. I think most reasonable Americans understand what that is all about. So very disappointed."

DHS later released an official statement under Chad's name.

"Mr. Taylor," he wrote, "was clearly pursuing a self-serving, self-promoting agenda while at the Department of Homeland Security. . . . I can attest that he never vocalized disagreement with the President's policies—and in fact expressed strong support. This charade is another sad reminder that not all who pursue public service are doing so for the public good."

I sent him a message. I thought we had a deal.

"I did not initiate this," Chad responded tersely. "I have [an] audience here I have to satisfy."

He didn't mean the DHS workforce. He meant the audience of one in the White House. I'd never lost a friend quite like that.

Around that time, a Trump aide visited the DHS front office with a screwdriver. The entryway is lined with plaques honoring former DHS secretaries and chiefs of staff. There, the appointee started unscrewing one of the gold metal rectangles.

"I'm removing the name of this traitor," he reportedly told colleagues.

The nameplate was mine.

★ ★ ★

People around the country reached out to say thank you after my video and op-ed were released, from everyday voters and small business owners to celebrities. Actor Ben Stiller sent his praise. Jennifer Aniston posted a supportive message on Instagram. One of my childhood idols—Mark Hamill, Luke Skywalker himself!—sent a note of gratitude.

I've forgotten most of it.

Positive memories seem to wane like sun-faded posters, while negative ones are chiseled in marble. Your brain reminds you of them again . . . and again . . . and again. That's what mine did anyway, as political operatives and social-media trolls combed through my personal life and sought out anyone who might have something bad to say about me.

A popular right-wing radio host dropped a creepy YouTube video, "How We Can Win the Election and Still Lose the Country: Miles Taylor." The commentator urged legions of followers to remember my name, repeating it throughout the program slowly and deliberately. His tone was sinister. I didn't think he was asking people to keep me in their thoughts and prayers out of kindness.

My older sister was visiting when the program came out. She barricaded herself in the guest room that night, placing her oversized luggage against the door. Family members like her were also on the receiving end of virtual harassment from dark corners of the web.

Nonetheless, they told me not to let the MAGA antagonists win. Voters needed to hear the truth before it was too late. So I went for broke. I agreed to as many interviews as possible to talk about who Trump really was, detailing as much as I could to anyone who would listen.

The growing media exposure led to a stream of angry messages from MAGA strangers. As a precaution, I went to the shooting range to practice with my concealed weapon. I didn't think I was in imminent danger, but if someone broke in at night, the Sig Sauer pistol was the last line of defense.

The firearm felt reassuring in my hand. Whenever I didn't have it with me, I found myself imagining the weight of it and mentally arming the weapon as fast as I could. Inserting the loaded magazine into the grip . . . the satisfying *click* once it was locked in place . . . pulling back the slide to chamber a round. Now it was ready to fire.

I used up my hollow-point ammunition at the range and found out that there wasn't any left to buy. Anywhere. A pandemic shortage was affecting the whole country, which also meant Americans were armed to the teeth.

A friend gave me a box of round-nose ammo as backup, the kind that might not be as effective at stopping an attacker. He didn't want me guarding the house with an empty magazine. Better to have range ammo than nothing.

I started drinking more to cope with the stress. Nothing too extreme, but I needed an escape from the mental noise. A bar down the street became my go-to spot for cocktails. Double gin martini, up, blue-cheese olives, filthy.

The week I released my missives, a top Biden advisor texted.

"Someone more senior than me is trying to reach you," he wrote cryptically.

The mystery caller could only be the Democratic candidate himself, Joe Biden. I told the advisor to pass along my number. I'd be waiting excitedly. Later that night, I saw the missed calls. I didn't feel the ringing in my pocket while chatting with patrons at the neighborhood bar.

At the end of August, a reporter called to say I was getting under

Trump's skin by not going away. Seeing me on TV was pissing him off. His associates were taking it up a notch. They started spreading rumors that I cheated on my wife the week of our wedding with a young personal assistant. Whoever was behind the whisper campaign clearly didn't know that I had been in Latin America then, no one from work was there, and my DHS assistant was actually a man nearly the same age as me.

No reporters took the bait. But it wouldn't have mattered. My would-be tormentors were wasting their time if they wanted to start rumors or dig up dirt about my private life. I didn't have one anymore. Amid the turmoil of the pandemic and the decision to come forward, Anabel and I had separated.

"We cannot pretend they are not shouting from the rooftops."

Late August sun filled the living room, illuminating the dust suspended in dead air. The nondescript high-rise blended into a nondescript street within a nondescript Virginia neighborhood. The apartment's interior was styled in slightly different shades of brown. Although the unit was fourteen stories above street level, I could still hear children shouting in the park below.

Divorced dads moved into places like this while figuring out their next moves. My situation wasn't far off. There was plenty of room for two, but I was there by myself. The safe house had been offered by a contact in the intelligence community who knew internet trolls were pursuing me and that my personal life was starting to deteriorate.

I grappled with the newfound discomfort of isolation. A lot of people lost marriages during the Trump years, so no one needed to play the violin for me, though the timing wasn't great. My relationship with Anabel crumbled just as I found myself badly needing a partner.

I rolled my bag inside and made a truce with the temporary apartment. I wouldn't begrudge the colorless space, as long as it returned solace. The safe house agreed wordlessly.

In the bedroom I unfurled a few blazers, wrinkled shirts, and jeans.

The toiletries in my backpack had reassembled themselves as haphazardly as I'd grabbed them on the way out the door. From below the pile I dug out black socks (adorned with white pineapples) and put them on the undergarments pile. The pair was still held together by a plastic thread.

"When it's time to do the right thing," the man who gave them to me had said, "don't get cold feet." Kelly's comment had picked up bittersweet irony in the years since.

Despite the initial enthusiasm, several household names who left the Trump administration had stopped answering my calls. They saw the attacks I was getting and didn't want to pick a fight with the president. Thankfully, other Trump aides told me they were prepared to speak out. The lesser-known appointees held positions similar to mine—as chiefs of staff, assistant secretaries, and White House advisors.

Elizabeth Neumann was among them. She had greeted me warmly on my first day at DHS with the confidence of a true Texan who thought we could course-correct the administration. Or lasso it. After more than three years trying, she quit in frustration. I told her about my plans. Elizabeth wanted to help and, to my delight, was willing to record her own testimonial.

As I unpacked my bags in the apartment, I was interrupted by a message from another former colleague.

"Can you meet?"

Olivia Troye wanted to get together. She'd recently left the vice president's office and the COVID-19 task force, and I assumed she wanted to talk about private-sector jobs. A number of people had reached out to see if there were openings at Google.

I would have to tell her to wait. Opposing Trump was now my full-time job. Just before my video was released, I had gotten approval to take several months of unpaid leave from Google for personal political activity. I wanted to devote my full attention to the presidential campaign, and there was just enough money in my savings account to get me through Election Day.

Olivia and I met for coffee in the Washington, D.C., Navy Yard neighborhood. She was nervous, since I was a pariah in Trump world, and she didn't want to get caught fraternizing with the opposition. I wasn't offended. We carried our drinks away from the coffee shop to a wooden walkway that hugged the winding Potomac River.

The pandemic made it easy to be discreet. Baseball caps, sunglasses, and face masks didn't seem unusual and made us hard to identify as we walked. On a bench, we removed our pedestrian disguises and appreciated the breeze off the water.

Olivia was exhausted after two years at the White House. But she told me that job advice wasn't what she was looking for. She wanted to do something about the president.

"Miles, I'm so scared for the country," she confided. "And I don't know what to do. I feel like I have to say something about what I've been through. They'll try to crush me, though."

I felt a jolt of excitement. Trump had badly bungled the pandemic response. To have someone on his inner team say so—publicly—would be devastating to his reelection. I told Olivia about the loose network of ex-Trumpers I was assembling. We could help amplify her message, I offered, and we'd protect her however we could.

Olivia was looking over my shoulder. Her face fell.

I turned and saw a woman we both knew, a prominent White House lawyer. She was coming over the footbridge and walking her dog. There was no use in getting up to move. It was too late.

She spotted us and waved. Olivia and I waved back, offering up an awkward hello in unison.

"Great," Olivia breathed sarcastically. "She's going to think we're conspiring."

"Well, we are conspiring a little bit," I said to tease her. She seemed rushed after that. We ended the conversation inconclusively, with Olivia promising to be in touch after she talked more about it with her husband.

Around that time, I was offered a part-time, temporary contributor role with CNN until the end of the year. The pay was modest, but the on-air spot would give me the opportunity to appear almost daily and share my concerns with a wide audience. I accepted.

I got flack from a few critics who accused people like me of "cashing in" at the time. I found the "grifters" label amusing. They had no idea how little money we were making. Indeed, many of the people I convinced to oppose Trump have been struggling financially ever since because the decision cost them lucrative jobs, resulted in mounting legal fees, and forced them to dig into savings accounts. Staying silent would have been much more profitable. A few times I sent people paystub screenshots to neuter their criticism. Otherwise, I ignored it.

Once I started, I reached out to CNN anchor Jake Tapper and a network executive to pitch an idea. I told them about the group of former Trump officials I was bringing together. If there were enough of us, could we do a televised town hall? Americans should hear from the people who worked for the president before deciding whether to rehire him. They said they'd get back to me.

In September, I got two messages that made my month.

"I'm in," and . . .

"You're on."

Olivia was ready to join us. And CNN was interested in my idea. That is, if I could deliver.

★ ★ ★

Trump Press Secretary Kayleigh McEnany strutted up to the White House podium on September 22 and read a terse statement. She mustered a look of forced disapproval, like a substitute teacher sending students to the principal's office.

"What we have here with this former disgruntled detailee and with Miles Taylor, as well, these are not profiles in courage. These are profiles in cowardice," she declared.

The detailee she was talking about was Olivia Troye. Her revelations had rocked the campaign. In a recorded video, Olivia shared firsthand recollections of Trump's callous mismanagement of the pandemic. In response, the White House unloaded on the two of us and our "club of Never Trumpers who are desperate for relevancy."

The dam was breaking. Elizabeth, Olivia, and I launched an organization called the Republican Political Alliance for Integrity and Reform, or REPAIR. We brought together dozens of Trump officials and GOP leaders to oppose the president, from a former White House communications director to a former head of the Republican National Committee. We also announced a legal defense partnership to support others who came forward.

"The price of admission into this club is fabricated smears and flat-out lies against President Trump," McEnany recited from her note card. "Troye joins the similarly irrelevant Miles Taylor. . . . Those who knew Miles during the administration knew he could not get results."

My feelings weren't hurt. If anything, I was thrilled. The White House was attacking us because our efforts were working, and the president was obviously nervous about the impact on public opinion. Polls showed disapproval of the COVID-19 response was a big threat to his reelection, and Olivia criticized him on that score with explosive force.

"When we were in a task-force meeting," she recalled in a sit-down interview, "the president said, 'Maybe this COVID thing is a good thing—I don't like shaking hands with people. I don't have to shake hands with these disgusting people.'"

Her emotion and sincerity were visible.

"Those disgusting people are the same people he claims to care about. These are the people who are still going to his rallies today, who have complete faith in who he is."

Video testimonials like hers garnered millions of impressions online, saturated television networks, and were plastered on billboards across America (thanks to Bill Kristol and Sarah Longwell's support at our parent organization, Republican Voters Against Trump). The president's cronies tried to say over and over that we were doing it for money. In reality, we were unpaid volunteers.

Elizabeth and I sought to recruit our original DHS team. All seven of us had felt similarly about Trump when we started. Unfortunately, Chad Wolf and Gene Hamilton had firmly put down roots in MAGA world—whether it was Stockholm syndrome or self-interest, I didn't know. Chris Krebs was trying to keep his head down to run the nation's domestic cybersecurity agency. And Kirstjen Nielsen was taking time away from it all.

That left General Kelly. He phoned me a few days after the press secretary's showy condemnation.

"What you're doing is noble," the chief said. His support buoyed me like a father's approval.

"I don't know how he's not in an institution somewhere, whether it's jail or a nuthouse," Kelly vented about Trump. "But he's a seriously sick guy. I never heard him saying anything that wasn't a lie."

I told General Kelly about the pending CNN special. I suggested that it would be a good platform for him to say something about the president. He said he'd think about it. We mused about the possibility of Trump's downfall.

"Nothing would please me more than if he chained himself to the Resolute desk, and they have to go in and cut the chains and carry him away in a straitjacket," he mused, only half joking. His premonition was eerily close to what would be the reality. I told him I'd keep him updated on our efforts.

The organization we set up, REPAIR, was targeting the voting bloc that would determine the electoral outcome: disenchanted Republicans. If enough turned away from Trump, he would lose. We felt well positioned to give GOP voters the justification to defect.

I spent the last six weeks of the campaign traveling to every battleground state. I did interviews, met with voters, and tried to rally Republicans and independents against the sitting president. I crisscrossed America mostly by car. New Mexico. Arizona. Pennsylvania. Ohio. Michigan. North Carolina. Virginia.

In between press conferences and radio interviews, I phoned ex-Trumpers to persuade them to appear on the television town hall. CNN officially green-lighted the development of an hour-long special. As October rolled around, the participant list grew longer, but there still weren't enough interviewees to fill out the program.

Friends in the FBI told me to be careful while I was in the swing states. The system was overwhelmed with politically charged threats.

FBI field offices were tracking violent plots against governors, congresspeople, local officials, and a range of political figures. The advice? *Keep your head down.* That would be hard to do on the campaign trail.

After an October event in Tucson, I drove to a taco joint to unwind. In the Southwest dusk light, I drank a margarita and scrolled through Twitter. Mobs of online detractors scuffled with me on the platform, a microcosm of the anger that consumed the wider presidential campaign.

A buzzing noise disrupted the solo meal. Feet above my head, a drone wobbled and steadied itself. I tried to act indifferent. But the incessant hum of the quad-copter was difficult to ignore. It dropped lower and lower. I looked up. The drone was inches away and apparently recording me, with an LED light and camera pointed downward at my face.

"Is that yours?" the waitress asked.

"No," I said, looking around.

Couples chatted at other tables, oblivious. None of them held a joystick. Much like the Twitter trolls, a drone operator was harassing me remotely from somewhere I couldn't see.

This was the downside of going public. People would occasionally say thank you in the street if they recognized me, while Trump supporters jeered as I waited in line at McDonald's or at the airport. Mostly it was harmless. Sometimes it felt invasive, as it did that evening in Tucson.

I paid for my drinks, and the drone buzzed off. I walked around the shopping area a few times to shake the feeling that I was being followed. MAGA hecklers weren't my biggest problem.

Exhaustion and anxiety were the main enemy. Long drives, late evenings, and early mornings steadily wore me down. The night Donald Trump was diagnosed with COVID, for instance, I was awake until 2:30 a.m. doing media to talk about the national security implications, and I was back on-air by 6:30 a.m.

Expressionless dark eyes stared back at me from graffitied rest stop mirrors.

Solitude didn't help. You forget what real silence is like when you're in a relationship. The absence of noise isn't nerve-racking if a reassuring sound can interrupt your thoughts anytime. Your name is hollered by a warm voice in the doorway. A shower turns on down the hall. A laugh leaps from the woman reading next to you, causing her to apologize before she recites an amusing line from her book.

Real silence is deafening like train tracks. Mostly, the iron mass of time just sits idly with its rails stretching onward and out of view. Occasionally, a rumble signals runaway thoughts, then you're startled by the locomotive's piercing horn when it rounds the corner. The infernal noises that follow can only be waited out, not ended, until the relief of the last car rattles past. Even when it's over, the tracks are still there.

That's how my anxiety attacks felt. I had no choice but to be alone with my thoughts when I was on the road, as my mind drifted inexorably toward something I'd been delaying. Dreading, really. A few times the racing thoughts spiraled, and I was forced to pull the car over while I caught my breath.

I starting getting edgy before TV hits, as if I was going to pass out. I drank to ease my nerves and refilled my Xanax prescription at a pharmacy somewhere in the Southwest. The mugs of coffee I sipped on the air sometimes held beer or whiskey. If you saw me on television in October 2020 on the campaign trail, there's a good chance I was lightly inebriated. Once or twice, close to drunk. You wouldn't have known it, or at least I don't think you would have, because I considered myself the high-functioning type.

The confidence that came with a clear conscience was getting replaced—ever so slowly—by doubt. Was anyone listening? Were we breaking through at all? Or was I setting myself up to get destroyed by Donald Trump for another four years?

My mood lifted on October 18, a few days before the final presidential debate. CNN was ready to air the program we'd spent so long assembling: *The Insiders: A Warning from Former Trump Officials*. I watched it from the road, streaming the program from the phone on my lap while I drove through the dark to another swing-state stop.

Jake Tapper's introduction spoke volumes.

"The world has never before witnessed so many former top U.S. government officials warning about the president for whom they once worked. It's just never happened before," the anchor intoned solemnly, "not in these numbers, and not with the same stark conclusion that President Trump in their view is unfit for the office he holds—the office he's asking you to return him to for a second term."

Tapper also read a damning statement about Trump from someone else. My former boss. I smiled.

"The depth of his dishonesty is just astounding to me," John Kelly was quoted as saying about the president. "The transactional nature of every relationship, though, it's more pathetic than anything else. He is the most flawed person I have ever met in my life."

The hour-long program featured a representative sample of our growing ranks. Interviewees included my former colleagues Olivia Troye, Elizabeth Neumann, and DHS General Counsel John Mitnick; Robert Cardillo, former director of the National Geospatial Intelligence Agency; Admiral Paul Zukunft, former commandant of the Coast Guard; and John Bolton, Trump's former national security advisor. They added their own descriptions of the president's extensive faults.

Trump's manipulation of intelligence: "Whenever [Trump] would bump into something that was inconvenient or went against that core vision that he had, he would deflect or deny it," Cardillo said.

Trump's handling of domestic terrorism: "White supremacist groups have been emboldened. They are chattering and talking about taking up arms in preparation for the election. . . . We're in a very, very dangerous space right now," Elizabeth advised.

Trump's antidemocratic tendencies: "Trump will not leave graciously if he loses. . . . Whether he carries it to the extreme, I don't think we know," Bolton warned, explaining the constitutional danger the man posed. "And I think that's important for people to understand, especially conservatives."

For me, Tapper's closing felt like a bookend to several grueling months in the public eye.

"You have heard a lot this hour from people who have worked with President Donald Trump who believe he should not win re-election, that he is uninterested in governing, that he is motivated only by his self-interests, and that the United States of America is less secure with him in the Oval Office.

"Now in every presidency, there are people who disagree with various policies of a president for whom they serve. But as a historical matter, we cannot ignore the sheer number of officials who worked for this president and are now sounding a very public alarm about his fitness for the job. You can listen to them, or you can ignore them. That is entirely up to you. But as journalists, we cannot pretend that they are not shouting from the rooftops."

With weeks to go until Election Day, we'd said everything we could about Donald Trump. Almost. I still had a confession to make, and the internal stress reached a breaking point.

"We are not enemies, but friends."

Mobile TV studios proliferated during the pandemic. Rather than inviting people on set, news networks sent modified vans to their guests' neighborhoods, such as the one Chad Wolf had disappeared into the last night we saw each other.

The first time I sat in one of the mini recording studios, in August 2020, I realized it was a claustrophobe's nightmare. Small, windowless, and quiet—so completely sound-dampened that no one outside could hear you scream. What's worse, the sweltering afternoon outside and the TV lights inside conspired to make it hot, particularly because the driver turned off the air-conditioning when the news segment went "live."

The only noise was Anderson Cooper's voice from an earpiece tucked into my right ear. He could see me. I couldn't see him. I looked straight into the camera, at the nothingness, nodding along with his questions as if we were sitting across from each other.

The veteran anchor brought me onto his show right after I went public. I don't know how many viewers were watching live, but millions saw the interview—months later—when it got replayed. Anderson used the half-hour appearance primarily to ask me about my disclosures, but he posed a question at the end.

"There was an op-ed, a book, by someone calling themselves Anonymous. Are you aware of who that is?" he asked.

I was sweating in the hot van.

"I'm not," I responded. "Look, that was a parlor game that happened in Washington, D.C. . . . I've got my own thoughts about who that might be, but I want my focus to be on the president. And I certainly don't want to—"

"You're not Anonymous?" Anderson interjected.

"I wear a mask for two things, Anderson: Halloweens and pandemics. So, no."

For the hundredth time, I lied.

Anderson Cooper wasn't the first person in the media to ask, or the last. My anonymity would've survived only fifteen minutes if I'd confessed to the first person who inquired after the 2018 *Times* op-ed came out. D.C. reporters interrogated everyone.

"If asked," Anonymous told readers, "I will strenuously deny I am the author."

You don't wear a mask if you plan to brag that you're undercover. So when Anderson raised the question in August 2020, I stuck with the plan, knowing I'd eventually make the revelation.

A few months later, I still hadn't done it. I was on a cross-country truth crusade against the President of the United States, yet I was maintaining a lie about my identity. The contradiction was splitting me open. I needed someone to talk to about it. But who?

Anabel and I were separated. My agents had a financial interest in whether I revealed myself (the revelation would surely affect book sales). And I wasn't going to phone Jim Dao at the *Times* and ask him if I should blow up my life. There was one person I thought I could trust, partly because she already suspected me.

On an October evening weeks before the 2020 election, I drove to a brewery and stuffed a book in my backpack. At a table in the corner— out of earshot from other patrons—I sat down and ordered a drink alone. I remember the tart guava beer because I had several.

A blond-haired woman in her late twenties walked in, drawing stares from the men at the bar. Her magnetic confidence and designer outfit contrasted with the table partner she sought out. From the corner, in my black running clothes, I waved to her.

"How are you?" Hannah asked. There was a knowing empathy in her voice when we hugged, and she held the embrace for an extra beat. Hannah had clearly heard about my relationship.

"I am . . . tired." I feigned a laugh.

"I bet. You've been everywhere. I'm really proud of you guys." Hannah had worked with several of the Trump dissenters—me, Elizabeth, Kelly, Olivia.

"Thank you. It's been a ride."

"I heard about Anabel. You probably don't want to talk about it, but I just want to say I'm really sorry."

"Yeah, I'm getting by. It is what it is."

"My boyfriend and I broke up earlier this year. We were together for five years. So I get it. Staying busy is the best thing you can do, and it seems like you've got a full plate."

I didn't want to talk about it.

"Hey, I have something I want to tell you," I lowered my voice.

"Okay . . ." She mirrored the hushed tone.

"You remember when we met up last winter?"

"Yeah, of course."

"And you asked me if I wrote something . . ."

She looked at me curiously. My hands shook as I withdrew the copy of *A Warning* from my backpack. I put it on the table. Hannah looked down, and her already wide eyes got impossibly wider. My heart beat against my hoodie like a fist hitting a door.

"You were right," I told her.

"Wow," she replied, ". . . wow."

She stared at the book for a long moment, shaking her head in disbelief, before cracking a smile.

"I told you. *I knew it.*"

"Yes, you did."

I flipped the book over to hide the title.

"I hope you know that it was a very powerful message," she said.

Hannah asked all the questions I expected. When did I decide to do it? How did I pull it off? Did anyone else in the administration know? And why was it still a secret?

"I decided not to say it when I came forward in August," I explained. "I didn't want the distraction about 'Anonymous' to overshadow everything."

"I guess that makes sense. So why not do it now?"

"Well, our effort is going better than I expected. I mean, it's working. I think. If I say I'm Anonymous, won't that confuse everyone? I want your opinion."

"I disagree. I think now is probably the most important time to re-up your message—that it's up to the voters to stop Trump. Also, didn't you say you'd do it by now?" Hannah asked.

She was referring to an online interview from a year prior.

"Yes and no," I admitted.

I told her about the "Ask Me Anything" session on Reddit. How I wore a disguise, holed up in a hotel room with my agents in Old Town, and answered questions about the book behind a virtual wall. When a user asked whether I'd reveal my identity, I wrote a very carefully worded response: "Trump will hear from me, in my own name, before the 2020 election."

Technically, I followed through. Trump had heard from me. In my own name. For months. I didn't specifically promise to reveal that I was Anonymous.

For the first time, Hannah looked at me critically.

"Don't get me wrong, I admire what you're doing. But that feels misleading. You should just say it."

This is why I wanted to talk to her. Not just to disclose my anonymity, but to confess a deeper truth: I didn't want to give it up. The "secret within a secret" was that I was afraid. I hid the fear from everyone, including myself, burying it under layers of delay and indecision and shifting justifications for why I shouldn't tell the world who I was.

"I don't know if I'm ready."

"I don't understand," Hannah replied. "You're already out there talking about Trump. You're on TV every day. You're traveling the country."

"Because Anonymous has taken on a life of his own. To some people, he's a resistance superhero—and to others he's this sort of villain. I don't think I measure up to either of those. If I unmask myself, who the hell is Miles Taylor?"

"Look at the response you've had so far. It's made a difference, really. What are you most afraid of happening?"

I searched for the right words.

"The reckoning," I told her.

Hannah's face insisted on a better explanation.

"Announcing it won't be that hard," I explained. "It's everything that comes after that."

I'd met the public mob already. Twice. First at Google, when left-wing activists assumed I was a MAGA foot soldier and pilloried me, then again in August, when I attacked Trump and the far right came for me. If I revealed I was the president's elusive critic, everyone would pile on.

"It's a life sentence," I told Hannah. "Of being praised, punished. Probably both."

"Well, what if you don't do it? If you let the election go by and then say it publicly in some splashy announcement, how will you feel?"

"Not good."

"Exactly. And what if you keep the secret forever?"

I considered it for a while. The answer became obvious to me when I was back home in La Porte. I hadn't voiced it aloud yet.

"I think I'll feel like a coward."

★ ★ ★

Back on the campaign trail, I made my way to another swing state. North Carolina. I had a few days on the road to mull over Hannah's advice. Before we parted ways, she had made the case that unmasking myself would create a final opportunity to send a message. If I decided against it, Hannah said she'd respect my decision and keep the secret.

I didn't doubt her trustworthiness for a minute, but it didn't matter. Hannah had held up a mirror so I could see what should have been strikingly clear from the outset. Hiding was untenable, politically and personally.

I released a statement the morning of October 28, 2020, from my hotel room in Asheville.

"Donald Trump is a man without character," the social media post read. "It's why I wrote A WARNING . . . and it's why me & my colleagues have spoken out against him (in our own names) for months. It's time for everyone to step out of the shadows."

I linked to a longer statement that confessed everything. Why I went into the Trump administration, why I quit, why I wrote cloaked critiques, why I chose this moment to take responsibility. People could dismiss me, but they couldn't disregard all of the other officials who'd told the truth about the Trump presidency. I listed their names.

"These public servants were not intimidated. And you shouldn't be either. As descendants of revolutionaries, honest dissent is part of our American character, and we must reject the culture of political intimidation that's been cultivated by this President. That's why I'm writing this note—to urge you to speak out if you haven't."

Beyond my revelation, it was a closing argument about the need to get rid of Donald Trump and the political turmoil affecting our democracy. I ended with a few lines Lincoln delivered when the country was nearing civil war.

"We are not enemies, but friends. We must not be enemies. Though passion may have strained it must not break our bonds of affection." If we didn't heed the martyred president's words and repair our republic, I wrote, America wouldn't endure.

Even I was surprised by what happened next.

Within minutes of my posting the statement, a burst of notifications and "BREAKING NEWS" alerts made the calm hotel room feel like a packed stadium. My face appeared on the wall-mounted TV. Every favorable and unfavorable opinion you can imagine—about my political views, my choices, my character—arrived in a ceaseless series of warring dings and vibrations on the desk.

I spoke to a few people on the phone, including John Kelly—"I'm proud of you," he said. His approval should have meant a lot to me in the moment, but once again, the negative reactions stood out in starker relief than the words of encouragement.

Trump went on the attack at a campaign event.

"You know 'Anonymous'—this 'Anonymous' everybody has been looking for? That law enforcement could've found?" he asked the crowd to widespread booing. "It turned out to be a low-level staffer, a sleaze-bag, a disgruntled employee!"

Never mind that Trump's own White House had referred to me as a "senior administration official" whenever they sent me out to speak publicly.

"There should be major criminal liability for some scum like this!"

People cheered and whistled.

"And you know for a year everybody walks into my office—Secretary of State Pompeo—I could name every one of them. All good people. And I'm looking at 'em saying, 'I wonder if that could be the one.' And it turns out to be this lowlife."

The audience laughed.

"This is a disgrace to our country. It shouldn't happen. And he should be prosecuted. Are you listening to me back in Washington? He should be prosecuted!"

Grown men leapt to their feet and pumped their fists in the air, as the crowd roared with approval. They weren't rally-goers. They were worshippers.

"Bad things are going to happen to him," the president concluded. ". . . It's like a horrible, treasonous, horrible thing that you can do this and get away with it."

His comments were classic Trump incitement, a not-so-subtle *wink-nod* to followers that they should make "bad things" happen to his enemy. I'd gotten used to shrugging off his personal attacks and rhetorical excess. This was different. It felt insidious.

I agreed to do a CNN interview to explain my decision. The network ran a countdown clock in the corner of the screen, ticking off the minutes until my remote appearance with anchor Chris Cuomo. The hotel room dimmed as the sun went down, and the backdrop was an exposed brick wall and a bed. Unfortunately, the setup reinforced the image of a man who'd been in hiding.

When we went on air, Cuomo was firm but fair. He grilled me on why I'd misled Anderson Cooper. I explained my reasoning.

"We have seen over the course of four years that Donald Trump's preference is to use personal attacks and distractions to pull people away from criticisms of his record," I explained. "I wrote anonymously to deprive him of that opportunity and to force him to answer the questions on their merits."

The president's reaction to my revelation was proof. He wasn't engaging me in a debate about the charges I'd made against him. Instead he resorted to petty slurs and wanted his followers to do the same.

The TV connection almost failed because the phone I was using to patch into the studio was overwhelmed with calls. MAGA supporters had found my number. With people around America tuned in, I tried to finish the discussion as the signal went in and out. Cuomo gave me the chance—in the waning days before the election—to explain what made Trump's re-election so dangerous.

When I got off the air, my phone was filled with text messages and emails. My voicemail inbox was maxed out, and I made the mistake of listening to several of them before bed.

"Miles, we are going to dox you," a guy with a Boston-like accent said, gloating. "You're not going to be able to walk down the street! You're an *anti-American*. Leave the country. You're not welcome here anymore."

"What you are doing to President Trump is disgusting. You are disgusting people. You're evil, and you're going to go down," a female caller threatened.

"Hi, Miles. I'm calling from South Texas. Just calling to see if you're a loyal person. . . . If you're working for the Communists, you're in big trouble."

"Your name's going to go viral because you are treasonous ilk to our country."

"Miles Taylor, what the fuck are you thinking going against Trump? You, my friend, are a piece of shit. You are a traitor."

"We will fight for President Trump until the very end because he loves us and he loves the country. . . . You're probably getting paid off somehow, some way."

"God help you, because you will deserve the wrath of hell. . . . I am disgusted by you all. And I think you will get what's coming to you. God willing."

"You duuuumb motherfucker," a man drawled in a lengthy, curse-filled diatribe that ended with "You know what? We will squash you like a fucking peanut, bitch. . . . You're done. You're done. . . . So eat a dick and die."

The texts were more concise: "Keep your head on a swivel, bitch."

Top Gun actor Miles Teller later sent me a message to say people had mistaken his name for mine.

"I've never woken up to more notifications on Twitter," he joked. "Even though all those hateful comments and death threats were actually meant for you and not me, it was nice to feel that important to people, if only just for a few [hours]."

A day-and-a-half later, I finally left my hotel room. I was out of food and needed to get breakfast. On the way back, I eyed someone standing next to a truck, watching me.

Rather than go back inside, I walked leisurely to my car. I went for a drive and tried to keep cool as the truck stayed on the same route. The man appeared to be tailing me.

I punched it, trying to lose him on unfamiliar streets. I pulled off onto the shoulder near the edge of town and the car whizzed past indifferently. I drove to a parking garage. No one followed. I thought I was being stalked at first, but it was more likely I was being an alarmist.

Then a friend in the Secret Service told me to get a protective detail—immediately. Based on the online chatter, he didn't think I was safe and suggested changing locations. I followed his advice, packed up my bags, and headed for Charlotte, booking a hotel there under a different name.

On the drive, a lawyer I knew connected me with a well-known

Silicon Valley billionaire. The man offered to supply a bodyguard for however long it was needed. I refused at first, but his team insisted on helping however they could. I was on the phone with a security firm before I got to my next stop.

"Hang tight, my friend," an executive protection coordinator said. "We'll have you covered soon."

Running out of money, I made sure my accommodations were cheap. The hotel room smelled like a spilled milkshake dried out on concrete. Settling in for the night, I picked up the rubber doorstop holding the bathroom entrance open and jammed it under the front door. Then I wedged an angled chair under the handle to be safe. I loaded my gun and placed it under the pillow next to me.

There's a difference between being "pursued" and being "hunted." For months I'd dealt with pursuers. People looked me up to send mocking messages or smears, and I got used to it.

Hunting is different. That's when someone wants you dead. And in the eyes of some rabid supporters, Donald Trump had turned me into a hunting trophy.

Still, I thought a bodyguard sounded like overkill. As I lay in the hotel, I was confident I could defend myself and that the threats would subside eventually, although the words were still on a loop in my head. *Bad things are going to happen to him. . . .*

It turned out that Trump was right. Bad things were about to happen.

PART II

In the early days of the pandemic, the President of the United States tweeted, "LIBERATE MICHIGAN!" Trump was responding to the controversy over stay-at-home orders. He was at odds with Michigan governor Gretchen Whitmer, who enforced strict policies while health officials scrambled to develop a vaccine. Eerily, he tied his rallying cry to gun rights.

"Save your great 2nd Amendment. It is under siege!" he added in a series of messages urging voters to "liberate" other states, too.

His supporters listened. In the weeks and months that followed, a dozen men in the Midwest started talking about a kinetic plan of action. They chatted on encrypted messaging apps and gathered in discreet locations in rural Michigan and Wisconsin throughout 2020 to develop their plot, including organizing several live-fire exercises.

Meeting on the edge of a lush green farm one day, the men suited up in the summer sun. They strapped on bulletproof vests and combat boots, adding extra loaded magazines of ammunition to their tactical belts. The mock attack commenced. Bobbing and weaving between obstacles, they fired dark gray assault weapons at homemade targets and coordinated their movements.

The "Wolverine Watchmen," as some called themselves, ratcheted up planning as the election drew closer. After meetings in the basement of a vacuum repair shop in Grand Rapids, they settled on a target: the Michigan governor. The men decided to kidnap the state's leader, and maybe kill her.

The militants explored mounting an assault near the governor's vacation home along the placid waters of Lake Michigan. Scouts traveled to the area, taking pictures of her home and identifying a bridge nearby as a potential attack site. They could detonate the structure at just the right moment. One group explored bomb construction, while another calculated the response times of local police.

When the FBI disrupted the plot in October 2020, it was far along the path to execution.

I remember seeing the news break from the campaign trail. The attack planning looked similar to complex, coordinated terrorist plots I'd seen hatched by groups like al Qaeda overseas. The case proved what many of us had been saying in the national security community—that the president was cultivating a dangerous terror threat environment in America's own backyard.

THE NEXT TRUMP WILL EXACERBATE POLITICAL VIOLENCE AND PUSH THE NATION TO THE BRINK OF A SECOND CIVIL WAR.

After the Michigan terror plot came to light, I caught up with Sue Gordon, the former deputy director of national intelligence under Donald Trump, over the phone. She had spent decades monitoring the stability of foreign governments inside the CIA and knew the indicators of political deterioration as well as anyone. Specifically, I wanted to know what the implications would be for democratic stability during the presidency of "Trump 2.0" or a MAGA successor.

Gordon answered in the language of a seasoned intelligence analyst, who prognosticates in terms of "low, medium, and high" confidence. Spy assessments are based on data from sources in the field and the uncertainty level of information they don't have.

"I would assess with 'low confidence' that the United States reaches its three hundredth birthday in any recognizable form," she stated without emotion, using the distant civic anniversary of 2076 as a marker.

Gordon elaborated on her dire forecast. Her pessimism wasn't because the Next Trump would succeed in breaking every democratic guardrail, per se. But in *attempting* to do so, he or she would stoke unprecedented division in the country and set off a slow turn toward despotism.

"People don't trust government institutions anymore or each other," she said, "and when the world gets tumultuous, they're more open to authoritarianism."

That's where it becomes a self-fulfilling prophecy. As public trust breaks down, social disorder goes up. Some people run to the safety of a populist strongman to protect the country from the chaos. Antidemocratic leaders then stoke further discord to justify retaining power, under the false pretense of maintaining "law and order." That, in turn, increases the potential for widespread armed conflict.

The process can take decades to unfold. If history is any guide, though, it might come to a head suddenly, with the literal pull of a trigger. And the odds of that happening in the not-too-distant future are historically high.

Political assassinations and civil unrest will become more likely.

According to U.S. Capitol Police, in the five years after Donald Trump was elected in 2016, the number of recorded threats against members of Congress increased more than 400 percent, to 9,625 in 2021. Lawmakers told news outlets that they were living in a state of fear and some were changing their votes for safety reasons. Many representatives retired after Trump's presidency, publicly citing the danger to their families.

We are witnessing what appears to be the largest spike in threats to U.S. public servants in modern history. In terms of volume, it's worse than the chatter we saw in the period following the September 11, 2001, terrorist attacks on the United States. The list of near-death incidents is growing.

The year after Trump left office, a man showed up outside the home of Representative Pramila Jayapal, allegedly brandishing a firearm and threatening to kill her. After a campaign event against MAGA Republican Mike Lee, independent U.S. Senate candidate Evan McMullin was reportedly chased by a man in a truck holding a pistol. And in November 2022, a man broke into the home of House Speaker Nancy Pelosi with the hope of killing the woman second in line to the presidency. She wasn't there. Instead the suspect beat her husband close to the edge of his life.

The MAGA movement's embrace of antigovernment rhetoric and violence toward public officials is elevating the risk of political assassinations. The invective is broadcast openly on the far right.

"When do we get the guns?" a young man asked to applause at a large gathering of nationally known conservative activists in late 2021. "That's not a joke. . . . I mean, literally, where's the line? How many elections are they going to steal before we kill these people?"

The danger doesn't stop with national figures. A survey by the Brennan Center for Justice found that one in three local election officials felt unsafe on the job. Half of that cohort said they'd received threats. Community leaders say they're getting death threats with regularity.

The Trump presidency unleashed a domestic extremism pandemic that swept the country. We are still dealing with it today, and it will lay the predicate for future civil unrest under the Next Trump. The surge is being driven by many of the conspiracy theories referenced earlier, such as the Great Replacement Theory, QAnon, and the Big Lie. Don't believe me. Just look at the data.

During Trump's first year in office, the FBI investigated roughly one thousand domestic terrorism cases. I remember writing congressional testimony on the subject. The number was shocking because—for the first time in my career—the volume of domestic terrorism cases was roughly equal to foreign terrorism cases. There were as many white supremacist and antigovernment plots as there were ISIS militant schemes monitored by authorities. At the time, DHS officials privately warned that the president's rhetoric and permissive attitude toward militant groups could drive an uptick in violent attack plots.

Then the caseload almost tripled. The year Donald Trump left office, FBI Director Christopher Wray told Congress that the Bureau was investigating almost three thousand domestic terrorism cases. DHS called it the number one threat to the United States. The "Global War on Terror" that had driven so many of us into public service after 9/11 officially shifted from foreign deserts to hometown streets—like the vacuum repair shop where potential assassins hatched a plot against the Michigan governor.

I call this an extremism pandemic because it's spreading beyond the fringes and into the mainstream.

The University of Chicago's Project on Security and Threats released a shocking study in 2022 that found Americans were more favorable toward political violence than in any time in recent memory. The survey revealed that 10 percent of American adults—or roughly 25 million people—agreed with the statement that the "use of force to restore former President Trump to the White House is justified."

Respondents didn't fit the stereotype of uninformed backwater country types. The majority lived in urban areas and reported consuming cable news and mainstream media. What set them apart from the rest of the population was that around half or more of those polled believed in conspiracy theories like QAnon and the Great Replacement.

What's more, support for violence has spread beyond just the political right wing. A survey by the COVID States Project found that one in four Americans believe violence against the government is "definitely" or "probably" justified. Liberals and conservatives agree in roughly the same numbers. The researchers compared the results to other periods of instability in places like Northern Ireland, Spain, and in the United States in the 1960s and '70s. They found that "community support for violence" was the warning sign. When people believed physical attacks were justified, all they needed was a "spark"—a major assassination or violent incident. Then the situation would explode.

In that sense, America is a powder keg.

Under the leadership of the Next Trump, nationwide discord could lead to a literal fracturing of the country once more.

Former U.S. president Ulysses S. Grant spoke to a group of military veterans in 1875, a decade after the Union and the Confederacy fought over the future of the country. Grant offered a prophecy about what might happen if America was split in two again. The divergence wouldn't be North versus South.

"If we are to have another contest in the near future of our national existence," he offered, "I predict that the dividing line will not be Mason and Dixon's, but between patriotism and intelligence on the one side, and superstition, ambition, and ignorance on the other."

In the wake of the Trump presidency, the term "civil war" that often gets thrown around in politics has taken on all-too-literal meaning.

Jason Van Tatenhove invoked the shadow of national conflict in testimony on Capitol Hill in July 2022. The former spokesman for the Oath Keepers, a pro-Trump militia group, quit the organization because of its support for violence.

During questioning, Representative Jamie Raskin asked Van Tatenhove why the head of the Oath Keepers wanted Donald Trump to invoke the Insurrection Act in 2020. The ex-spokesman responded that it was because they wanted Trump to use the military to remain in power, regardless of the election outcome.

"This could have been the spark that started a new civil war," Van Tatenhove said matter-of-factly. "We need to stop mincing words and just call things what they are. It was going to be an armed revolution."

A month after his testimony, something chilling happened.

The FBI raided ex-President Trump's home in search of missing classified documents. Talk of "civil war" exploded on social media. Twitter posts with the term skyrocketed nearly 3,000 percent in the hours after the raid, and the same happened on conservative sites, where "civil war" and "lock and load" became trending topics. Media monitors saw a doubling in usage of the phrase on radio and podcasts, according to *The New York Times*, as the president's allies equated the law-enforcement action with a declaration of war.

If I've learned anything in counterterrorism, it's that you should listen to the other side. You don't assume what they'll do or what they believe. You listen carefully to their words and take them seriously.

Several years after 9/11, I picked up a copy of *Messages to the World: The Statements of Osama bin Laden* and kept it on my desk. The terrorist leader of al Qaeda had laid out his plans and intentions—extensively—in the years leading up to the attack and afterward. Many observers made false assumptions about bin Laden's motivations and kept underestimating him, which resulted in costly setbacks in the effort to counter the group. Yet bin Laden's own words proved to be a fairly reliable guide to the group's anti-imperialist quest and messianic aims.

Similarly, domestic extremists have made their goals clear. Rebellion. Civil war. Secession. They believe that our democracy is so damaged and that the other side is so evil that conflict is inevitable. They are preparing for it, and in doing so, they might actually precipitate it.

The actual numbers are striking. Over 50 percent of self-described "strong Republicans" reported believing that civil war was "likely" in the next ten years in the United States, according to polling by *The*

Economist and YouGov two years after Trump left office. Some want to manifest it. During the same period, 66 percent of Republicans in the South said they supported "leaving the United States and forming a new country"—i.e., seceding from the Union. Only 20 percent of Democrats felt the same way, according to the poll by Bright Line Watch.

Two leading academics put together a risk measurement for political instability. Peter Turchin and Jack Goldstone (who previously led a CIA task force on the subject and developed a model that claimed to predict civil wars and democratic collapse with over 80 percent accuracy) developed the "political stress indicator," or PSI. According to the two researchers, the chart today looks similar to how it did in the 1860s.

"If Trump had been reelected, we would have had a civil war," a former Senate-confirmed Trump official said to me. "By that I mean, not artillery divisions firing at each other across an open field—but extreme, continuous civil unrest. Massive numbers of people killed or injured in said unrest."

He predicted it would happen under another MAGA presidency.

"It will be a rolling or creeping civil war. There will be secession movements. Whether those will succeed or fail is unclear, but there will be movements in that direction. There will be a legal state of war between the federal and state governments."

It doesn't help that GOP leaders are amplifying the civil war talk. "We need a national divorce," wrote Representative Marjorie Taylor Greene. "We need to separate by red states and blue states and shrink the federal government. Everyone I talk to says this."

When it comes to dividing America, the Next Trump will probably receive help from the outside. America's enemies are keen to see the country split in two. According to Joan O'Hara, Trump's former chief of staff on the National Security Council, rival nations will seek to make it a reality.

"Our foreign adversaries are taking advantage of political and cultural polarization in the U.S.," O'Hara noted. "Indeed, they're stoking tensions. During my time at the White House, intelligence indicated that adversaries intentionally fostered discord on both the right and the left. . . . It's about causing internal conflict. If you can get us to tear each

other down, it's much better for you as an adversary than investing resources in doing it."

★   ★   ★

What can we do about it? Traditionally, the citizenry would be viewed
as the final guardrail of democracy. The people themselves are the ones
who choose government leaders and ultimately decide whether the
country remains united. But I believe their ability to save the republic
from self-destruction depends on something more fundamental, something which is also at risk.

Chapter 8

THE ANGEL

But what is government itself, but the greatest of all reflections on human nature? If men were angels, no government would be necessary. If angels were to govern men, neither external nor internal controls on government would be necessary.

—JAMES MADISON, FEDERALIST NO. 51, 1788

PART I

November 3, 2020

"**M**eet Dennis," Bill said, gesturing at the imposing figure emerging from the driver's seat of the SUV.

A handsome black man in his early fifties, Dennis looked more like an NFL linebacker than a security agent. He towered over his boss, Bill.

"Good to meet you, sir," Dennis said, shaking my hand, which was compressed within his like a child's.

Bill finished the briefing.

"Effective noon today, your protective detail starts. Dennis will be with you wherever you go. He's able to call backup if it's needed," he explained. Bill was a former Secret Service agent who now managed private security operations for celebrities and foreign dignitaries. Dennis was a former Marine.

I certainly couldn't afford a bodyguard. But thanks to a Good Samaritan (who ironically wished to remain anonymous), I had a team providing digital and physical overwatch amid the death threats. The assignment was open-ended, basically until things cooled down.

I told Bill I'd spent a lot of time around Secret Service agents, so he didn't need to tell me the usual: *Don't distract Dennis while he's scanning for threats. Don't make plans without telling Dennis in advance. Don't even go for a walk without Dennis.* But he felt compelled to add a note about something that peeved agents.

"Just don't ask him to pick up luggage or a bag or anything like that. He needs to remain hands-free while he's with you." What he was really saying was that Dennis needed to be able to pull out his gun.

"Of course," I told him.

Bill left, and my new bodyguard studied me, as if waiting for orders.

"Well, uh, I'm going to go back up to the apartment for a bit," I told Dennis. "No need to join. I'll text you my plans for the day. Really appreciate what you're doing."

"Yes, sir. I'll be in the car, sir," he said.

I went back inside the building, up fourteen floors, and into the lifeless apartment. It was Election Day 2020, one of the most important days of my life, but I didn't have much to do.

I had tried to play the role of happy warrior on the outside, rallying the REPAIR alliance of GOP figures for a burst of last-minute statements and advertisements against Trump. But the Anonymous revelation had created too many distractions. What I had wanted to do on voting day—leave the apartment and go door-knocking to boost turnout for Biden—was a bad idea, the security people said. Better to stay put.

What they didn't realize was that in the false comfort of the "safe house" that night, someone would try to put a gun to my head.

"The counting continues."

Going public in the social media age is a dignity-destroying onslaught. Everyone shoots their opinion at you. They take aim with a grudge or belittling comment, fire, and move on to the next target, indifferent to the human toll.

I woke earlier that day, admitting to myself that I missed anonymity. I was becoming a punching bag in a political war, not a person. If you think years in D.C. prepared me to take the blows, you're wrong. In the final days of the campaign it got worse. Every swing I took at Trump resulted in a thousand face shots back, to the point that I couldn't look at Twitter anymore without seeing trolls spreading lies:

"Miles Taylor championed Trump's worst policies!"

"He's doing it for fame!"

"He's cashing in!"

In reality, I had little income. I had followed through on my plans to pledge almost all the royalties from *A Warning* to charity, and in weaker moments, I wondered whether I should have forfeited the potential of a million-dollar payday. Meanwhile, I was still on unpaid hiatus from work.

Republican friends in Washington were hesitant to be seen with me. I was radioactive in GOP circles. A White House aide—whose wedding I had attended as a groomsman—went radio silent, while others who shared my strong views about the president sent bizarre messages, pretending to be aghast.

"Very surprised by what you did," a former colleague texted. "And disappointed. I never thought of you as sneaky. Or underhanded. Or as a betrayer."

Inside the administration, the woman had privately spoken of her disgust toward Trump, but now she distanced herself, lest I threaten her MAGA credentials.

The situation affected my wider family. My brothers and sisters passed along supportive messages from friends and strangers, but I knew they

were still getting hate mail. Eventually the FBI and multiple police juris-
dictions got involved, after far-right extremists and stalkers shared my
siblings' street addresses, pictures taken outside their homes, and photos
of children in our family.

"Free speech" didn't feel so free anymore.

When I got back from North Carolina, an ex-military buddy reached
out to suggest wearing a Kevlar vest in public.

"You think it's that bad?" I asked.

"Yes," he said, assuring me the garment would be discreet. If I wore
loose-fitting clothes, no one would notice.

Over beers at his place, I tried one on. My clothes were slim-fitting,
not loose. As I struggled to conceal the bulky body armor, a button
popped off my shirt.

"Yeah, there's no way I'm doing this," I told him. However, I kept my
concealed pistol with me everywhere I went, tucked in a holster inside
my waistband, even after the bodyguard started.

I texted Dennis his first afternoon on duty to let him know I was
going to get lunch.

"I'll be down in about 5–10," I wrote.

"Copy standing by," he responded immediately.

It was the perfect fall day. Sunlight broke the clouds, and a cool
breeze carried the dry smell of autumn. Trees lining the sidewalk
glowed a vivid orange and yellow, punctuated by occasional red.

The linebacker waited for me outside the building in sunglasses,
hands folded in front of him. I had assured Bill I knew how to interact
with a security team, but I had never been the actual protectee, just the
staffer. On the way to a nearby taco joint, I didn't know whether to walk
alongside Dennis, in front of him, or behind him as we made our way
out into the world. He answered the question with his body language.

Dennis let me pass and then trailed behind. The silence of his presence over my shoulder felt awkward, so I made a few phone calls on the
walk. I rang two separate lawyers who were helping me on different
cases.

The first was an attorney preparing to defend me against whatever lawsuit Donald Trump might file. "He should be prosecuted!" Trump raged, calling on the Justice Department to come after me.

"Don't worry," the lawyer assured me, "if it happens, the lawsuit would probably be frivolous. Your comments about him are fully protected by the First Amendment."

It was still the President of the United States and the Justice Department I was facing. The prospect of being sued by the government—and the financial cost—was intimidating. The lawyer could tell I was anxious and changed the subject.

"How are you feeling about tonight? Doing any TV?" he asked, unwittingly touching another sore subject.

"I'm cautiously optimistic," I told him, knowing it wasn't how I was really feeling about the election. "No media. I'll probably just watch the returns from home."

The truth was that CNN had effectively benched me after the revelation about my true identity. They clearly didn't want me on air telling the story of the final days of the election when I was so wrapped up in it personally and in the president's cross hairs. Trump and his aides were relentless in calling on Google and CNN to let me go.

"They should fire, shame, and punish everybody . . . associated with this FRAUD on the American people!" the president declared in a tweet storm about the Anonymous revelation, tagging both of my employers.

This was my last day on unpaid leave from the tech company. Tomorrow, the day after the election, I was set to return to work. I had a call scheduled with a Google executive that evening in preparation for coming back on board. I was ready to return to work and step back from the political fray.

In the meantime, I made what I expected would be among my last public comments before going dark again. I wanted to flag my remarks for a second attorney—the one who was reviewing threats made against my family. I called the veteran former prosecutor next.

"I put out a statement today," I told him, as Dennis continued to stroll behind me. "I'll send it to you in case any of the MAGA wackos get spun up about it."

Earlier that day, *Politico* had reported that Trump was making ominous comments about the fairness of the election. He was laying the groundwork for contesting the vote. They quoted a strongly worded statement I'd provided:

"'For months the President has questioned the integrity of the election, and now at the 11th hour, he's signaling prematurely that he'll declare victory before the result is certain, setting the stage for further discord,' said Miles Taylor, the former chief of staff at the Department of Homeland Security who recently unmasked himself as Anonymous, the internal Trump critic who published a scathing op-ed in *The New York Times.* 'I think it's destructive to the democratic process. I think it could potentially lead to civil unrest and even violence in the country, and it's wildly irresponsible for a president to do.'"

I sent a screenshot to my lawyer for awareness. When I tweeted or spoke to news organizations, inevitably I received a swell of angry responses from the right, most of them innocuous, some of them darkly threatening. My lawyer said to stay on the lookout, and I got off the line.

At the taco spot, I asked Dennis if he wanted anything. He shook his head and eyed the seated patrons skeptically. To me, none of them appeared ready to abandon their burritos and attack a perfect stranger.

On the walk back, I tried to reply to a few messages on my work phone, but the email was down. I pocketed the device to handle later. Technically, I didn't have obligations to respond to anything until 12:01 a.m., but I was stir crazy and needed something to do.

When we got to the apartment building, I told Dennis that I planned to go to the grocery store mid-afternoon. I turned to head inside.

"Yes, sir," he said. "Which grocery store?"

"Um," I stopped. "Probably the Safeway close by."

"Can you send me the address?"

"Yeah, of course." I turned again to go.

"And what time?"

"Maybe 3?"

"Okay, sir. I will stage the vehicle in the parking garage on G1 at 1500."

"I'm fine just coming out front here." I gestured to the street.

"I'd prefer not, sir. We should load up in the garage."

"Okay," I said, getting his drift, and went upstairs.

When I came down to the parking garage later, Dennis had the vehicle parked closely to the elevator bank and was already standing with the back passenger door open, ready for me to enter. I did. He closed the door firmly and got into the driver's seat.

On the way, we deviated from the main thoroughfare and into a winding little neighborhood. This was not the route Google Maps had recommended to get to the nearest Safeway. I gently corrected Dennis's directions.

"Sir, I'm supposed to vary our routes for security," he explained.

Nauseous in the back seat, I decided not to protest. It was the first day. At the grocery, I told Dennis I was happy to go in alone, but he came in anyway. If the goal was to blend in, we failed.

The place was as busy as it was before the Super Bowl. Everyone was buying food for election watch parties. I was shopping for a night inside alone.

Customers gawked at the six-foot-six bodyguard and he gawked back, daring them with his planted feet to come near the produce section, as I bagged iceberg lettuce and celery. I tried to act oblivious, but I still felt the eyes pointed in my direction. The checkout line was weirder, as Dennis stood and faced the people behind us while I paid. They looked rightfully confused.

We rolled a full cart of bags out to the car. He opened the back hatch of the maroon SUV, and I remembered Bill's counsel. I told Dennis I could handle all of it. One by one, I filled the trunk. He surveyed the parking lot like we were on a safari and vigilant about predators. The winding route home felt like a safari, too.

Back at the apartment, I hopped on my catch-up call with Google, and I noticed several people were in the virtual meeting room. Names I didn't recognize. My colleague's tone was oddly stiff.

"Miles," he said, "I want to welcome someone from People Operations to join us on this phone call."

My heart sank into my stomach. He didn't need to say anything else.

The woman introduced herself, and while I didn't catch her title, it didn't matter. I had been on the other end of enough of these phone calls to know right away what this was.

I was being let go. There wasn't any use in protesting or asking for answers. The HR shop wouldn't be able to provide any.

I was disappointed in myself. I hadn't seriously expected this outcome, yet the political turmoil was obviously unappealing for a major company. After all, they had no way of knowing if Trump would win or not. If he did, another four years of harboring an anti-Trump fugitive would be risky, particularly because it was my job to liaise with the executive branch.

They had to make a decision before midnight, before I was back on payroll. With seven hours to go, they cut me loose. The call was formal and brief, and the company execs were gracious.

"I've really enjoyed my time at Google." I fumbled for words when it was my turn. "Sorry it has to be this way. You all were amazing to work with, even during the rocky start."

"Thanks, Miles," a woman I'd never met said. "We'll mail you a postmarked envelope so you can return your hardware."

"Of course. Thanks."

When I was off the line, I sat still. Another one of those deafening silences filled the apartment, the kind followed by a rumble on the train tracks. My chest was tight as I stared through the smudged glass of the dining room table at my running shoes. I needed to get up.

I searched the unopened grocery bags on the counter. When I found the olives, I opened the jar, poured two thimbles of brine into a drinking cup, and scooped a handful of ice from the freezer and dropped it into the glass. I filled it with gin, then splashed in vermouth. I took a long drink.

Staying in the apartment alone was unwise, so as I sipped my second makeshift martini, I decided to go to a friend's election party in D.C.

I changed clothes. The bulk of my wardrobe formed an island on the bedroom floor, and standing on one of the promontories, I scouted a pair of jeans and a shirt. The grip of my pistol poked out from the holster clipped into a pair of Levis. I left the gun and took the denim.

Before walking out, I realized I was supposed to give Dennis a heads-up first. I told him about the plan.

"Sir," he texted back, "if it's OK with you, I'll pick you up in the garage at the same door I dropped you earlier."

"Perfect," I told him. "Sorry for the short notice . . ."

"No problem, sir."

Downstairs, Dennis was ready again. Car staged, door open. We drove into Washington just after sunset, as the last light raked the sky. Dennis said nothing.

The Capitol Hill row house was a block behind the U.S. Supreme Court, and I remembered as we rolled up that my friend's place was next door to Steve Bannon's. The two shared a tiny alleyway. I scoured the property through the car window because I had no interest in stumbling into a MAGA get-together by accident. It appeared Bannon's lights were out.

"Sir, would you like me to come in with you?" Dennis asked.

"No, no. It's fine. Just checking something out. I'll text you when I'm done."

"Yes, sir."

I got out and went up the steps, knocked, and waited. Most of these people hadn't seen me in months. Since I went public, since I went on the campaign trail, since I unmasked myself. Since . . .

"Hey! Good to see you! Where is Anabel?" My friend greeted me, not knowing the news.

"Eh, she stayed home. Too worried about the outcome tonight." I deflected.

"Well, come on in. We're just getting started."

A dozen people milled about drinking beers and eating, most of them journalists. Everyone was hoping to see Trump lose. I knew some of them, and the ones I didn't seemed to know me.

"Miles, right?" a large man in his early forties asked. He was a reporter at a major newspaper.

"Yes," I said, shaking his hand.

"You've been busy!"

"Yeah, something like that. But I'm looking forward to all of this being over."

He offered me his seat and a beer. I obliged. Jake Tapper's voice filled the room after CNN declared that my home state, Indiana, had been called for Donald Trump. Soon polls closed in Florida, Georgia, North Carolina, and Ohio, four crucial battlegrounds that could affect the outcome—and among the most pivotal states of the night. The network said they were too early to call. Opinion polls favored Biden in three of them.

We drank and watched for a few hours. Not much happened. Then bad news arrived in rapid succession. The *New York Times* "needle"— which showed who was favored to win each state—started pointing Trump's direction.

North Carolina. "Probably Trump," the *Times* predicted.

Georgia. "Probably Trump."

Florida. "Very likely Trump."

Analysts were shocked. Biden had an edge in a lot of the earlier Florida polls, but as the votes were counted, it wasn't even close. Trump was outperforming in traditionally Democratic areas. Experts speculated that there might have been a nationwide "polling error" that artificially favored Biden, because in all of these key places the race was trending toward Trump.

The president's chances of winning a second term were starting to look good as the evening wore on. We drank more.

"Don't worry, the counting continues," a lone optimist advised.

Meanwhile, NBC reported that the atmosphere was "great" in the White House's East Room, where hundreds had gathered to watch the results. Officials with the Trump campaign were confident they'd clinch those three swing states leaning his direction. They were waiting on more data out of Ohio but felt good. We did a round of shots for consolation.

"I should be wrapped here in about 20," I texted Dennis. I wanted to go home.

The reporter who had offered me his seat was as tipsy as I was.

"Well," he said, "I guess we plan for another four years of our adrenal glands being shot, but I don't know if I have any adrenaline left."

"I'll probably be in an orange jumpsuit," I replied.

"Maybe 15," I texted Dennis.

"Copy, I'm here," he wrote back. "Staged."

I left without saying goodbye, pretending to slip out to make a phone call. On the way home, the commentary on my newsfeed was so bleak I sent a picture of the screen to a friend.

"I don't understand my own country," wrote former CIA officer and political commentator John Sipher. Beneath that . . .

"The incredible thing is that, with 230,000 dead from COVID, this is where we are as a country," posted columnist Susan Glasser. Beneath that . . .

"Wtf. That's it. That's the tweet," wrote Asha Rangappa, a legal and national security analyst. And on and on.

We arrived once more at the Virginia high-rise. Dennis pulled into the concrete parking garage, circling deeper until we arrived at the lowest level. He opened my door by the elevator bank.

"Thank you," I told him. "Have a good night."

"Good night, sir. Let me know if you need anything," he said. He would be clocking out soon. A night shift would be on call.

I made another martini in the apartment and watched the returns on mute, scanning the subtitles for good news. There wasn't much. Florida, Georgia, and North Carolina seemed all but assured for the Trump team.

Then at 12:01 a.m., news outlets projected Trump would win the fourth swing state of the bunch. Ohio. Renowned pollster Nate Silver reminded readers on his popular *FiveThirtyEight* blog that there were still other states hanging in the balance.

"But it's certainly not a great sign for Biden," he wrote. As the counting progressed, Trump signaled that he was prepared to claim victory. I turned off the TV.

★ ★ ★

In the early morning hours of November 4, I was drunk. Negative thoughts rolled at me in waves, as I sat on the outer peninsula of clothing on the bedroom floor doing my own tallying. I was counting up and down, trying to neatly and numerically sum up the moment. I was proud of myself for conjuring an opening cadence.

One. The number of days since I'd been let go from my job.

Two. The weeks since my unmasking, which had magnified the online hate.

Three. The months since I had to leave my home.

Four. The years since I gambled my reputation on the false hope of an "Axis of Adults."

Five. I didn't have a five.

So I skipped to six. That was the number of relationship anniversaries Anabel and I shared before our untimely end.

Okay, now I was stuck.

The mental accounting of self-pity wasn't necessarily about a Trump second term—either way, my life would never be the same—but I survived and thrived on having control. I was starting to feel powerless when my thoughts drifted to a darker place.

Fourteen. The number of floors above street level. I pondered the distance to the ground, which was more than enough.

Twenty. The exact number of rounds of ammunition. I found the pistol lying in the pile, and my thumb was raw from loading and unloading the clip. The cartridges popped out with a satisfying metallic *snap.*

Sixty-plus. I hadn't refilled my prescriptions lately, so I was guessing. But it seemed like a good estimate for the number of pills on the nightstand.

Like brand-name cereals in a grocery aisle, I weighed my options. I drank the martini and the remnants of a warm beer. A banging noise outside the bedroom interrupted.

I brought the gun as I got up to see who was at the door. No one was visible through the blurry peephole. I unlatched the deadbolt and slid back the chain lock, cautiously peering out and keeping the gun in the apartment. The hallway was empty. I locked everything and returned to the bedroom.

In reality, there wasn't any need to fret about an intruder. The most dangerous person—the someone who would try to put a gun to my head that night—was me. There wasn't anything a bodyguard could do about it.

I fiddled with the cold cartridges again on the floor, wondering about the collateral damage. What if the anticipation of the recoil—or blowback—caused me to flinch and miss, and only cripple myself? That's when I realized something.

The bullets were not hollow-point. I had used up all of my home defense rounds at the range and had only the round-nose ones my friend gave me. Whether or not I misfired, the projectile might not be fatal and it would probably travel through the wall into another apartment, which also wasn't good.

Fuck. I couldn't help but let out a laugh. I didn't even have the right ammo to kill myself.

Sometime after three in the morning, I moved my watery martini to the nightstand and lay on the bed with my phone, a distraction from the morbid musings. A lot of people online were talking about mail-in ballots and the crucial state of Arizona, which hadn't yet been called. The election wasn't over.

Hundreds of unread messages beckoned in my social media apps. The majority of them were days and weeks old, from a time when I was trying hard to tune out unsolicited messages and too worn down for hate mail. For some reason I decided to open my inboxes. The notes weren't what I had expected.

"I know you will probably never get a moment to read this," a New York woman direct-messaged me, "but I wanted to write to you anyway." She explained that she lived with her mother, and they had watched me on CNN throughout the campaign talking about my time in the Trump administration.

"The night you said that you basically had to leave your position . . . because you couldn't live with yourself staying in such a problematic situation, my mom and I cried and had a long discussion," she said. "We applauded you and understood your explanation of 'Anonymous' and anyone who listens with an open mind would realize you didn't want the story to be about 'you,' it was about the 'facts.'"

I scrolled to another.

"Hi Miles! I'm the mom of a 7-year old Miles in———" (I'll leave out her hometown). "I showed him the recent article about you in the NYT and he wrote you a letter about the meaning of your name. . . . I'd love to actually send it to you—for him, and for you to keep nearby, as you go forth saying truths. Lord knows there will be plenty of people slinging nasty things back at you; keep it as one more reminder that so many of us have your back. . . . We need people like you."

They were interspersed with sillier comments.

"The most handsome Trump-Troll ever!" a user wrote.

"Your hair is so much better post Trump," one teased. I appreciated it nonetheless, and I read a few more as I got drowsy.

I usually slept with the gun inches away on the nightstand. Before I turned out the light, I released the magazine from the grip and pulled back the slide, coaxing the pistol to spit out a bullet onto the desk. I slid the weapon under the bed and went to sleep.

"We came home safely . . ."

Chalky and dry. That's how my mouth and my hands felt when I woke up. I staggered to the fridge for water, forgetting at first about the election. Back in bed, I saw that the contest was still undeclared. Arizona and Pennsylvania were shaping up to be the deciding states, but they hadn't been called for Biden or Trump.

A text message buzzed. "Good Morning, Sir. I'm on deck."

Shit. I was supposed to go to my old place on Capitol Hill to move out remaining belongings. I felt too hungover. I told Dennis there was a logistical mixup, and I wouldn't be able to go until 2:30 p.m.

"We're going to have to adjust fire and head over there then. That OK?" I wrote back.

"Sir, I'm here for you," he said. "Time isn't an issue, ever."

I don't know why, but the comment made me pause, like Dennis sensed I was going through a tough time. I shook it off. We'd only known each other a day.

I showered and put myself together for the drive back into the District, throwing on sunglasses to cover bloodshot eyes. I wasn't talkative on the ride, and the unsmiling bodyguard followed my lead. We pulled up to the blue-brick row house just after three in the afternoon. Dennis parked on the street in front and stayed in the car.

Inside the lights were off. The place smelled like fresh cardboard boxes, and the Reconstruction-era floorboards creaked loudly, as if someone else were there with me, but I was alone surveying the accumulation of things. The oddest aspects of the place jumped out. An empty fireplace. A guest room with a perfectly made bed. The memories were small land mines planted everywhere, so I resolved not to linger. I carried the crates of my belongings out to the SUV, and Dennis jumped out of the driver's seat to open the back hatch.

"Here, give me that," he insisted.

"No, it's all right," I said, but Dennis took the box anyway.

We took turns walking into the house and carrying duffel bags and boxes to the car. We got creative, tucking Christmas decorations and winter coats into the spaces between the seats and on top of luggage until the vehicle was full. We ferried the collection back across the river to Virginia, riding again in silence, save for the clattering melody of trinkets whenever the car hit an uneven spot in the road.

Then Dennis started talking.

"I grew up around here," he said.

"Where at?" I asked to be polite, but I didn't want to chat.

"Maryland. The other direction."

"Oh, nice. Did you like it?"

"Home, or Maryland?"

"Either."

"I liked Maryland, not home. My dad was a mean guy. Mean guy. He had a bad temper and liked to take it out on me."

"I'm sorry," I said.

"Don't be, that's life, you know? I don't know if you've ever had someone wale on you, but they never seem to care what it is, so long as it's something. So I didn't take it personally. It was drugs and stuff."

He told me about how he moved out after his father passed away. Dennis lived on the streets as a teenager and struggled with substances before joining the Marines. He moved to Georgia, got married, and had kids, thinking life was stable. Then it was upended by his exit from the military and a difficult divorce. Dennis was forced to start over. This was his reset.

"Anyway sir, I read up about you. I usually leave my politics at the door. If someone hasn't said it to you lately though, I think you did the right thing. I'm sure it hasn't been easy. But there's something else to hustle for on the other side of it."

The sunglasses hid my eyes from view as they welled up.

"I really appreciate that, Dennis. Thank you."

"Yes, sir. Let me know if we have anything else planned for this evening."

His words sounded like a recommendation. We arrived at the high-rise and wound our way down into the garage with my belongings. I knew I shouldn't spend another evening alone, drinking, so I responded to someone who reached out to check up on me.

★ ★ ★

There was a loud banging on the door. Not quite a knock, more like kicking. Through the peephole, I made out the shape of a blond woman in leggings, an oversized winter jacket, and two armfuls of groceries. She looked impatient. I opened the door, and she walked right in.

"I'm making you blueberry pancakes. *And* hash browns. *And* bacon!" she announced, walking past me with her supplies. "You're welcome."

It was the morning of November 7, the third day Hannah had come by to check on me.

The day Dennis and I packed up boxes, Hannah texted to see how I was doing and if I wanted to grab food. I agreed. When I showed up at a Japanese restaurant to meet her that night, puffy face and red eyes, Hannah got way more than she bargained for.

"I've had some big life events lead to depressing places," Hannah told me over sushi. "And you had, like, six of them at the same time. I'm surprised you're even eating."

She checked on me for the next few days. Though we'd never had a particularly close friendship, I trusted her with the most sensitive information in government—and later—the secret about my identity. My reticence to personal questions collapsed quickly as Hannah pressed to see how far down the rabbit hole I'd gone.

I told her about the conversation with Dennis. People like him got dealt a bad hand and played it anyway, enduring life without thinking there was an option to exit. I felt awash in shame, like the specter of suicidal ideation was some selfish luxury I'd been contemplating. An easy way out.

We talked about it for hours. We talked about everything—social media harassment, breakups, anxiety and depression, the country, and what types of bad takeout I should order to fashion a grungier safe-house aesthetic. Hannah took the role of accidental counselor seriously.

But she also kept it light. When I confessed that I felt like I was drinking too much and might have an addiction problem, she didn't miss a beat.

"Miles, you know there's a really good Alcoholics Anonymous joke somewhere in there."

I laughed.

"That's a big deal for me to say that out loud," I told her. "So I'm gonna need some kind of confession from you in exchange."

"I've kept something to myself for a long time," she replied, looking into my eyes with the utmost somberness. "I have always, always wanted to be a redhead."

Hannah met Dennis and told him to get me out of the house more. One of the days, she proposed a short hike on Teddy Roosevelt Island to get fresh air, knowing I was anxious about the continued ambiguity surrounding the election. (Arizona had been called for Biden; now all eyes were on Pennsylvania.) The three of us trudged through the muddy paths realizing we'd all worn the wrong shoes.

I was partway out of my funk by the time she came over on Saturday morning.

Hannah smoked up the kitchen with pancakes and hash browns and bacon, while I did things I'd been putting off. I looked up how to file for unemployment, and I searched for my own apartment. Frankly, I didn't want to be holed up in a place that wasn't mine, and Hannah insisted a scenery change was needed. While I was scrolling through listings trying to find something affordable, she let out a gasp.

"Oh my god!" Hannah was looking at her phone in shock.

"What?" I looked up. She covered her mouth, and I worried someone had been shot.

"It's over," she said, reading to me from her phone. "Pennsylvania. 'NBC says . . . Biden is the projected winner.' We did it, Miles. You guys did it! It's over!"

Hearing those words got me. I hadn't cried in years, but for the second time in days, tears ran down my cheeks as Hannah walked over and hugged me at the dining room table. I covered my face as she sneaked a picture of me.

You could hear the news alert spreading outside. Within minutes, people cheered on the sidewalks below and drivers honked, again and again. An overwhelming sense of relief filled the sunny apartment.

"We have to go celebrate. Tell Dennis we're going down to the National Mall," she declared.

I called him.

"No, no, no, no," Dennis said. "Sir, there could be dangerous people who show up and want to ruin the party."

"Dennis, we're doing it," I told him, "whether you come with us or not."

On the ride over a few hours later, Hannah was reading me news and Twitter posts. Data suggested that Biden wouldn't have won if not for moderate Republican defectors. One poll showed 8 percent of people who voted for Trump in 2016 had flipped sides, voting for Biden in 2020. Easily the margin of victory.

"You all persuaded them!" Hannah exclaimed.

It was impossible to prove, but that had been my hope and the hope of many others who'd done the same. We wanted to give GOP voters a rationale to switch sides. And they did. In key swing states in 2020, the defectors were apparently enough—just barely enough—to tip the balance.

"Thank you, @MilesTaylorUSA for keeping the porch light on for us during these dark times," Hannah quoted. "We came home safely, and now it's up to the American people to continue Her fight for a fair Democracy."

"I don't think I can do more," I told her.

We arrived at the Lincoln Memorial just as the sun sank. Dennis tailed at a distance. Hannah and I walked around to the back of the memorial and sat on a marble ledge with our legs dangling off the side. The cloudless horizon just above the Potomac River was orange sorbet fading into plum.

We went to the other side and read the enormous inscriptions etched into opposite walls of the Memorial's interior. In between, Lincoln sat stoically. On one side, the Gettysburg Address is carved into stone. On the other, the former president's second inaugural address, which reads famously, "With malice toward none, with charity for all, with firmness in the right as God gives us to see the right, let us strive on to finish the work we are in to bind up the nation's wounds . . ."

Jubilant revelers strolled alongside the reflecting pool. We sat and watched them from the memorial steps. The last warm strokes of autumn were mirrored by the water, lighting Hannah's face and hair like a cigar. We smiled at each other, and she laid her head on my shoulder. A happy nervousness ran through me, which I hadn't felt in years.

"The nightmare is over," she sighed wistfully, harking back to Nixon's departure. She was wrong, unfortunately. For the next seventy-four days it got worse.

"The last line of defense . . ."

The momentary hope of the post-election period was soon replaced by fear and turmoil. Donald Trump rejected the results, claiming the election had been stolen. D.C.-watchers rolled their eyes at another Trump lie, but this was something different. Tens of millions of Americans bought the myth that their votes had been nullified, and the president launched an all-out effort to prevent the transfer of power by suing states, cajoling lawmakers, and pressuring officials to change vote tallies.

Our REPAIR alliance tried to stay active. We criticized Trump's last-minute purges of top officials, especially in the Pentagon, where the firings seemed designed to destabilize the government. Our cohort went on television and radio to refute Trump's claim the election was rigged. Part of me felt called to push back against what appeared to be a soft coup.

At the same time, I wanted to take a sabbatical from public engagement while I put my life back together. So I declined most media engagements. What's more, if I stayed in the fray, it would mean continuing to attract the attention of creeps, like the drunken patrons who heckled me as D.C. got more tense.

"Hey Anooooonymous, get your ass over here!" a guy hollered one night at a restaurant, as his buddies walked toward me pulling out cell phones to film the encounter.

Dennis stepped in to physically block them while I walked to the car. The scene repeated itself nights later when MAGA protesters interrupted dinner with friends.

"Sir, it's time to go," he implored me, as I offered my friends an apology for the commotion and for leaving early.

"SPOTTED," a line item in *Politico* read. "Miles Taylor at Mission Navy Yard with a private security guard." The photo was of me and Dennis exiting the scene.

I continued the search for a new place to live. Apartment hunting was an elaborate exercise, since the security people had advised me not to use my real name on rental applications. My previous address was already all over the web, and someone had recently mailed a hair-raising collage of personal photos—all somehow pulled from my private Instagram account—which arrived at my forwarding address in a soiled envelope. I supplied pseudonyms to property managers, filled out applications through a shell company, and offered up not-so-believable explanations for why I was touring buildings with a guy twice my size, who looked like a nightclub bouncer when he told strangers they couldn't ride the elevator with us.

"This is my boyfriend, Dennis," I informed one landlord, finally eliciting a grin from my stone-faced bodyguard.

On November 14, I had a dozen or so apartment tours lined up in downtown Washington. When I shared the list with Dennis in the morning, he balked.

"Sir, I think you need to cancel these," he said.

"What? No way. These are hot listings," I responded.

"There are protests planned in D.C. today. A lot of people are expected. I don't think it's a good idea, sir."

"No one will notice us."

Dennis was paranoid that I'd get followed, but I shrugged it off. I was eager to get out of the soulless Virginia suburbs and back to somewhere busier, somewhere I could be distracted.

When we got into Chinatown, I saw what Dennis was talking about. There were obvious Trump supporters everywhere. MAGA caps. Trump-Pence flags. American flags as capes, with Trump's name written across the stars and stripes. A truck was covered in the words "STOP THE STEAL! Trump 2020."

"Yeah, okay," I conceded. "I'll wear a hat."

We toured the apartments anyway, and I was glad I did. I got a great deal on a tiny but new unit a few blocks from the Senate side of Capitol Hill, near stores and restaurants.

Meanwhile, I reached out to my former colleague Chris Krebs. The slick-haired advisor I'd met on my first day at DHS ("Ride the wave," Chris advised) had stayed behind to run the DHS agency in charge of cybersecurity and election integrity. He needed to be vocal in countering Trump's falsehoods, though doing so would surely put him on a collision course with the White House.

I urged him to "simply speak the truth about the security of the election, fraud, disinformation, etc.," which fortunately Chris was already doing. "Goad them into firing you," I added.

Then the president did. He tied the dismissal directly to Chris's recent public assurances that there was "no evidence that any voting system deleted or lost votes, changed votes, or was in any way compromised."

"The recent statement by Chris Krebs on the security of the 2020 Election was highly inaccurate, in that there were massive improprieties and fraud," Trump tweeted. "Therefore, effective immediately, Chris Krebs has been terminated as Director of the Cybersecurity and Infrastructure Security Agency."

I was proud of him for standing up at such a crucial moment, while some of our other colleagues who'd stayed inside were silent. Chris was immediately on the receiving end of MAGA ire, and Trump-friendly outlets were giddy to tie us together to magnify the hate.

"Foes claim he's close to former DHS chief of staff Miles Taylor, who recently outed himself as 'Anonymous,'" the *New York Post* wrote. The president told DHS Secretary Chad Wolf "to fire Anonymous's best friend."

Soon after, Trump's campaign lawyer and former U.S. attorney Joe diGenova went on right-wing radio to say Chris should be executed.

"That guy is a class A moron," diGenova remarked. "He should be drawn and quartered. Taken out at dawn and shot." It led to more death threats, and Chris sued the Trump lawyer. (Four months later, diGenova issued a public apology.)

I rallied a cohort of former DHS officials to put out a declaration that none of us ever thought we'd need to sign.

"The President has wrongfully called into question the integrity and security of the 2020 U.S. election and is now inappropriately abusing his office to undermine the democratic process," we wrote. "He has also embarked on a spree of dismissals of senior national security officials. . . . Such behavior currently ranks among the most serious threats to the national security of the United States."

That week I moved into my new apartment and said goodbye to the safe house, hoping my own security situation was improving. Aside from getting accosted by a guy at an Ikea (whose repeated attempts to get in my face spiced up an otherwise boring day for Dennis), it was uneventful. The building was quiet and modern. A guard sat in the lobby.

After I moved in, I got a notification that I had received a package, which was strange. I hadn't given the address out to friends or family yet. Downstairs in the mail room, I fetched the shipment. Inside a grimy box, someone had sent me cheaply made winter clothing. No note. No return address. The package was followed by several more, including a glove, a knitted cap, and other assorted items.

The packages were all dated the same. November 14, 2020, the day we'd toured apartments during the first "Stop the Steal" rally. I should have taken Dennis's advice and stayed home that day. Someone had clearly followed me to the new address, despite painstaking efforts to keep it under wraps. Within days of move-in, the place didn't feel like a sanctuary. It was just another target.

Nevertheless, I decided to stop carrying my handgun for a while, for mental health reasons. I had started going to therapy again and was on a low-dose antidepressant. I locked the pistol in a metal gun safe and gave Hannah the key.

Dennis didn't ask why I stopped carrying. But one evening as I prepared to head in for the night, he stopped me to offer up a self-defense alternative.

"Sir, I have a small gift for you," he said, digging in his backpack, pushing aside extra magazines of ammo and a trauma kit. He handed me a small box.

"What's this?" I asked.

"Open it."

Inside was a gray ballpoint pen with a cap.

"My favorite weapon," he replied. He could tell I was confused. "It's made out of carbon fiber."

"So it's an indestructible ballpoint pen?" I replied, not catching on.

Dennis removed the pen from the box and pulled off the cap to reveal it wasn't a pen at all but a shiv, sharpened to a fine point. The shaft was hollowed out, like a soda straw with a knife at the end.

"If a bad guy comes your way, you plunge the sharp part into his neck, chest, or wherever," he explained, "while keeping your thumb over the end of the straw."

He made a stabbing motion in the air.

"The attacker has got two options: A, he can hold still, keep this inside him, and stay alive until help arrives. Or B, he can throw you off and bleed out," he said, lifting his thumb off the end of the shaft to demonstrate.

"Dennis, I don't know what to say," I remarked. "What a graphic gift."

"Don't mention it," he responded. "Just keep 'Little Dennis' with you, especially when I'm gone."

★　★　★

The morning of January 6, 2021, I woke up with only one in-person meeting on my calendar: "TSCM Sweep." 2 p.m. McLean, Virginia. I looked on the map. The office building I was scheduled to visit was about six minutes away from CIA headquarters, which made sense, because I was meeting former spooks.

The security firm that employed Dennis had arranged for a technical surveillance countermeasures sweep of my vehicle. For reasons I won't get into, they were concerned someone could have planted a location tracker or listening device inside the car. Former law-enforcement and CIA technicians were scheduled to comb through the interior and exterior with sophisticated tools to ensure it wasn't bugged.

I granted myself a slow start that day. The evening prior, I had joined a friend and top House aide for my first non-drinking night out in a long time. I was attempting a "dry January" and had a great time, sans alcohol, albeit a very late night. The next morning I answered emails from prospective employers and scrolled through job listings. I was looking to return to the private sector once Trump was gone. Then I could put politics out of my mind, maybe for good.

In the early afternoon, I left to grab coffee on the other side of Capitol Hill before heading out to Virginia. I might pop in to see my friend in his congressional office, too.

Happy to be behind the wheel, I was driving myself again for the first time in months. The security detail had wound down at my request, with the expectation that the threat environment would probably ease in the lead-up to Biden's inauguration—and as long as they didn't find a tracker stuck to my car. Admittedly, the days were a little lonely without Dennis.

Outside the air was chilly and overcast when I parked. I knew there was a rally planned at the White House, but as I passed within a block of the U.S. Capitol, I heard chanting.

"USA! USA! USA!"

Protesters had gathered at the east front of the building with Trump flags, pressing against pedestrian barriers as Capitol Police stood guard. I steered clear of the scene and continued on to the coffee shop. When I emerged maybe fifteen minutes later, the situation had deteriorated considerably.

"We want Trump! We want Trump!"

The chanting was louder. More protesters were pouring into the area. A man-and-woman couple walked past me wearing dark green bulletproof vests, while another group in winter coats and MAGA beanies marched across the street. They were headed for the same place, like a magnet pulling them to the Capitol. I decided against visiting my friend's office.

At the corner, police officers held us in place as the area went into lockdown. At first I was annoyed. I was late for my appointment, but it quickly dawned on me that I had a higher priority: avoiding notice.

Staffers streamed out of a nearby congressional building, crowding my route back to the car. They were evacuating. The aides were as bewildered by the scene as I was when they emerged onto the sidewalk, watching in the distance as protesters climbed over barricades and into the secure zone.

If those people see me, my head will be on a fucking pike.

Hard adrenaline shot into my system. Head down and walking quickly, I turned from the crowd and made my way to a side street. I gripped Dennis's carbon-fiber pen in my pocket, feeling a bit ridiculous but prepared to pull it out of the cap. I elbowed past an odd mix of staffers and protesters until I was clear of the foot traffic and back at my car.

I locked the doors and breathed. Police vehicles zipped by in every direction, emanating a deep bass and sirens as they passed. Roadblocks and cop cars complicated the drive away from Capitol Hill. Stop. Go. Stop. Go. Finally I reached the highway and scanned the newsfeed on my phone.

Back at the Capitol Building, protesters were now smashing windows and some had reportedly breached the facility. Oddly, on C-SPAN I saw that members of Congress were still speaking on the House floor.

"I rise for myself and sixty of my colleagues to object to the counting of the electoral ballots of Arizona," Representative Paul Gosar proclaimed.

Clearly he wasn't aware that the building was being stormed. The Republican stood at the microphone in the U.S. House chamber, clad in an American flag mask, rattling off the reasons Arizona shouldn't certify the 2020 election results. He suggested "cover-ups" and "fraud" had taken place.

At the crescendo of Gosar's speech—just as the Republican peddled data alleging voting irregularities (". . . with odds *so rare* and *unlikely* that winning the Mega Millions lottery is more probable!")—he was interrupted by commotion. Security agents crossed the floor quickly. Loud banging noises filled the chamber.

"Without objection, the chair declares the House in recess," the presiding officer announced hastily, banging the gavel.

The live feed was cut. I switched back to CNN. Barely focusing on the road, I watched as the mob swarmed into the U.S. Capitol Building.

★ ★ ★

That night, a curfew was imposed across the nation's capital. I returned from Virginia as everything began to shut down. The TSCM sweep found nothing unusual in my car, so I parked it back at the apartment and quickly ran to the grocery before the stores closed.

The streets were empty of people, like the desolate European boulevards you see in war movies. Instead Washington was filled with haunting sounds. Screeching tires in the distance. Helicopters. The guttural howling of the Earth, as cold wind took over the roadways.

Much as I'd done on 9/11, I rewatched the footage when I got home and saw new pictures. The scene on the House floor was horrifying. Plainclothes officers with earpieces had scurried to move furniture— a desk and benches—in front of the main entrance, creating a makeshift barricade as legislators and staff were rushed to the exits.

"The whole country hates you! We hate you!" voices yelled from beyond the doors.

The sound of broken windowpanes signaled a partial breach. A half-dozen officers in suits drew their pistols and aimed at the entrance, as would-be intruders peered through jagged glass. From the gallery, a photographer snapped a photo of the moment that defined the whole day. I squinted at the computer screen.

Was that what I thought it was? Something unusual about the scene caught my eye. There was a person I wanted to see about the image. I reached out, and he agreed to dinner the following night.

Hannah worked on Capitol Hill. In the emotional aftermath—of her friends and colleagues sheltering in place and fearing for their lives—she was on the verge of quitting. This wasn't a protest gone wrong, which is what her boss was already saying. The Republican Party she worked for had instigated it by promoting Trump's lies, right up until the moment the barbarians were at the gates.

"I hope people finally realize this is more than the president," she said.

"Yeah," I agreed. "It's not over. I feel like this is just beginning somehow."

"You should say that."

"How do you mean?"

"Like you should get back out there, publicly."

I told Hannah I'd been wrestling with it. Earlier in the day, my friend Evan McMullin—the former GOP official who'd been opposing Trump since the very beginning—called to urge me to "stay in the fight."

"There will be a time to retreat to the private sector," he said. "It's not now."

Evan put a proposal on the table. He wanted me to consider joining his nonprofit organization, which was focused on reducing political extremism. Specifically, he was looking at ways to counter MAGA forces after the president left the White House.

I was torn. Entering the fray again would be triggering, resurfacing the pain of recent months. On the other hand, it felt like necessary atonement. I had the chance to try again and listen to my conscience from the start. My bones ached that night, like they do when you get sick—or when you're about to do something you're afraid of doing.

Early the next morning, on January 7, I agreed to a request from CNN to go back on the air.

"This is an absolute five-alarm fire for democracy," I told the anchors. "This is the ultimate outcome of Trumpism—the defacement of democracy."

Later in the day, I had a similar conversation with Nicolle Wallace on MSNBC, who was covering breaking news that Trump's cabinet was considering his removal with two weeks left in office.

"The talk of the Twenty-Fifth Amendment didn't just—poof!—come out of nowhere today," Wallace told viewers. She said someone had raised the subject years prior, warning about the president's instability. Wallace quoted directly from my 2018 op-ed, and noted that this was all foreseeable.

Why, she asked, didn't more people stand up?

The question bothered me throughout the Trump years. I didn't have a satisfying answer until I dealt with my own demons. But I knew if we didn't get to the source, the long-term consequences would be devastating.

"This will be the civic cause of our time," I told Wallace. "But it's not going to happen in Washington, D.C. . . . As the tide of Trumpism is receding, we're starting to see all of the damage, and it's not just in the United States Capitol Building where the broken glass is. The damage extends all the way into our own communities and our own homes."

That night, I arrived at a regal brick building just blocks away from the vice president's mansion in Northwest D.C. I knocked on the tall door of a condominium. It swung open to reveal the face of a longtime mentor, former Republican congressman Jim Kolbe.

"Hi there," the man greeted me with a frail hug. Jim was almost eighty and swayed gently as he stood, like the gray wisps atop his head. "You doing all right?"

"As much as can be expected," I told him. "You?"

"Well, to see that building trashed and vandalized and desecrated by these people breaks my heart," he confided, beckoning me inside.

The Arizona lawmaker had served for more than two decades in the House. He was best known for his independent streak—staking out positions on abortion, the environment, and immigration that diverged with the Republican Party—and in retirement he was still speaking out. Jim was the person who had asked me years prior whether I was sure I wanted to go into the Trump administration. He was one of my last living mentors.

"You want a drink?" he asked.

"No, I'd rather not."

We sat at an oval dining room table. His Christmas decorations were still up.

Jim had been close friends with John McCain and carried on the mantle of "maverick" after McCain's death. He bucked the GOP and vocally opposed Trump's re-election, for the first time in his life endorsing a Democrat for president.

"I don't get emotional that much," Jim told me. He hadn't even cried during his mother's funeral. "And then I saw this."

He showed me a picture on his phone. It was the chaos on the House floor, the exact same photo I wanted to show him. Plainclothes police. Guns drawn. Makeshift barricade in front of the House doors.

"It's the page desk," he remarked incredulously. "The last line of defense was the page desk."

Like me, the ex-congressman had gotten his start in public service as a congressional page. He worked for the original maverick, U.S. senator Barry Goldwater, in the late 1950s.

"I saw it, too," I responded. "I couldn't believe it."

The table and bench blockading the chamber had once been my workspace. From that perch years ago, I watched members of Congress like Jim Kolbe argue and joke and negotiate bipartisan deals to propel the nation forward. Now the front-row seat to democracy was the final bulwark against a pitchfork mob.

"Do you know the last time something like this happened in the House?" Jim asked.

I knew where he was going. Jim had told the story many times. In fact, one of my first weeks on the job, the congressman gave the pages a tour, telling us little-known tales of the chamber.

"You see that?" the lawmaker pointed to a penny-sized hole in the wood on a desk. "That's from a bullet."

In March 1954, Puerto Rican nationalists had stormed the House and opened fire in the worst terrorist attack in its history, up to that point. Lawmakers were wounded in the shooting.

"And you know who carried them to safety?" The group of sixteen-year-olds listening did not. We shook our heads. "Pages. They carried the shot members out of the room amidst a hail of gunfire."

The metaphor felt too literal—America being saved by the next generation. The night of January 7, Jim told me the story again. He'd gone to Washington several years after it happened.

"I never thought I'd live to see the place attacked again."

The seasoned lawmaker fretted that GOP leaders were already changing their tune. Yesterday, they were starting to turn against Trump. Today, some were defending him. If a domestic terror attack on Congress wasn't enough to wake up the GOP and the country, it would happen once more. That's the beautiful and terrifying truth of the human experience. It doesn't rewind but it often repeats.

"It's up to your generation to decide whether this happens again, you know, whether the doors are still defended next time."

I told him about the offer to go work for Evan's nonprofit. He knew some of the struggles I'd been through in recent months and the reluctance to stay in the arena. I wasn't fully recovered by any stretch.

"I'm leaning toward it," I said, "but I don't know if I'm ready yet."

"Well, I certainly wasn't ready to go to war. I went to Vietnam when I was a kid. We didn't get to pick that fight, but we went anyway."

After dinner, I thanked the Arizonan for hosting me, and for being a mentor all these years. The ranks of people like him—willing to put country over party—were thinning in Washington. I thought about it on the drive home.

"Don't meet your heroes."

That's what my first boss had told me, knowing that an overeager cub reporter would be disappointed by his idols. He wanted me to understand that real caped crusaders don't exist, and the good guys are imperfect. After years in the nation's capital, I realized he was right about all of that, but I decided he was wrong about avoiding those people.

To be clear, looking up to the Adults in Washington had been a letdown. I witnessed their calculating timidity over the course of many years, and I spent fearful nights wondering whether I'd inherited the same flaws—the defect of indecision and the morality of convenience. Even still, the failures of those people who precede us are more instructive than their triumphs. We *should* meet our heroes. Yes, they will disappoint us. But when they do, we have an opportunity to learn from their mistakes, to see what they did not, and, hopefully, to speak what they could not: the truth.

PART II

What guardrails protect democracy against autocrats?

A healthy polity is safeguarded by the moderating forces within the political parties; law-abiding public servants; the balances of the justice system; the checks of the legislature; the constitutional commitments of the nation's security forces (in dire circumstances); and the people themselves. Neglecting these guardrails can backfire, enabling a potential autocrat to weaponize them against the country.

Truth itself is the final, foundational guardrail of a free society. It is the angel on overwatch.

I learned this unexpectedly in a place where very few people discover knowledge these days: a college classroom. The seminar was aptly titled "Liberty and Its Enemies," and we were required to read John Stuart Mill, the nineteenth-century British philosopher and author of the timeless tome *On Liberty*.

I won't attempt to retrace Mill's work, other than to highlight two key sentences. In the faded copy I still have, the passage is double-underlined and starred in blue pen on page 21:

> *The peculiar evil of silencing the expression of an opinion is, that it is robbing the human race; posterity as well as the existing generation; those who dissent from the opinion, still more than those who hold it. If the opinion is right, they are deprived of the opportunity of exchanging error for truth: if wrong, they lose, what is almost as great a benefit, the clearer perception and livelier impression of truth, produced by its collision with error.*

Put another way, contrary opinions are a two-fold gift. If we're wrong about an idea ("The Earth is flat!"), the expression of a contrary opinion gives us the chance to change our minds. If we're right about an idea ("The Earth is round!"), an objection can lead us to a stronger defense of the truth. We might set about to *prove* the Earth is round and, in doing so, further confirm the truth and disprove the lie.

This was Mill's argument for a competitive "marketplace of ideas." He mounted one of the strongest defenses in history for maximizing free speech, even the sharing of bad ideas. Mill drew an important conclusion about the silencing of dissent. He observed that freedom cannot survive without truth and vice versa. So when open societies self-censor, democracy's self-destruction is all but assured.

THE TRUTH IS IN DANGER FROM AN INTERNAL MENACE.

The volatile civic climate in the United States could careen into a period of violence, as previously outlined. By talking about a Second Civil War, experts are using terminology that would've been unthinkable at the turn of the millennium. To reverse this hostility, we must ask hard questions, starting with:

Why has the vitriol jumped the tracks to violence?

"There's a very simple reason for the trend toward political intimidation," democracy scholar Lee Drutman explained. He's one of the country's leading, nonpartisan scholars on political reform. "People feel like the normal channels of politics are broken. Their vote doesn't matter, it won't be counted anyway, and the elections are 'rigged.' So they feel like they have to go outside the system in order to break and reset the system. That means violence."

In 2017, a *Washington Post* poll found that more than 70 percent of Americans agreed that the political system had reached "a dangerous low point." In 2019, nearly two-thirds of voters said "significant changes" were needed to the "fundamental design and structure" of American government, according to a Pew survey. Even after Donald Trump left office, a majority reported that U.S. democracy was "in crisis and at risk of failing," according to an NPR/Ipsos poll, which raises the question—

Why do people feel like the normal channels are broken?

Americans say that the two major parties no longer adequately reflect their views. Roughly half of Americans now identify as "political independents" and not as members of either major party. They are turned off by the polarization. Data since the early 1970s shows Democrats in Congress becoming more liberal, Republicans becoming "much more conservative," and moderates nearing extinction.

"The polarization in today's Congress has roots that go back decades," the Pew Research Center wrote in 2022. "There are now only about two dozen moderate Democrats and Republicans left on Capitol Hill, versus more than 160 in 1971–72."

What's more, hardcore partisans are holding on to their seats. On average, 85 to 95 percent of sitting members of Congress are re-elected. Only a fraction of congressional districts today are seen as genuine toss-ups, which raises another question:

Why has democracy gotten less competitive?

The short answer is that the extremes have taken over the electoral system, thanks to structural factors and increasing polarization.

Think of structural factors as the vehicle. A combination of voting laws, partisan primaries, and gerrymandering has handed the nominating process and king-making power to the parties, which have worked hard to keep the other side from taking their seats away. Data shows that they've been successful: Republican localities are getting redder and Democratic localities are getting bluer.

Think of polarization as the fuel. A CBS News poll found that a majority of both Democrats and Republicans no longer described each other as "political opponents" but as "enemies." It's so bad that these Americans see *each other* as "the biggest threat" to their way of life—more than foreign countries, military threats, natural disasters, environmental factors, viruses, or economic forces. With moderates and independents fleeing the two major parties, the problem has gotten worse.

What is causing higher polarization?

The obvious culprit is social media. Social psychologist Jonathan Haidt has cataloged it better than anyone. "The dart guns of social media give more power and voice to the political extremes while reducing the power and voice of the moderate majority," Haidt wrote in *The Atlantic*. He pointed to research which found that people on the far-left and far-right fringes—who make up only slivers of the population (8 percent and 6 percent, respectively)—are the most prolific "sharers" on social media. The two extremes represent the "whitest and richest" parts of the country, "which suggests that America is being torn apart by a battle between two subsets of the elite who are not representative of the broader society," Haidt explained.

But I believe there is something more troubling. Americans aren't just silencing each other. They are choosing to silence themselves. U.S. voters are afraid to share their beliefs because of reprisal attacks or getting socially canceled—or even fired from their jobs. A groundbreaking study by nonpartisan think tank Populace Insights found that respondents often presented to others very different views than they actually held about hot-button topics.

"The pressure to misrepresent our private views—to offer answers on politically and socially sensitive questions that are out of sync with our true beliefs—is pervasive in society today," the report concluded. "Across all demographics every subgroup had multiple issues with at least a double-digit gap between public and private opinion." Political independents were "the least comfortable sharing their private views in public."

So what does self-censorship mean for truth?

Taken together, these findings are bad news for democracy. Independents represent the largest voting bloc in the United States. If they are increasingly afraid to share their views, or speak up at all, it has ominous implications for a free and open society. If we accept John Stuart Mill's way of thinking, it means the broader marketplace of ideas will become less competitive. The result is there will be fewer opportunities for "truth" and "error" to collide, and we will be more liable to stumble into civic danger and national decline.

We need to make it easier to dissent by making democracy competitive again.

When I speak to student groups around the country, I use an example from economics to describe the situation. The conversation goes the same way almost every time.

"How many of you have taken Econ 101?" I ask. Most of the hands go up.

"And how many of you remember supply and demand curves?" The hands stay up.

"What do these charts tell us? Any volunteers?"

Someone will raise his or her hand and explain: "The curves show us that prices change based on two factors, supply and demand—how much of a product is available and how badly people want it."

"That's right," I say. "So if something is really expensive—let's say, vegetables—what are the two ways the price might go down?"

The same student usually jumps in: "You can decrease demand for vegetables. If less people want them, the price will go down. Or you increase the supply by growing more, or introducing different varieties."

"Correct. Now I want to talk about something I experienced the past few years . . ."

I tell them about my decision to speak out against Donald Trump and the aftermath. I discovered the "price" of dissent was higher than it's ever been in America. The decision nearly cost me everything, which everyone would consider unaffordable.

"So let's think of politics as a marketplace. What are the two ways to *lower* the price of dissent, to make it less costly?" I ask, looking to the precocious student for an answer.

"Uh, you can decrease demand . . ." he or she might say.

"That's one way. But do we really want to *decrease demand* for dissent? Do we want fewer ideas and less free expression in the marketplace?"

The student jumps in. "Or you can increase the supply?"

"BINGO. If you want the price of dissent to go down, the best way to do it is increase the supply. Get more of it out there on the store shelves—a more competitive market of ideas. And you know who produces that product? *You.*"

The point isn't lost on students who grew up as digital natives. They're used to self-censoring, whether it's in the classroom or online in the face of crowd-sourced pressure to say the right thing and not to offend. They'll look first to see if someone will have their back before speaking up, so they don't pay a high price alone.

Put another way, there is strength in numbers, which applies as much to courage as it does to cowardice. When we are silent about antidemocratic behavior, especially within our own political tribes, it will flourish and get costlier to oppose. When more people stand up against it, the consequences become less severe. The hard part is making people feel comfortable expressing their true opinions.

The Founders believed a thriving democracy of many competing sides would prevent any single group or movement from becoming too powerful and "make it less probable that a majority of the whole will have a common motive to invade the rights of other citizens." Competition would allow people to speak up without fear of oppression from one side. Unfortunately, as we've discussed, political choice is floundering.

We must make democracy competitive again. Right now it rewards extremism and scares off alternatives, particularly dissenting views.

"The longer-term picture requires changes to our electoral system," offered Stanford's Larry Diamond, regarded as one of America's leading "democracy doctors." He's an advocate for something known as ranked-choice voting (RCV). "Reforms like ranked-choice voting are essential to swing the pendulum away from these perverse incentives to nominate and elect the most radical figures."

Ranked-choice voting is a tool to give voters more say in who their elected representatives are. And it's steadily gaining popularity nationwide. Rather than choose just one candidate, the system allows voters to rank candidates in order of preference. The first one to win a majority wins the election. If no candidate receives a majority on the first round, the one with the least votes is eliminated and voters' *next* preferences are factored in until a winner is determined. The process requires candidates to appeal to a broader base of citizens, rather than relying on a single, extreme faction.

Imagine a MAGA Republican running in a GOP primary today for Congress. He or she would prioritize turning out the base, getting as many far-right Republicans to the polls as possible. If others are in the race and split the vote, the MAGA candidate might be able to win with, let's say, only 32 percent, from the hardcore conservatives.

But in an RCV primary, catering to the extremes wouldn't cut it. To win, the MAGA Republican would need to appeal to a broader group than the MAGA base. If the candidate couldn't get 50 percent of voters to rank him or her "#1," the candidate would need to rely on enough to rank him or her "#2." That requires attracting broader support from the electorate, not just a single ideological wing.

"This is the method most likely to marginalize extremists and elevate moderates," Diamond noted. And for voters, "RCV means your vote is no longer a 'throwaway' vote."

This isn't the only method for reinvigorating a majority view and giving Americans the opportunity to dissent with their votes. A range of electoral reforms are being hotly debated and considered across America, including nonpartisan primaries and independent redistricting.

The current primary system is obviously dysfunctional. The vast majority of congressional districts in the country are "safe" (i.e., either the Republicans or the Democrats have a stranglehold). That means the winner of a primary race is basically guaranteed to win the election—before most voters have a chance to make their voices heard. In that sense, the most ideological 10 percent of voters tend to select the representatives for the rest of us, the other 90 percent.

Nonpartisan primaries rejigger this process to allow for wider participation. Everyone who wants to run for a specific public office enters the same primary. *All* voters can participate, regardless of their political affiliation. Then, the top vote-getters proceed to the general election. This vastly increases participation and ideological diversity in the selection process.

Democracy reformers are also hoping to make districts less "safe." The two major parties have spent decades drawing districts that make it nearly impossible for the other side to win. Independent redistricting eliminates the influence of political interests. When nonpartisan or bipartisan groups of officials are put in charge of drawing voting districts (rather than state legislatures), boundaries are drawn in a way that doesn't favor a particular party.

Electoral reforms like these can safeguard democracy from the Next Trump. The structural changes will make it harder for extremists to win elections and will give sensible leaders more avenues to succeed. Reforms can also create the conditions for depolarization; when the voices of the common-sense majority are restored, the fringes are put back in their places and dissenting doesn't seem so dangerous anymore. Finally, fixing the democratic process will open the door for fresh voices, including third parties.

"For many years, there was a sense that the two-party system was a stabilizing force in the U.S. political system. Now we're seeing the opposite," noted Lee Drutman, who has drawn national attention for his analysis of Americans' growing interest in new political parties. "The strongest evidence is that two-thirds of Americans say there should be more than two choices."

The Next Trump will rise if we remain anonymous.

A group of top Republicans gathered in secret in February 2021— only weeks after Donald Trump left the White House—with a mission: to stop it from happening again.

More than one hundred current and former officials participated in the multi-hour session. They spanned generations of elected leaders, party chairs, lawmakers, governors, cabinet secretaries, operatives, and appointees from the Trump, Bush, and Reagan administrations. I helped organize the gathering after taking my mentor's advice. Jim Kolbe, the former GOP congressman, was right. Whether I was ready for it or not, the struggle for the soul of our political system would continue, so I stayed in the fight.

It was an unlikely group. The Trump presidency pitted GOP figures against one another, ruining many friendships and straining others. Some in our group had opposed the New Yorker from the start, while many had hoped to help the man govern. A few had been true believers until the shock of the insurrection at the U.S. Capitol. None of them wanted to experience another four years like it again.

The discussion centered on whether to launch a movement to rebuild the Republican Party internally by bolstering the ranks of "rational Republicans" against the MAGA movement, or to break away from the GOP altogether and form a new political party. There were enormous risks to both options. The debate was civil but impassioned.

During the second hour, a virtual poll was sent to each participant, asking whether a reformist "faction" or a "new party" was the right answer. When the results came back, there was an even split. Fifty-fifty. Half supported staying in the GOP to defeat MAGA candidates from within, while the other half said it was time to quit the Republican Party and create a new home for disaffected conservatives.

I was sympathetic to both positions. But I was concerned about ending the meeting divided, with everyone going his or her separate way.

"We might disagree on the tactics," I interjected, "but I think we need to align on the strategy, which is to create a countermovement. Can we unify around that?"

Other speakers echoed the sentiment, noting that Donald Trump had emerged by dividing and conquering the moderate majority. Then he intimidated it into silence. We had to stay together, regardless of party affiliation.

★　★　★

Anonymity symbolizes the greatest threat to democracy.

This is the "hidden threat" to our republic that I referenced at the outset of this book. To be clear, I am not speaking about individual whistle-blowers. Our legal system rightfully protects people who want to disclose wrongdoing without disclosing their identities. For example, the intelligence community whistle-blower whose revelations led to the impeachment of former president Trump remains anonymous and has been able to protect his or her family and career as a result. This is as it should be.

What concerns me is a different and broader kind of anonymity. Social fear is creating a mass bystander effect in our politics. Psychological research has shown that pedestrians are less inclined to help a victim who is being attacked if others are present. They will stay to the edge of the crowd and watch, waiting for someone else to act. In today's political climate, as democracy is being bludgeoned, citizens are shrinking in the face of intimidation, standing on the sidelines, and hoping that someone else will come forward to end the villainy.

If there is any lesson from the Trump years, it's that this is preventable. The business tycoon's abuses of power could have been averted if more people within the Republican Party and his own administration had stood up and told the truth sooner. The anecdotes detailed in this book of immoral policies, conspiracies and lies, illegal acts, assassination plots, and sedition could have been thwarted—all of them—by a minimal amount of civic bravery. Instead, people who knew better acted like bystanders. I similarly fooled myself into thinking so-called Adults would step forward so I didn't have to.

A multitude of people risked their careers and safety in a hostile political climate to break from the Republican Party and encourage citizens to oppose Donald Trump. For that, they have my enduring gratitude. In my own case, I wish I had come forward and spoken the truth sooner to provide cover for others.

Just in writing this book, I have been reminded of the extent of apprehension at the highest levels. Many people I interviewed wouldn't use their names out of fear of retribution. They are people who could still help convince fellow Republicans to oppose MAGA forces, but they are effectively in moral hiding.

Several senior former Trump officials, each of whom declined to be identified, provided revealing statements in our interviews:

"People are scared for their livelihoods. I don't attach my name to anything because I want to live my life. . . . We are all on an island together. Just because many of us don't like each other doesn't mean we're not all on an island."

"[I] can't go public because they will take everything from you. I have a family and no safety net. What do I do? My family will basically be destitute if I swing at these people."

"The job environment has been horrible, almost doubly for dissenters. The left is scared of your Trump association. The right will never welcome you back if you oppose them."

★ ★ ★

Representative Adam Kinzinger was one of the handful of Republicans who came forward and called for a change in the party's direction after

Trump left the White House. He organized a summit in South Carolina for right-leaning reformers in August 2022, continuing some of the discussions we started after Trump left office. As we sought refuge from the afternoon sun, Kinzinger and I talked about progress—or lack thereof.

"The future of the country is on the line," he said, "but people are still scared to poke their heads out."

Nearby, his wife Sofia chatted with supporters under the shade of a palmetto tree, holding their eight-month-old son. They'd been on the receiving end of graphic death threats. He later released a string of voicemails, similar in tenor and tone to the menacing threats in my own inbox.

"I hope you die as quickly as fucking possible, you fucking piece of shit." "Hey you little cocksucker. Going to come protest in front of your house this weekend. We know where your family is, and we're going to come get you." "Gonna get your wife, gonna get your kids." "Coming to your house. We're gonna get you and Liz Cheney."

I asked Kinzinger if he thought his colleagues were still withholding their true opinions because they wanted to avoid being similarly terrorized.

"Sure, but they have a bigger fear than that," he insisted.

"Bigger than their families getting attacked?" I asked.

"Yeah. They're scared to get kicked out of the tribe," he explained. "These people fear getting booted from the Republican tribe more than death. Their entire identities are wrapped up in it. That's how powerful the tribalism is."

His point stuck with me. Comedian Jerry Seinfeld had a joke along these lines.

"According to most studies, people's number one fear is public speaking. Number two is death," he opened. *"Death is number two.* Does that sound right? This means to the average person, if you go to a funeral, you're better off in the casket than doing the eulogy."

Conservatives feel the same way about speaking up. It's why they only whisper the truth.

I saw it so many times. In Congress, representatives who were terrified of Trump's impact on the party decided to cheer him on anyway. In the White House, the president's aides warned about his corrupt behavior behind closed doors yet waxed about his "genius" to the press. In the Department of Homeland Security, some of my closest colleagues discussed how Trump's rash decisions endangered American lives, only to stay behind until the end, hailing him as "bold and decisive."

Adam Kinzinger wasn't one of these people, but the post-Trump period didn't go the way the congressman hoped. Several months after our conversation, a MAGA-led GOP retook the U.S. House by a slim majority. Kinzinger was forced to retire from Congress, gerrymandered out of his district and censured by the Republican Party. One of the GOP's last vocal dissenters was booted from the tribe, while most others held their tongues.

★ ★ ★

Whatever you want to call it—anonymity, the bystander phenomenon, self-censorship—the reluctance of people to stand against extremism is putting our republic in danger. Too many Americans are donning figurative masks, preferring the safe harbor of obscurity to the discomfort of reality. A broken system perpetuates it.

This is how the most dangerous president in American history ascended to power in the first place.

To save democracy from the Next Trump, we must avoid anonymity and the blowback that comes with it. Authoritarians thrive on chasing their rivals into the dark, which is why nothing is so caustic to an autocrat as a critic who stands unmovable in the light. Truth is the final guardrail of our collective democracy, and we each individually control its fate.

Washington is a town obsessed with external enemies. Here you're trained to focus your mind and actions against another person, a president, a political party, or perhaps a foreign nation state. All the while, you lose sight of the fact that the most formidable enemy is within, and if you don't confront the self-delusion of your vices and the tendency to deny the truth, the internal conflict will rage eternally.

My journey to that realization was long and fraught and painful. It required unlearning the conventional lessons of my chosen profession. I concluded that in politics, as in life, the real struggle is not us-versus-them. It is us-versus-us.

EPILOGUE

November 1, 2022

We drove fast out of Washington, but not in a hurry. As we entered Virginia, the light ignited the countryside. It was the week—or maybe the final day—before the trees would begin shedding until they became skeletons.

The last time I'd seen an autumn afternoon like this, my life was different. I was alone and looking over my shoulder and had just been assigned a bodyguard. Now a passenger with flowing red hair sat next to me as we drove home. We appreciated the scenery, knowing we might not see it again for a while. A drifting melody called "Harmonia's Dream" played on repeat, and she said I was running it into the ground.

Back home, I got a message from my younger brother. He was in Mexico City with friends for el Día de los Muertos, the Day of the Dead. The holiday was a celebration of the departed, and Patrick sent photos of his cohort in a rainbow of spectral costumes, their faces painted as bone.

It gave me an idea for how to mark the evening, so I made a trip to the corner store to pick up firewood.

At dark I scouted the map for an open field. I found a place that looked like it might give us almost as much open air as land, and I packed the car with supplies. I convinced my companion to bring the dog, ironically named Martini. I'd gotten sober since then.

On the road, the once-colorful trees had become tall silhouettes, forming a nocturnal hallway to our destination. We drove for a while in contentment but quiet. The hum of the motor was a steady white noise behind my thoughts.

"What guardrails protect us against vices?"

The question was on my mind, as I relived the past few years and conducted a sort of spiritual accounting.

Had I been a healthier person, I would've been safeguarded by the faction of my subconscious that raised doubts; the moral deputy who cautioned me; the judge who knew I was at my limit; the assembly of confidants who held up a mirror; a thin shield of inhibitions; the sword of self-defense; and the citizen in my soul that served a final notice.

But I wasn't. I was distracted by secrets that I kept from others and from myself, which almost ended up destroying me. An angel on overwatch—the truth—saved my life.

I thought about the woman next to me. She spent many months gently helping me build myself back up and was now living a clean life with me. Her ring pressed against my skin as we held hands, the way it probably would on long drives like this to come. Earlier in the day, we had decided that we would soon embark on a yearlong journey across the country.

We pulled up to a dark field, parked the car, and unpacked. I carried a fire pit into the expanse, as a distant circle of maple trees stood sentry. My passenger set up two folding chairs in the grass, and Martini scouted the area in zigzag fashion with the aid of clear skies.

I arranged the kindling and wood in an upright pile. Kneeling down, I placed the tinder in the center and lit it. The blaze warmed my face as it grew, and I stepped back to take my seat.

We talked for a long time, as we always did. About our parents and siblings. The future. The dog. And as you do around a campfire, we found ourselves reminiscing about the past and the peculiar fact that the lights we were peering at above were thousands of years old.

When I look at art, I don't want to be thinking about the artist, but it's not the same way with nature. Mysticism is for people who can't make sense of the world. I spent two years directly coming to terms with my own impermanence and finally accepted it. The conclusion caused me to treat my life with greater care than ever before and to better understand its foundations, which made me grateful for—and almost reverent of—the pain that it took to get there.

I wasn't mourning past losses. Tonight was a celebration.

I got up from my chair and walked across the leafy park back to the car. In the trunk, there was a briefcase. The metal box was cold to the touch as I scrolled the combination on two separate dials. The password was the answer to a math problem from school—why I still remembered it, I didn't know.

I slid the buttons to the side and popped open the latches with a soft click. I lifted the lid. Inside, there were several loose papers, a few charging cords, and the corners of cash peeking out from beneath it all. What I wanted was on top. A newspaper clipping yellowed with age, and a hardback book with a sparse white cover. I pulled them out and closed the lid, snapping the latches shut.

I walked back over and told my fellow traveler what they were. She asked if I was sure about it. I said I was, and she smiled. I placed the only copy of the newspaper clipping that I had into the fire pit and watched it curl up and disappear within seconds.

The second item took longer. I set it on top of the pyre, and for a moment it didn't catch. A thin circle of flame lazily enveloped the cover. Like the border of a closing wound, it shrank toward the center until the words were gone. The blaze caught hold of the spine and consumed the book from within, causing the pages to flutter in the heat like butterflies. They fell away in charred flakes.

"Nobody ever tells you that books burn so pretty," she said.

The remaining pages became fire, and after a while, the last wooden support collapsed into the heap. Briefly, the embers blended with the stars as they drifted into the night sky.

A NOTE ON SOURCES

The anecdotes and analysis contained in this book are based on interviews with dozens of current and former U.S. government officials, personal recollections, contemporaneous notes, emails and text messages, public records, and other sources. Where notes or records did not exist for a particular conversation, I have reconstructed the exchange to the very best of my recollection and/or in consultation with subjects who were involved in or aware of those conversations. Some names and identifying characteristics have been changed.

INDEX

ABOUT THE AUTHOR

Miles Taylor is a national security expert who works in Washington, D.C. Taylor previously served as chief of staff at the U.S. Department of Homeland Security, where he published an "Anonymous" essay in *The New York Times*, blowing the whistle on presidential misconduct. He later published the #1 national bestseller *A Warning* (2019), revealed himself to be the author, and launched a campaign of ex-officials to oppose Donald Trump's re-election. He has worked as an advisor in the George W. Bush administration, on Capitol Hill, and as a CNN contributor, and he is cofounder of a D.C.-based charter school and of several democracy-reform groups. Taylor received his M.Phil. in international relations from Oxford University as a Marshall Scholar and B.A. from Indiana University as a Truman Scholar.